PASSION & CLARITY

PASSION & CLARITY

THE ART OF

JOSEPH JEFFERS
DODGE

Debra Murphy-Livingston

THE Cummer
MUSEUM OF ART & GARDENS
JACKSONVILLE FLORIDA

Publication made possible by the estate of Joseph Jeffers Dodge.

The Cummer Museum of Art & Gardens is recognized by the state of Florida as a Florida Cultural Institution and receives partial funding from the State of Florida Department of State, the Florida Arts Council, the Division of Cultural Affairs, and the City of Jacksonville.

  AMERICAN ASSOCIATION OF MUSEUMS

Title page and above:
Detail: *The Artist and Muse*, 1992, Oil on canvas

ISBN 0-915135-13-2

For more information please contact the Cummer Museum of Art & Gardens, 829 Riverside Avenue, Jacksonville, FL 32204.

www.cummer.org

Designer's Note

In *The Gallery* section of this book, on the top edge of the page, the reader will note a discreet number that corresponds to the plate number. This number will facilitate finding «*pl.*» reference pages.

All works are by Joseph Jeffers Dodge unless otherwise noted. All measurements are given in inches; height precedes width.

Incomplete information is available for unlocated and destroyed works. They are cited here without dimensions and supports. Some tolerance is required with a few of the reproductions due to the rare archival material found to make this book as complete as possible.

To EmmaJean and Queenie

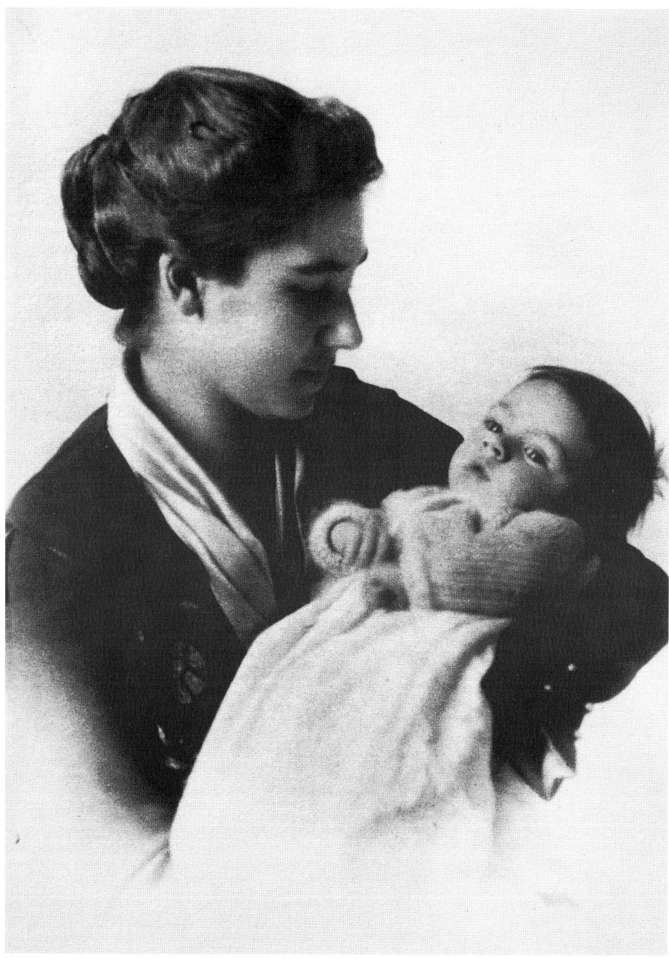

Fig. 1—Jerry as a baby, held by his mother, 1917

Joseph Jeffers Dodge was a man of many talents: accomplished museum director, inveterate traveler, discerning connoisseur, engaging conversationalist, occasional curmudgeon, graduate of Choate and Harvard, and, most enduringly, a highly talented painter. This monograph celebrates the passion Jerry Dodge felt for the art of painting and the clarity with which he rendered his vision in paint.

Dodge once said of his own art, «I've simply painted what I saw—told it like it is, so to speak, have tried to make the art 'The Mirror of Nature,' as Leonardo said.»[1] One look at Jerry Dodge's work, however, makes it immediately clear that creating art is never that simple. One may recognize the subject matter and describe the painted scene in fairly accurate terms, but much more is going on beyond the surface of the canvas.

Debra Murphy-Livingston performs a magisterial job charting Dodge's life and career and analyzing his paintings. She is extremely adept at noting the mysterious and occasionally ominous character of Dodge's work. Murphy-Livingston knew the artist well. This familiarity gives her valuable insight and enables her to find Dodge's voice. The quotes chosen from Dodge's writings are pertinent and eloquent, providing a context for the artist's aesthetic system, although Dodge would no doubt have frowned at the use of this term. He preferred to call his art «a poetic visual fancy in which your imagination could roam.»[2]

Florida played a very important role in Jerry Dodge's art. He spent thirty-five of his almost eighty years living in Florida. Locale and its accurate representation formed a crucial component of Dodge's painting. Florida's marshes, beaches, and Intracoastal waterway were favorite backdrops for many of his canvases. Murphy-Livingston's description of Dodge's life in Florida becomes more than an artistic biography. In those pages the artist's life metamorphoses into a socio-cultural history of Jacksonville, the artist's chosen residence. Gallery exhibitions, opening nights at the Cummer Museum, and the many people who interacted with Jerry Dodge are depicted. The portrait that emerges from these pages is one of a man who possessed a remarkable capacity for friendship and engaged his friends in a profound and lasting bond.

I wish to express my gratitude to the Estate of Joseph Jeffers Dodge for its generous support of this publication; to its executor and Dodge's close friend, Jeffrey Dunn, for his unfailing encouragement of this project; to the author of this lovingly researched and timely monograph, Debra Murphy-Livingston; and to the family and many friends of the artist. This book is a triumphal tribute to Jerry Dodge's long life and enduring art.

Maarten van de Guchte, Director
Cummer Museum of Art & Gardens

Acknowledgements

It is indeed a pleasure to acknowledge the many debts I have accrued in completing this manuscript. Joseph Jeffers «Jerry» Dodge was my friend and I admired the breadth of his knowledge about art and many other topics.

Conversation with Jerry was reliably exhilarating and delightful. I appreciate his confidence in entrusting me with the bulk of his records, documents, and other autobiographical materials. They form a poignant corpus ranging from Dodge's baby book lovingly compiled by his mother, to his Harvard diploma (he graduated with honors in the same class as President John F. Kennedy), to countless clippings, photographs, reviews, and catalogues, all reflecting a life well lived. These will be deposited in the Cummer Museum of Art & Gardens in Jacksonville, Florida, as part of the Joseph Jeffers Dodge Archives.

I wish to convey my gratitude to Dodge's family: sons Joseph Morrell Dodge II and Jeffers MacArthur Dodge, and daughters Julia «Julie» Dodge and Lisa Morrell Dodge, for their patience and cooperation. Both Joseph and Julie read the manuscript and made important contributions.

Mr. and Mrs. Edward Klempf have been gracious in their hospitality and generous with their encouragement. Mrs. Klempf, Jeanne, one of Dodge's closest friends, the artist's primary model, and as the artist often said, his muse, read the manuscript numerous times making useful suggestions, constructive criticisms, and important corrections. She argued rightly for a broader treatment of the personality of Dodge.

Jeffrey D. Dunn, Dodge's attorney and close friend has been stellar in his counsel and unfailing in his generosity, good humor, and patience throughout the entire process of writing and research. Jeff has read the texts so many times that he can probably recite passages by heart. He was closely involved in every aspect of the book's publication and it is a stronger work for his devotion to the endeavor. I salute his commitment.

In addition, Dodge's old friends attorney David N. Mills and architect Taylor Hardwick provided useful insights and corrected inaccuracies. Mr. Mills and Jerry were friends for sixty-five years and his knowledge of Dodge's life and many other areas was invaluable. To these gentlemen, each so important to the artist, I give my thanks.

As early as the 1970s Dodge dreamed that there would be a book about his life and career. This project grew partially from the artist's vision of a monograph, but its real impetus came from the dedication of Maarten van de Guchte, director, and Jeanette Toohey, chief curator, of the Cummer Museum of Art & Gardens. They recognized the quality of Dodge's work and the significant roles he played in the early formation of the Cummer and in the development of the cultural life of Jacksonville.

It has been a delight to work with the current Cummer Museum staff in the final phases of production. Maarten van de Guchte brought his tremendous experience and connections to the task; he also made astute comments regarding the organization of the text. Jeanette Toohey was tireless in her encouragement and wise in her suggestions. Both displayed an impressive professionalism and warm collegiality for which I am grateful. Vance Shrum was indispensable in converting and translating computer files. Jennifer Lisella wins kudos for tackling the Herculean task of securing rights to reproduction of images, contacting owners, establishing the Cummer database on Dodge, and for too many other contributions to list here. The entire team appreciates the indefatigable work of editor Jeannie

Theriault and designer Kym Staiff, who also collaborated on the index. Thanks also go to the owners of Dodge works who generously agreed to share their paintings for illustration in this text.

Special acknowledgement goes to my colleagues at the University of North Florida, especially to Paul Karabinis with whom I co-curated two exhibitions of Dodge's works and selections from his collection at the University Gallery. My first lecture on Dodge was held at the gallery in 1995 at Karabinis's invitation. Former chairman of the Department of Communications and Visual Arts Robert Bohle, and current chair Oscar Patterson III, were also enthusiastic advocates of this undertaking. I would like to recognize the cheerful and dependable assistance of Donna Oxford and Jozsef Szeremi as well. I received a University of North Florida grant under the administration of the late provost Alan Ling that provided travel support to Glens Falls, New York, where Dodge had served as curator of The Hyde Collection.

In Glens Falls, I was welcomed by former Hyde Collection director Kathleen Monaghan and her assistant Tammy Zaroff. Dodge's old friends Morton Raych and Shirley Patton assisted in expanding my understanding of this important period of the artist's life. It was also a pleasure to meet Mrs. Hyde's granddaughter Mary Whitney Renz and her husband, Franklin Renz.

Giving lectures and reading papers on Dodge's work and career helped clarify the text. In addition to Karabinis and Monaghan, I appreciate the hospitality of the former and current museum administrators who welcomed me to their institutions: Henry Adams, Kahren Arbitman, Sally Metzler, Aaron De Groft, Jean Hall Dodd, and Hope McMath at the Cummer Museum of Art & Gardens, and Steve Lotz at the University of Central Florida in Orlando. I have also delivered papers on the patronage of Mrs. Hyde and Mrs. Cummer and on Dodge's work at the 1998 and 1999 meetings of the Southeastern College Art Conference in Miami and Norfolk, Virginia, where I benefited from colleagues' responses to my research.

Student assistance has been of tremendous help over the last few years. Kathy Filiatreau and Catherine Richardson were indispensable in the transcription of Dodge's autobiographical tapes, and more recently, Jennifer Nicolason, Tonya Lee, and Erika Thompson have lent their energies to the project.

My colleague and friend, John A. Elliott, has been steadfast in his encouragement of this project, as have Ivy Bigbee and Mary Gaylen Phillips. My mother Jean Howe Ashline has been an ardent admirer of Dodge's works and of this project from its inception. She read the manuscript early on and made useful comments. Her late husband, Edward F. Ashline; my father and his wife, James E. and Laura Murphy; and my mother-in-law, Emma L. Penny, have always provided good cheer and reassurance.

My husband, Felix Rex Livingston, read the manuscript with his experienced and keen editorial eye. He also lent selfless support in countless ways on the domestic front. I wish to express my loving gratitude to this wonderful man.

Finally, this adoring mother wishes to dedicate this book to our daughters, EmmaJean Murphy Livingston and Florence Regina «Queenie» Livingston.

Debra Murphy-Livingston

Fig. 2 —Detail: **Jerry, Jeanne and** *Portrait of Jeanne* at the Art and Culture Center, Hollywood, Florida, *Florida 10 plus 5* exhibition, September 10, 1977

Fig. 3 —Joseph Jeffers Dodge's studio at his Silversmith Creek home

Table of Contents

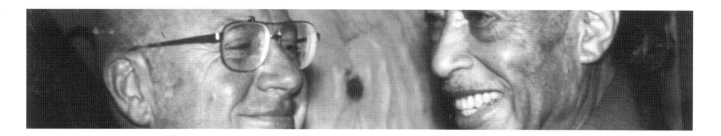

Introduction

Jerry Dodge had a healthy ego, certainly not a bad attribute for an artist whose work would be subject to the review of critics. He took great pride in his artistic accomplishments, but realized he would only be a footnote in the annals of art history. One of his favorite quotations was «*Vita brevis. Ars longa*»—life is short but art endures. Dodge had a keen sense of art's ability to transcend mortality and had great confidence that his body of paintings and drawings would continue to represent him well and forcefully after his death.

As early as the 1970s Dodge dreamed there would be a book about his life and career. *Passion and Clarity: The Art of Joseph Jeffers Dodge* is primarily a study of Dodge's paintings. Although this book also documents aspects of the artist's life, it is not nor was it ever intended to be a biography in the conventional sense. Certainly major biographical facts are reviewed, but the emphasis is on what Dodge believed his true legacy would be—the works of art themselves. Throughout Dodge's career he was inspired by his surroundings. His early paintings include a series from a quarry near Glens Falls, New York, and views of Hudson River factory towns, (pl. 35). In addition, the early paintings often reflect his deep love for jazz, especially for the work of Duke Ellington who was a friend. Later paintings and drawings reflect new artistic territory for Jerry, many of which depict views of Florida: vistas of Washington Oaks Park south of St. Augustine, Florida, and rich in coquina formations; renderings of Fort Clinch, pl. 42, at the mouth of the Amelia River in north Florida; and cypress trees and swamps. Dozens more works are responses to Dodge's travels to the New England and Pacific coasts, the American Southwest, the Yucatán Peninsula, Greece, Italy, France, and Egypt. The themes of the artist's subjects sometimes overlap, but more often they are easily divided into classic modern versions of the *fête champêtre* or the *fête galante*, beautiful women clothed or nude, landscapes, coastal scenes and seascapes, monuments inspired by travel, and still lifes.

Although Jerry Dodge often relied on photographs, slides, or even pages torn from magazines, he was never a photo-realist. As he explained it, he strove to make an imaginary world real. Dodge's works are often small in scale and detailed. They require perusal and contemplation. Steve Lotz, an artist, professor, and friend of Jerry, once remarked that his mentor's works were almost devotional in the sense that they were often tranquil compositions that invited close and quiet scrutiny.

Largely self-taught, Dodge's early works were influenced by a number of artists including Pablo Picasso and Salvador Dalí. Jerry Dodge was always drawn to French painters such as Nicolas Poussin and Camille Corot, whose inherent classicism matched Dodge's own preferences and approaches to composition and subject matter. He also admired the Venetian school and sought to evoke the idyllic ambience of works by Giorgione and Titian, and was inspired by the French Rococo artists Watteau and Fragonard.

Jerry Dodge once referred to himself as a visual glutton. His obsession with images is evident in his tireless photographing; his steady production of paintings and drawings spanning a career of more than fifty years; his devouring of journals, magazines, and catalogues; his attraction for popular culture; his numerous exhibitions at home and abroad; and his delight in the scenery surrounding his residence and studio on Silversmith Creek in Jacksonville, Florida. Furthermore, Jerry was an impassioned collector of paintings, drawings, photographs, porcelain, glass, and a wide variety of *objets d'art*. He surrounded himself with beauty and sought to create it in his own works.

Dodge had a very close cadre of friends both in Glens Falls, New York, where he was curator of The Hyde Collection for twenty-one years, and in Jacksonville, Florida, where he was director of the Cummer Gallery of Art for ten years and where he retired in 1972. Dodge also remained lifelong friends with school chums David Mills, William French, and William Swift. During his years in Jacksonville, Jeanne and Edward Klempf, attorney Jeffrey Dunn, and architect Taylor «Cinder» Hardwick were the artist's closest confidants. Dodge had lunch with Hardwick nearly every Friday and he spoke to Jeanne Klempf and Jeff Dunn almost daily. In a newspaper article about the role Jeanne Klempf played as the painter's primary model, she recalled that the day had not begun if she and Jerry had not exchanged belly laughs.[3]

Dodge laughed readily and often. He was a man of many interests and much enthusiasm and maintained a *joie de vivre* throughout his life. Jerry enjoyed his friends and family; loved reading mysteries and a wide variety of journals, magazines, art books, and catalogues; and liked watching tennis and a variety of sports. He reveled in spending time alone, a prob-

able extension of his upbringing as an only child. Dodge once noted that the only times he felt bored were when in the company of others. He also relished traveling. Sometimes he traveled alone, but more often, Jerry preferred to travel in the company of his close friends or family members. Dodge could be intimidating, for he was highly intelligent and opinionated, and as his brother-in-law Dugald MacArthur once observed, he carried himself with a patrician hauteur at times. For all of his achievements, Dodge could also be shy. To his friends, Jerry was generous, interested, loyal, fun loving, and always interesting

An accomplished photographer, Dodge shot literally thousands of rolls of film in his lifetime. Hardwick, Klempf, and Mills share vivid memories of Jerry on trips where he spent hours, sometimes days, photographing sights. He would wait tirelessly for precisely the right light or for the clouds to move into a desired position. Hardwick recalls traveling with Dodge from Boston to Maine. A trip by car that would normally have taken several hours took two days as the enraptured Dodge photographed countless aspects of one of his favorite coastlines. David Mills remembers many such instances from their travels together, such as the time Dodge spent the better part of a day sitting in a public plaza in Quito, Ecuador, shooting rolls of film of the passing spectacle of humanity. Dodge carefully screened, labeled, and filed his slides for possible use in future compositions.

Fig. 4 (*top left page*) —Detail: **Joseph Jeffers Dodge and Duke Ellington**, Jacksonville University, March 7, 1974

Fig. 5 (*above*) —**Wedding photograph**: (L-R) Joseph M. Dodge, Joseph J. Dodge and Dorothy M. Dodge, 1949

Fig. 6 —Detail: **Dodge lecturing at The Hyde Collection**

Fig. 7 —*TIME* cover of Joseph Dodge, January 24, 1955

A major source of information on the artist's life leading up to 1962, when he and his family moved to Jacksonville, Florida, is a series of tapes recorded by the artist in 1995.[4] These autobiographical musings, transcribed and to date unedited, provide insights into his past as well as reminiscences of childhood through the college years at Harvard University. They recount eloping, embarking on a career, the birth of his first son, and a failed marriage. Dodge describes romances; the heady New York scene with Alan Jay Lerner and Duke Ellington; friendships with luminaries such as sculptor David Smith and his wife, artist Dorothy Dehner; a second marriage, to Dorothy MacArthur; and the forming of a new family. In these recordings Dodge also remembers fondly the generosity of Charlotte Pruyn Hyde, who with her husband, Louis Fiske Hyde, formed one of the great private art collections in New York. During his twenty-one years as curator for The Hyde Collection, Dodge was instrumental in assisting Mrs. Hyde in transforming the collection into a public resource. Dodge's accounts of these years reflect an astonishing variety of activities that call to mind a court artist working for a great patron.

In addition to the autobiographical recordings, two unpublished and untitled lectures provide a tremendous amount of information about Dodge's works until about 1970. The first of these lectures was delivered at the University of Florida on April 2, 1969, in conjunction with an exhibition of his works.[5]

The second, similar to the 1969 lecture, contains a few alterations and additions and was presented at the Jacksonville Art Museum on June 28, 1990.[6]

Dodge not only exhibited consistently over the years; critics reviewed his work consistently, and most often, positively. The artist was fastidious about saving clippings. During the last half of Dodge's life in Jacksonville, several local critics wrote about him, most importantly Elihu Edelson, Cynthia Parks, Judy Wells, Catherine Enns, and gallery owner and art dealer Jacqueline Holmes. Their writings form a body of contemporary criticism that reflects the general esteem in which Dodge's work was held in northeast Florida.

Joseph Jeffers, «Jerry,» Dodge was admired and celebrated for his contributions to the cultural legacy of Glens Falls, New York, and Jacksonville, Florida. He left his own works and those from his private collection to numerous institutions including Choate, Harvard University, The Hyde Collection, and the Cummer Museum of Art & Gardens. His paintings and drawings are housed in private and public collections in this country and abroad. It is the goal of this volume to chronicle and document the achievements of this widely respected artist and man.

Joseph Jeffers Dodge—The Life of the Artist

From Detroit to Glens Falls: 1917-1941

The only child of Julia Jane Jeffers (1891-1970) and Joseph Morrell Dodge (1890-1964), Joseph Jeffers Dodge was born in Detroit, Michigan, on August 9, 1917. Both father and grandfather were Josephs, and because neither Joe nor Joey was particularly to his parents' liking, this redheaded baby was called Jerry practically from birth. The boy lived a life of advantage, yet in later years Jerry Dodge would insist he was never spoiled. This life of privilege, of the private schools Choate and Harvard, was in part the result of the illustrious achievements realized by his father, Joseph Morrell Dodge, whose stellar career was characterized by hard work, outstanding accomplishments, and national prominence.

Jerry Dodge's father, Joe, was born in Detroit on November 18, 1890, and died there December 2, 1964. He worked as the vice president and sales manager of the Thomas J. Doyle Dodge Automobile agency in Detroit. The Joseph Morrell Dodge family was not related to the famous automobile Dodge brothers, but being in the same business in the heyday of Detroit exposed the bright and ambitious Dodge to a wide variety of people from numerous walks of life. Dodge decided he needed to make a move because Doyle was not going to retire and did not plan to sell.

After considering going into business for himself, Dodge received and accepted an offer from the First National Bank, thereby becoming the youngest bank examiner in Michigan.

Although Jerry's father never attended college, the elder Dodge rose to the position of bank president and served under four United States presidents. In occupied Germany between 1945 and 1946, Joe Dodge served under Generals Lucius D. Clay, Dwight D. Eisenhower, and John J. McCloy, and oversaw financial reforms leading to the creation of a new German monetary policy. President Truman appointed the senior Dodge in 1947 as a United States minister representing the United States at the Austrian Treaty Commission in Vienna. Dodge was Deputy for Austrian Affairs to Secretary of State (General) George C. Marshall at the Council of Foreign Ministers meeting in London in 1947. In another appointment by President Truman, Dodge served as United States Minister and Financial Adviser to General MacArthur in Japan between 1949 and 1951, where he «overhauled the government's budget and currency and cut the highly inflated Japanese economy down to size.»[7]

Under the Eisenhower administration Jerry's father was the first man appointed to cabinet level. As Director of the Bureau of the Budget, Joe Dodge was the first budget director asked to attend all meetings of the Cabinet and the National Security Council. The elder Dodge appeared on the cover of *TIME* magazine, January 24, 1955, and was the subject of numerous articles and editorial cartoons because of his fiscal policies and cost-cutting measures.[8] From the mid-1930s until his retirement a few years before his death in 1964, Joe Dodge was Chief Executive Officer of the Detroit Bank, which is now Comerica Bank.

The senior Joseph Dodge met his future bride, Julia Jane Jeffers, when he was the bank examiner in Michigan at First National Bank. She and her older sister lost both parents at an early age: their mother as the result of complications from giving birth, and their father several years later. Their mother's sister, Eliza Foote Packard, took in Julia Jane. The Packards operated a prosperous farm and feed business near Charlotte, Michigan. Mr. O. E. Packard, Eliza's husband, was also a bank director. While Dodge was examining the books of the Charlotte bank, he impressed Mr. Packard, who invited the promising young man home for dinner. Thus began the Julia Jane Jeffers and Joseph Morrell Dodge romance. They married June 28, 1916.

Dodge remembered his mother as:

> ... a very warm and loving person. I wish I had her completely unselfconscious and genuine enjoyment with meeting people and getting along. She could walk into any room, any situation and be completely at ease. She wasn't what I would call an intellectual by any means. She wasn't stupid but she wasn't interested in anything like that particularly. She made friends easily.[9]

His father:

> ... on the other hand was shy, standoffish, and a little bit awkward. You could tell when he was forcing himself to be sociable. He learned to tell a few jokes and learned to be gracious, but it was an effort. He was extremely self-disciplined and self-controlled, perhaps cold in some ways. He couldn't express his feelings, and I guess people thought he had none. He made a point of remembering names and knowing something about people. He wrote thank you notes and remembered birthdays. He was very organized in that respect. He wanted to be liked but he didn't know how to do it in that easy, genuine, and relaxed way that Mother did.
>
> There were lots of very fine things about my Father. The common denominator, or basis of his achievements was his sense of organization. Whether it was business, the National Budget, a diplomatic mission, the banking business, arranging his bureau drawers, his clothes in the closet, or his books in the library, everything was logically ordered.... He did it for a purpose, because things worked better that way.... I learned a great deal from that. I think that's one of the principal good qualities of my painting and a lot of things I do. If I've inherited anything from him that has affected my art and my life, it is this instinct for order.[10]

Jerry's father was committed to exposing his son to a rich variety of experiences and to the very best of everything, which included attending performances by the classical pianist Paderewski and the jazz great Duke Ellington; seeing the legendary Barrymores perform Shakespeare; witnessing the staging of a Stravinsky Ballet; and of course, rooting for the hometown team, the Detroit Tigers. Jerry also met Tom Mix, the cowboy star. In 1926 the young Dodge had the privilege of visiting the Ringling Brothers Circus the day before it opened to the public. The nine year old was invited to have lunch with the clowns and watch the elephants pull up the tent posts. The older Dodge enjoyed watching the Indianapolis auto races, something his son found infinitely boring, and took his son to the Dayton air shows and races to which airplanes came from all over the world to compete. Jerry also attended boxing matches with his father who was an ardent boxing fan and had been an amateur boxer in school.

Joseph Dodge senior was an enthusiastic and voracious reader.[11] His large library of books devoted to economics, biographies, history, and philosophy provided his son with a wealth and readily accessible source of knowledge. The library was also peppered with mysteries, which Joseph senior delighted in reading as a form of relaxation. Here the young Jerry discovered Agatha Christie, Dashell Hammett, and Georges Simenon. Reading good mysteries was a hobby he would pursue throughout his life.

As the senior Dodge's career advanced, the family moved to a house at 375 Washington Road in suburban Grosse Pointe in 1927 or 1928. The younger Dodge left the public school system and began the fifth grade at the Grosse Pointe Country Day School, where there were about twenty children in his class. English instruction was quite good and Jerry recalled that students in the ninth grade routinely excelled in the college board examinations.[12] As a schoolboy Jerry Dodge played the usual sports: baseball, basketball, and football. He made close friends with the Mills brothers, David and William. Sadly, William died in WWII. Dave, however, became Dodge's roommate at both Choate and Harvard and remained one of Jerry's closest friends for more than sixty years.

Jerry Dodge spent a considerable amount of time drawing as a youngster. This childhood interest was not surprising, given that relatives on both the Jeffers and Dodge sides of the family had been involved in the arts.[13] Dodge's maternal grandfather, Alvord Pomeroy Jeffers, was a newspaper illustrator who specialized in sketching courtroom activities. His maternal grandmother, Mary Veronica Foote Jeffers, created small oil paintings in the 1880s of white roses, some of which are still in existence. One such painting titled *White Roses* (1887) is in a Dodge family album, along with a portrait drawn by Edward A. Foote, Mary Veronica's father.[14] It was typical of families during this era to pursue drawing and painting, which were considered refined and cultured activities.[15] Jerry remembered with fondness an uncle, Paul Crow, from his father's mother's side of the family. Uncle Paul was an artist, craftsman, and musician who made and played violins. He was also an accomplished chess player and it was he who took his great nephew, Jerry, at an early age to see an exhibition of works by Picasso.[16] In addition, the artist's paternal grandfather, Joseph Cheeseman Dodge, was a sign painter who taught Jerry Dodge's father, as well as his uncle Irving C. (Pete) Dodge, how to draw. Pete Dodge became a designer of small buildings and gas stations and enjoyed a successful career in southern California without ever becoming a licensed architect. In turn it was Uncle Pete who taught the young Dodge the rudiments of drawing.

As an only child Jerry spent hours reading childhood classics and sought out illustrated editions, which inspired him to draw. Uncle Pete also introduced his nephew to *Fix Bayonets!*, by Colonel John W. Thomason Jr., U.S.M.C. The book was a record and

illustrated account of Thomason's wartime experiences. Even late in life Dodge remembered vividly the collection of lively sketches by the author.[17] Other literary influences on Jerry included *Treasure Island, The Three Musketeers* and its sequels, and *The Count of Monte Cristo*. Dodge, who especially enjoyed French fiction, treasured an edition of *The Three Musketeers* that had illustrations by Maurice LeLoir.[18] Dodge noted about LeLoir's work, «He did very good, kind of French Academy, Meissonier-like illustrations every two or three pages. Some were vignettes and some were full page, and they were wonderful.»[19] In addition to LeLoir's vignettes, Dodge appreciated the great illustrations found in *The Saturday Evening Post*, the *New Yorker*, Rockwell Kent's *Moby Dick*, and N.C. Wyeth's *Treasure Island*. Dodge also admired the work of Frederick Remington, and another western artist and writer, Will James.

Of his childhood drawing hobby Dodge remembered:

> I used to draw ... a lot on scraps of paper and in the margins of my notebooks during school. I drew airplanes, cars, athletes, football players, baseball players and the teachers and my friends in class, and sometimes a movie star of the female variety. I also drew lots of maps and plans of imaginary places. One of the things I think was characteristic was that, although I would sometimes draw particular airplanes or particular cars, as often as not I would try to make improvements on them, redesign them, or make fantasy cars of my own. For a while I thought I might go into industrial design or automotive design, but I think I would have been better as an architect. I was never really content to draw things as they were. I was always trying to improve, change or make-up something out of whole-cloth, so to speak, or depict some fantasy or something imagined of my own.[20]

A list, handwritten by Jerry Dodge and found in his papers at his death, foreshadowed his mature habit of drawing as a ritual. It was titled «My Early Drawing, (As Best I Remember) more or less chronologically.» Upon reading the list later in life, he recognized the obsessive characteristics of his mature work in early artistic projects and added an important notation in the left margin (the underlining is Dodge's):

> [A]pparently drawing was very much a ritual, done over and over to perfection. The act was more important than [the] finished product, the working out, distilling and perfecting of the subject was the only consideration—an art of possession, a magic materialization of my fantasies or desires or interests, making it real, perfect and beautiful in itself and not as a work of art.[21]

When Jerry was ten, his father was so impressed by his son's artistic creations that he thought the boy should receive some professional art instruction. The father enrolled Jerry in the downtown Detroit

Scarab Club, signing him up for a life drawing class. The young Dodge, however, was completely out of place, because it was an adult class and he was already very shy. Mortified, he only attended the class a couple of times. In thinking about his parents' reaction to their son's enthusiasm for art, Jerry remembered:

> My parents were certainly not against [my] being in the art world. They were supportive and were pleased when I did well. My father was very conservative. There was no money in his family and certainly none in mother's. He just wanted to make sure that I had a good education, the best that he could provide for me, and that I could do something that was self-supporting. So he was never against [my] going into the arts, but he was always making sure that I really wanted to do it and that I knew what I was doing. And he insisted that I have enough of a general education so that, if it didn't work out, I could do something else.[22]

Interested in art and influenced by his Uncle Pete, Jerry aspired to be an architect. Dodge recalled how these aspirations were dashed when his eyesight began to weaken. A doctor informed Jerry's parents that the eyes of their very myopic child, who had already worn thick glasses for some time, would not stand the intense strain architectural study would demand. In retrospect this is quite ironic, for scrutiny of Dodge's paintings reveals his meticulous attention to minute and painstaking detail.[23] Dodge recollected:

> I think I might have been pretty good as an architect or designer; but, on that single judgment—perhaps right, perhaps wrong, the focus of my life changed, and for several years after, I had no particular direction or goal.[24]

Yet even with this disappointment, the young Dodge had what in retrospect seemed like an idyllic childhood. While he continued to develop his drawing skills, Jerry was also developing an intense interest in jazz and swing. In the early thirties he was captivated by the music of Duke Ellington:

> For some reason my grandmother [Gertrude Crow Dodge] was sympathetic to this. When Ellington came to Detroit around 1931-32, he played at one of the downtown movie theaters. In those days, there were often big elaborate stage productions between the movies. The movie, newsreel, and one-reel comedies would be shown, and then the bands or some other stage acts would play for an hour or so, and then the films would be repeated, and so on. My grandmother, knowing my interest, took me on the bus downtown to this theater. You can imagine this fluttery, genteel Victorian lady with her hat and her gloves and this barely teen-age kid, possibly in knee-pants, taking a long bus ride to downtown Detroit, to see a Negro jazz band— amazing! She took me to see Ellington twice. I'm eternally grateful to her for that.[25]

Fig. 8 —Detail: **Jerry and his father in Carmel, California**, 1926

Dodge actually met his musical hero several years later in what would turn out to be a defining moment in the teenager's life. He recalled that about:

> ... 1934 maybe, Ellington came through the Midwest and went to the ballrooms and big amusement parks. There was one on our side of town called Eastwood Gardens.... Ellington would broadcast on local radio from these places at night. One time, I must have been fourteen or fifteen, Mother and Dad took me out there and left me.... I went in this large ballroom and just stood by the band, by myself. I had a little Brownie camera and took some pictures, which I still have.... It was very exciting and I did it a couple of nights. My parents would come and pick me up about 11:00. I remember the second night I was there I got to talk to Duke for a little bit. I stood in front of him and I guess he realized I was interested and appreciative and he said, «You should have been here last night.» I said «why?» and he said, «Well, we rehearsed a new thing that's kind of interesting, it's a little bit different.» I think he gave me the title of it then and it turned out to be his longest and most ambitious composition to date. It came out a bit later on four sides of two records called *Reminiscing in Tempo*. It was quite revolutionary and caused a big stir in the Jazz and music world. A lot of people were saying it wasn't Jazz and he was betraying his tradition. It's still one of my favorite things.[26]

This meeting thrilled the young Dodge and planted the seed of what would eventually become a long friendship.

Another major influence in the life of the artist occurred when Jerry was about eleven and he traveled out west by train with his parents. He remembered:

> [T]wo things absolutely bowled me over. The first was a stop by train at the Grand Canyon. I didn't know what to expect. When I walked up to the low stone wall, along the

rim and looked over ... well, there [are] no words to describe the sensation. The only experience I've had to compare was when I first walked into Chartres Cathedral, but that was much, much later. The other experience was the California coast, near Carmel, especially at Point Lobos. The Grand Canyon was overwhelming, but the Carmel coast was more human in scale, and awoke all sorts of romantic feelings, perhaps some dim echo of the south English coast, near Devon, where my family originated centuries ago. Who knows? Anyway, I've made a point to return to Carmel every chance I get and have never been disappointed, and for years afterwards, I fantasized living there in a house of my design.[27]

Dodge had a great affinity for rocky coastlines and for rock formations in general, including them in many works inspired by his travels. He was especially drawn to the western and eastern shores of the United States, most notably Midway Point near Carmel, California. These rocky coastlines and formations would become recurring subjects in his work.

Throughout high school Jerry continued to draw, producing illustrations for the Detroit University School newspaper for which he was editor and artist. He also provided portrait sketches of his senior class in the 1935 edition of *The Helicon*, the Detroit University School yearbook.[28] During these late teenage years Dodge would draw portraits of famous people, usually based on photographs, including Duke Ellington, Joe Louis, Henry Ford, and President Franklin Roosevelt (pl. 2).[29] Dodge managed to have all of the portraits autographed, but unfortunately, all but the portrait of Roosevelt were stolen during one of his moves. Dodge noted jokingly that he had «to assume that the thief was a Republican.»[30] Furthermore, the mother of his life-long friend and college roommate, David Mills, made arrangements for the young Dodge to visit the scaffolding to watch Diego Rivera paint the murals of *Detroit Industry* in The Detroit Institute of Arts sometime between 1932 and 1933.[31]

After high school Dodge attended Choate in Wallingford, Connecticut, for the 1935-36 academic year. As he had done in high school, Jerry turned out illustrations and vignettes for the yearbook, among them a portrait of the headmaster, *The Faculty*, and *The Alumni*.[32] Dodge was also active in contributing to the literary magazine, which published a short illustrated poem of his titled «*Jazz*» (1935, pl. 1), inspired by the sights and sounds of the Duke Ellington orchestra.[33] In 1965, thirty years later, the poem was included in a Choate memorial anthology, which also published entries by John Dos Passos, Edward Albee, Paul Mellon, and Avery Dulles.[34] The illustrated poem remains a fitting testimony to Jerry Dodge's enduring passion for jazz, especially for the music of Duke Ellington.[35] Dodge once observed, «I fell in love with the music of Duke Ellington ... and have been in love with it ever since.

It has been the one constant in my life, and the older I get, and the more of it I hear, the more of my musical needs it fulfills.»[36]

From Choate, Dodge went on to attend Harvard University. Dodge's files contain an interesting and telling letter written by his father. Responding to a request for information about incoming students from Delmar Leighton, the Harvard dean of freshmen, the elder Dodge's insights summed up many of his son's traits especially his «natural artistic ability» [see opposite page].

Harvard's eminent art history professors Edwin Forbes and Arthur Pope offered a sequence of courses in design and techniques. Pope's required design course covered the modes of painting and drawing as the techniques applied to art history.[38] Dodge remembers the course as being interesting, complete, and his favorite, despite his feeling that Pope was less than a compelling lecturer. Pope had been a protégé of Denman Ross, a well-known aesthetic theoretician in Boston, who had categorized systems of color after analyzing the palettes of numerous artists, including Giotto and Titian. Ross then assessed the painters' approaches to color.[39] Forbes, who was described as a «kindly, soft-spoken, rumpled, absentminded, and profoundly curious man,» taught historical techniques. His students made a fresco, or tempera; they also learned pointillism and gilding, among many other techniques.[40] Dodge enjoyed the course so much, he audited it again in his junior and senior years.

Being in these courses at Harvard taught Jerry Dodge the discipline to make quick thumbnail sketches of the hundreds of slides of great works of art shown in his art history classes. The skill served him well as an artist and he heartily recommended this practice to his own students years later. Incorporating the discipline in his work early on, Dodge's 1938 notebooks include thumbnail sketches of Asian art and a drawing of the interior of St. Peter's Basilica in Rome. The image of a fencing match, a sport that Jerry lettered in at Choate and Harvard, enlivens one page.[41]

Reflecting on his education, Dodge noted that if he could have added one experience to his training, it would have been that of spending several years as an apprentice in an artist's workshop like that of Bellini, Rubens, or David, or in an academy taught by a Gérôme or an Eakins, thoroughly learning the craft of painting. He was convinced that an early fluency in the vocabulary, grammar, and syntax of painting would have allowed him to concentrate more on what to do rather than how to do it.[42]

Until the young artist attended Harvard, he had seen «very little real art, but then, all at once, it seems, I was hit by the whole history of world art,

August 24, 1936

Dear Mr. Leighton:

This is in reply to your letter of August 13th requesting information about my son, Joseph J. (Jerry) Dodge. As your records will show, he is a graduate of the Grosse Pointe Country Day School, the Detroit University School and The Choate School.

At the Detroit University School he and another boy organized, edited and distributed a weekly school newspaper. At the Choate School he was on the Board of the «Literary Magazine» and also of «The Brief.» He was the art editor of the latter publication and had the unusual distinction of doing all the art work and illustrating for the 1936 edition. My recollection is that there [were] some dozen to fifteen full pages of black and white pen and ink and brush art work, plus the supplementary headings and minor illustrations. These included full page crayon portraits of the Head Master, Mr. St. John, and Mrs. St. John. As a result of this work, he was given the art prize at the school.

He seems to have a natural artistic ability, without being in the least bit «arty» as far as his personal characteristics are concerned. This ability is evident not only in his drawing and portrait work, but in photography, and extends into industrial and architectural design. It is apparently a self-acquired ability, which showed up in his early youth, and which he developed by himself without any regularly organized instruction. In the graduating book of the Detroit University School he had two full pages of portraits which he drew of the entire membership of the graduating class.

He has amused himself at odd moments with the drawing of portraits of prominent people on which he has obtained their autographs. These include Franklin Roosevelt, Henry Ford, Alexander Woolcott, Bing Crosby, Duke Ellington and Joe Louis. Quite a catholic collection.

His major sport interest is tennis. He started in at football and baseball but had to be denied those sports because of bad eyes. He is near-sighted and partially color-blind, which latter condition restricts his art to black and white. His eyes appear to have improved a great deal in the last two years. In this last year at Choate he apparently had very little difficulty although there was a period of time several years ago when his reading had to be strictly limited. This eye condition was reported to the Masters at Choate who kept him under observation to make sure he did not over strain them. We see he is supplied lamps for his room so he has proper lighting conditions for study. In every other respect his general health is excellent.

So far he has shown no disposition to be wild or unruly, and he has no taste for hard liquor although he will drink a little wine occasionally. One of the school requirements imposed by his family, to which he readily agrees, was that there was to be no whiskey or gin or cocktails. It can be fairly said of him that he has never given his family or anyone else we know of any trouble.

I believe his standings in English and Literature have been above average. It is a subject he apparently enjoys. He shows a disposition to read only the best of books. This vacation I noticed his principal reading has been *The Three Musketeers*, *Twenty Years After* and the *Forty-Five Guardsmen* (in French), the *Life of Cellini*, and books of that type, which are his own preference.

His selection of Harvard as his school seems to have been largely based on his intellectual standing. He is not a «grind» either in manner or attitude toward study. He seems to get his lessons easily and well. He has no ambition to be the best student but seems to rank high in the subjects which interest him, without much effort. He is very self sufficient and has definite ideas and definite interests. I have never known him to seek the association of second rate people. Social position or wealth apparently carry no weight with him unless the individual has something to offer.

I think his major fault is possibly a disposition to be too selective about the things he does and the individuals with whom he cares to associate. He will take an extreme interest in anything which appeals to him and has a tendency to disregard things which do not.

He is rather reserved in manner but apparently makes friends easily and has many of them. He is not at all inclined to run to «cliques» and seems to hold the respect and friendship of both boys and girls.

Ever since he was very young he has traveled extensively in the United States (never abroad). For the last two summers he has motored with two school mates through the West and is at present on a tour through Glacier National Park, Banff, Lake Louise and down the West Coast to San Francisco. Last summer the boys covered the district South of San Francisco.

Very truly yours,
Joseph Morrell Dodge[37]

Fig. 9 —Detail: **Joseph Jeffers Dodge and Jane Pike**

not only in the slide courses, but with the real thing.»[43] Dodge was immersed in and overwhelmed by the magnificent cultural and artistic resources in Cambridge and Boston. Thinking back on visiting Harvard's outstanding University Museum, the Fogg; Boston's all encompassing Museum of Fine Arts; and the eccentric but jewel-like Isabella Stewart Gardner Museum, Dodge remembered «I was like a starving person in a super-market and I really stuffed myself!» The rich artistic feast provided by these museums «took years to work its way through my system, but the residue of artistic vitamins, nutrients and fat has continued to nourish my work ever since.»[44]

Dodge's senior honors thesis, submitted in April, 1940, was titled *An Introduction to Landscape in French Eighteenth Century Drawing and Painting.* The thesis signaled his early love for French painting, especially the landscape. In 134 pages with 175 illustrations, Dodge considered the historical, social, and cultural backgrounds, as well as the varying categories within the landscape genre. It is interesting to see the thoroughness of his study knowing how Dodge's predilection for contemporary pastoral settings would develop in his own career as an artist.

Dodge recalled with deep appreciation his education at Harvard and realized he had had the privilege of studying with one of the most distinguished art history faculty in the world at that time. His tutor, acclaimed Renaissance art historian the late Sydney Freedberg, remained a lifelong friend. Dodge's training at Harvard introduced him to a philosophy that he often espoused: a college could not and should not attempt to produce artists in the same way it trains doctors and lawyers. Dodge noted:

> One can teach art as knowledge—where, in fact, there are things that are knowable, and one can train the skills, of course, but trying to teach, or measure for grades or diplomas, such things as imagination, sensitivity, and the like—the really important things about art—seems like wishful thinking at best—if not downright fraud.[45]

This viewpoint reflects the influence of his Harvard faculty, especially of Edward Forbes who remarked:

> The purpose of a university Fine Arts Department is not the creation of artists. It is in the first place to give a large number of men familiarity with the art heritage of our civilization and to arouse or create in them that love of the arts which is theirs by inherent right, and to make it an integral, vital part [of] their lives. In the second place it should give to a limited number of men the training and experience necessary to enable them to serve as curators and directors of museums, or connoisseurs, critics, and teachers of the arts.[46]

In 1938, Dodge eloped with Jane Holliday Pike (b. 1920) whom he had met through his cousin Betsy Lay. The Pikes lived in Indian Village, a residential area close to Detroit. The romance began one summer when the Dodges and the Pikes rented summer cottages near Charlevoix on Lake Michigan. Dodge recalled:

> We fell passionately in love, and having been brought up the way we were, getting married was the only solution to our desires and our passions. So we eloped.... We drove from Detroit and stopped at Charlotte, Michigan, mother's home town, where we were married by a Justice of the Peace who ... was a ... cousin to mother. We spent our honeymoon ... in Chicago.... when we came back, we tried to keep it a secret.... The news got out very quickly.... There was a gathering of the families and much discussion. It was decided that the marriage would be encouraged and provisions were made for Jane to come with me to Harvard. It was my Junior year.... In retrospect, I don't think it was such a great idea. My marks didn't suffer particularly. I was still able to graduate with honors.... But I think I missed out on a lot of things.[47]

After Dodge's graduation from Harvard with honors in 1940, the young couple returned to Detroit. Dodge began graduate studies, enrolling at Wayne State University for a master's degree. He also worked for a year in a bank «at the lowest rung of a ladder I had no desire to climb.»[48] A son, Joseph Morrell Dodge II, called Jamie, was born in 1941. Dodge applied for a position at The Detroit Institute of Arts but was the second choice. The director of the DIA at the time was William Valentiner, and it was he who would be instrumental in Dodge's appointment as curator for an excellent, little known, yet growing collection of art being amassed by a widowed heiress in Glens Falls, New York.

Glens Falls and The Hyde Collection

Glens Falls, New York, situated on the Hudson River, is the gateway to the Adirondacks and Lake George. It was there that Samuel Pruyn made his fortune in mining, lumbering, canal transportation, and paper manufacturing.[49] The eldest of his three daughters, Charlotte Pruyn (1867-1963) was born in Glens Falls in 1867. In 1888 she was sent to a finishing school in Boston and met Louis Fiske Hyde (1866-1934), a Harvard Law School student who was a tenant in the same boarding house. They married in 1901, thirteen years after they met. The couple lived in Boston and were friends of Charles Eliot Norton and Bernard Berenson.[50] They also knew Isabella Stewart Gardner and were quite familiar with her residence and collection on Fenway Court, which was opened to the public in 1903. The couple moved to Glens Falls in 1907 when Hyde was convinced by the elderly Mr. Pruyn to become vice president of the family paper business, Finch, Pruyn and Company, Inc.

In 1910 the Hyde House was commissioned and styled in the manner of a Florentine Renaissance villa. Boston architect Henry Forbes Bigelow designed the home, which has a central courtyard like the Gardner museum in Boston. The Hyde mansion was marked by restraint rather than flamboyance, however, a distinction that was characteristic of the Hydes' approach to philanthropy as well. They shunned publicity and unnecessary public display. «Unassuming to the point of self-effacement, they nurtured late Victorian proprieties.»[51] Hyde House overlooked the Hudson River in close proximity to the Finch, Pruyn lumber and paper manufacturing plant. It became part of a family compound that also included the homes of Charlotte's two younger sisters and their husbands.

By 1920 the Hydes had started to collect fine art in earnest beginning with the purchase of a small predella panel, the Botticelli *Annunciation*.[52] Relying on advice from the famed connoisseur Bernard Berenson, and also from William R. Valentiner, the couple made wise choices including the acquisition of *A Portrait of Christ* by Rembrandt, which has been called «one of the great Protestant religious expressions in the world.»[53] At the time of Louis Hyde's death in 1934, one-third of the current collection had been assembled.

Charlotte continued to collect judiciously and concentrated on the educational possibilities of her growing collection. She hired two curators. The first was Otto Wittman Jr. who had graduated from Mr. Hyde's *alma mater* Harvard, once dubbed as the «West Point of museum directors.» Wittman had been trained in the museum course taught by the almost legendary Paul J.

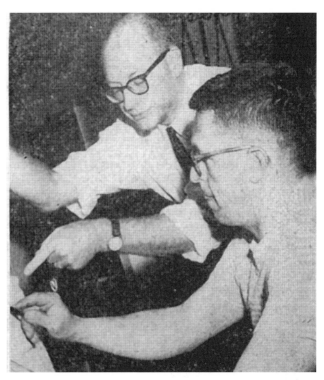

Fig. 10 —**Jerry instructing at The Hyde**

Sachs.[54] Wittman, however, was drafted into the army in 1941, where he helped in the restitution of looted art treasures. After the war Wittman became director of the Toledo Art Museum.

William Valentiner, an internationally known connoisseur, director of The Detroit Institute of Arts, and adviser to Mrs. Hyde, recommended the second curator. Valentiner had recently interviewed Jerry Dodge for a position at the DIA based on recommendations made by Harvard faculty members he knew. Dodge was a strong candidate for The Hyde because he was an honors graduate in Fine Arts, because of his recent marriage and fatherhood, and because very poor eyesight made him an unlikely candidate for military service. Mrs. Hyde hired him in 1941. Dodge remembered Mrs. Hyde fondly:

> She was kind of a funny woman in a way. She was very short and round. You could say that she was fat and jolly. She had thick glasses and dressed very plainly in simple black dresses and a cloth coat. Some dealers told me about this rather plainly dressed woman who would appear and look around and ask questions and so forth. Nobody took her seriously for a while until gradually word got around that she was building up quite an art collection.[55]

Charlotte Hyde was an astute collector who sought excellent counsel before acquiring works of art. Dodge advised her on purchases that included a Jean-Honoré Fragonard wash drawing, three works by Pablo Picasso, a Georges Braque Cubist painting, a Childe Hassam pastel, and a John Frederick Peto still life, among a number of other pieces.[56] Dodge

21

Fig.11 —**Dorothy M. Dodge at David Smith's**, Bolton Landing

noted, «she had an eye and an absolutely fantastic sense of color. She had what could be called the equivalent of perfect pitch» in terms of color.[57]

Mrs. Hyde had the business acumen to realize that because the great majority of the collectors at the time were men, portraits or representations of male subjects by important artists were often undervalued, especially when compared to paintings of female sitters.[58] The Hyde Collection includes *Portrait of a Young Man* attributed to Raphael, *St. James* by El Greco, the Tintoretto portrait of *Doge Alvise Mocenigo, Man in Armor* by Rubens, and *Portrait of Jan van den Wouwere* by Anthony van Dyck.[59] Mrs. Hyde also collected very fine examples of American paintings. In addition to purchasing works by Peto and Hassam, she acquired works by Thomas Eakins, Elihu Vedder, and Winslow Homer.[60]

In 1952 Charlotte Pruyn Hyde endowed a trust in order to establish the basis for transforming the Hyde House into The Hyde Collection. Even before the death of her husband, offers were made from the Metropolitan Museum in New York City and the Fogg Museum at Harvard expressing interest in securing the collection. Mrs. Hyde remained steadfast in her determination to offer the collection and the Italianate villa that contained it to the city and populace of Glens Falls. Until her death, the widowed Mrs. Louis Hyde, whose portrait

was painted by Dodge in 1944, lived in the mansion on the Hudson River amidst a whirlwind of classes, concerts, and tours of the very fine collection she and her husband had amassed. She died in her beloved home in 1963. In an article about her life and death, the local newspaper noted her art collection but focused on her as a «patron of music and a generous contributor to many other phases of the cultural life of the community. Her quiet philanthropy was known to few.»[61]

The Glens Falls Years: 1941-1962

During his twenty-one years as curator of The Hyde Collection, Dodge oversaw the transformation of the Hyde's private collection into a public art museum and cultural center.[62] His work at what has been called «one of the finest small art collections in America,» was significant.[63] Dodge «aggressively pursued an accessions policy of 'gap filling' ... he was firm in insisting that the collection include work by modern artists, and he was instrumental in the purchase of three Picassos.»[64]

The «one-man-band» at the Hyde, Dodge gave advice for purchases; arranged and installed exhibitions, especially at the Crandall Library in Glens Falls; and taught drawing, painting, art appreciation, and art history. During the summer of 1943, Dodge studied with Yasuo Kuniyoshi in Woodstock, New York, where he also met artist Eugene Speicher. Dodge had started painting in earnest by this time and Mrs. Hyde encouraged his participation in Kuniyoshi's workshop. Dodge offered art classes at The Hyde utilizing what he had learned in Pope's and Forbes's classes at Harvard and began to make colored compositions. He wrote a weekly column called «The Visual Arts» for the *Glens Falls Post Star*. Dodge also taught at several local colleges, including Hamilton College where he became friends with noted artist William Palmer.[65] Dodge exhibited his own paintings regularly in exhibitions throughout the upper Hudson area and in New York City at The Wildenstein and Hirschl & Adler Galleries.[66]

Dodge's first marriage to Jane Holliday Pike dissolved three years later in 1941 after their move to Glens Falls. They divorced in 1949. Dodge's son, Joseph «Jamie» Morrell Dodge II, went to live with his paternal grandparents. Due to the demands of public service, the elder Dodges traveled often during these years. Jamie spent those periods with David Mills's family in Detroit. In 1953, four years after Dodge remarried, Jamie returned to live with his father, stepmother, and baby sister in Glens Falls.

Jerry Dodge's participation in the Glens Falls Rotary Club provided him the opportunity to meet Stanley MacArthur, vice-president and managing director of the Portland Cement company. He remembered MacArthur as «bright, well-read, entertaining and opinionated—especially after a few drinks.» One evening when Dodge was playing bridge in MacArthur's home, he met MacArthur's daughter Dorothy who was home after graduating from Hood College in Maryland. Dodge married Dorothy MacArthur (1925-2000), September 24, 1949, and that union produced four children: Dorothy «Tia» van Orden (1952-1993), Julia «Julie» Jeffers (b. 1954), Jeffers MacArthur (b. 1955), and Lisa Morrell (b. 1956).

Dodge remembered his friendships during his two decades in Glens Falls as being rich and satisfying. His circle included noted illustrator Douglass Crockwell; internationally-renowned sculptor David Smith, one of his closest friends; and Smith's first wife, painter and sculptor Dorothy Dehner.[67] Crockwell, a nationally-known commercial artist, created illustrations for products like Welch's Concord Grape Jelly™. Dodge recalled, «because of obvious similarities in names, Douglass Crockwell, Norman Rockwell and Rockwell Kent all got kind of confused at times in people's minds.»[68] Crockwell worked entirely from photographs and used Dodge, Dorothy, and their children in several of his compositions.[69]

In the late 1930s Dorothy Dehner had begun working on small-scale paintings inspired by medieval books of hours.[70] Titled *Life on the Farm*, the series depicted Dehner's life at Bolton Landing. She included Jamie Dodge in one of these. Dodge's autobiographical notes from this time include fond memories of family trips to the Bolton Landing home of the Smiths:

> Dave's big studio was like a small factory with a lot of steel and machines to cut steel and welding machines and blow torches. It was … fascinating. Dave's sculpture would be out in the yard, down from the house in this big open field. Instead of trees there would be these six and eight foot sculptures rusting…. They didn't have kids of their own but liked young children, and they kind of adopted our brood.[71]

At one children's party, balloons were tied to Smith's outdoor pieces in festive celebration.[72]

Dodge also attended New York openings of musicals by his Harvard classmate and close friend Alan Jay Lerner, who was godfather to Lisa Morrell Dodge, the artist's third daughter. A torn clipping from one of Dodge's files, with the name of the famed gossip columnist Hedda Hopper scribbled across it in pencil, notes that Jerry Dodge was the inspiration for the main character in Lerner's conception of *An American in Paris*.[73] Dodge had traveled to Europe to meet his parents after his father «had been appointed United States Minister to the quadripartite treaty convention in Vienna to make a post-war

treaty with Austria» in 1947.[74] The younger Dodge also visited Paris and London. Apparently Dodge's adventures and flings abroad, in addition to his enthusiasm for jazz, inspired Lerner to name the central character in *An American in Paris*, Jerry, after his old chum.

Dodge and Lerner were to remain close friends until Dodge moved from Glens Falls in 1962, when their contact gradually lessened. Dodge remembered in particular two specific observations made by Lerner. In his 1969 lecture at the University of Florida, Dodge recalled Lerner's comments:

> … about individuality and how so many artists seem to think that it's so very important and try so very hard to be individual by being different. At any rate, he kind of closed the subject as far as I'm concerned by saying that, in this day of mediocrity, to be good at anything is to be individual enough.[75]

In a second reference to Lerner, Dodge recalled a conversation in which Lerner concluded that a certain novel would not make a good musical because, «There's not much in it for the characters to sing about.» Dodge went on to say:

> Now this has always stuck in my mind as kind of a guide for my own work; and I ask myself, from time to time, am I doing a particular thing for technical reasons? Or to impress someone? Or because it's a current fad? Or to sell? Or because there's really something for me to sing about, whether it's a happy song, or a sad one.[76]

Jacksonville and the Cummer Gallery of Art

Jerry Dodge was invited to become director of the Cummer Gallery of Art in Jacksonville, Florida, in 1962. The first director, John Parsons, had died suddenly before the new museum opened and there was a frantic search to fill the position. Dodge recalled:

> I got a call one day in the middle of winter. I was on the next plane. The job was perfect for me, because I had a general background in the same kind of collection. I was not a specialist or a scholar, but the job did not call for that kind of person.[77]

Although separated by much of the length of the eastern seaboard, the histories of The Hyde Collection in Glens Falls, New York, and the Cummer Museum of Art & Gardens, as it is now called, in Jacksonville, Florida, have much in common. Both museums are located in lovely spots on grand rivers; the Hudson in Glens Falls, and the St. Johns in Jacksonville; both occupy the site of the homes of the founders of the museums; both were

Fig.12 —*Art Celebration!*, 1987.
Left to right at top : Robin Shepherd, David Engdahl, Jeff Dunn, Ben'h Usry, Gene Roberds, William Marshall, Peter Rumpel, Allison Watson; middle row : Enzo Torcoletti, Marilyn Taylor, Jerry Dodge; bottom : Mary Ann Bryan and Mark Howard.

started by husband and wife teams; both were completed and opened to the public because of the tenacity and vision of the widows; and both museums were realized largely as the result of great profits made from the lumber business.[78]

The collection amassed by Arthur Gerrish Cummer (1873-1943) and his wife Ninah May Holden Cummer (1875-1958) began in 1906 while they were on a second honeymoon. The couple visited the Philadelphia studio of American painter Paul King and purchased *Along the Strand*.[79] After Arthur Cummer's death in 1943, his widow began collecting works of art in earnest. With the counsel of her attorney, John W. Donahoo, Mrs. Cummer planned for the creation and endowment of an art museum to benefit Jacksonville.[80] In addition, she worked diligently to expand the gardens on the riverfront, drawing inspiration from a visit to the Villa Gamberaia near Florence, Italy. Mrs. Cummer commissioned Ellen Biddle Shipman, known as «the dean of American women landscape architects,» and set out to add her own Italian garden to the riverfront estate. Shipman, who was familiar with the garden at Villa Gamberaia, designed what would come to be known as one of her most significant extant residential gardens.[81]

When Dodge assumed his new position as director of the Cummer Gallery of Art, he found a collection of about sixty works, comprised not only of paintings but also tapestries and antique furnishings, which were housed in a building that was only partially filled. Marcia Corbino noted in her 1983 article on Dodge that, «during his ten years in that position, he tripled the gallery's holdings while deleting the mediocre and the doubtful.»[82]

At the Cummer, Dodge continued the diverse activities he had engaged in at The Hyde Collection, with the exception of teaching classes. He organized exhibitions and gave lectures regularly, not only at the Cummer but also throughout the community and the region. The artist's files contain a record of his annual reports and the catalogues of exhibitions staged during his tenure.[83] From 1962 to 1972, Dodge gave 41 of the 142 formal lectures given at the Cummer. During the same period, there were 106 exhibitions; 60 were created and curated by Dodge and his staff. Dodge wrote the majority of the catalogues. He referred to the following as «pioneer exhibitions»: in 1964, *French Art of the 16th Century* and *Artists of the Paris Salon*; in 1965, *Artists of Victoria's England*; in 1969, *The Age of Louis XIII* and *American Paintings of Ports and Harbors*; in 1971, *Remnants of Things Past*; and in 1972, *Edmund W. Greacen, N. A.*

The Cummer made ninety acquisitions during Jerry Dodge's decade at the museum, including paintings, sculpture, decorative art, important period pieces of furniture, a seventeenth-century French Gobelins-style tapestry, drawings, prints, and sculpture. One notable sculpture is the gift by Mr. and Mrs. Edward W. Lane of the *Portrait Bust of Cardinal Richelieu* by the workshop of Bernini.[84] One of the finest paintings by William-Adolphe Bouguereau in the United States, *Return from the Harvest*, was added to the collection under Dodge's tenure.[85] Several of the purchases made for the collection were highlighted in exhibitions Dodge organized. For example, *Theseus Discovering his Father's Sword* by Levieux de Nîmes was featured in the 1969 exhibition titled *The Age of Louis XIII*.[86] In 1965 Dodge influenced the collector Ralph Wark to give the Cummer Gallery of Art his collection of Meissen porcelain, which is widely acclaimed as one of the world's finest and most exquisite of its kind.[87] After an impressive ten years as the Cummer Gallery of Art's director, Dodge retired in 1972 to paint full time.

The Jacksonville Years: 1962-1997

Throughout his years at the Cummer and until his death, Dodge was a prominent member of the Jacksonville community. Only four years after Dodge's retirement, one of his successors, former Cummer director Robert W. Schlageter, acknowledged Dodge's contributions in an introduction at the museum on December 5, 1976:

> It is a distinct pleasure to have with us this afternoon the gentleman, scholar, and artist who helped create this museum. It was his eye, hand, and heart that guided the formation of that large body of works known as the «Membership Fund Collection.» It is a singular achievement, when in a museum without a large staff of supportive curators one person can know, select, and acquire art objects across the board—that is 20 centuries of time, and from multiple, worldwide cultures. This Mr. Dodge did with success, taste and style.

> He holds a unique place as a dean of artists in this community ... he maintains an active exhibition record, and continues to make his presence, taste and judgment felt both here in the Cummer and the community.[88]

Involved in a wide variety of community activities, Dodge served on the Fine Arts Committee for the Chamber of Commerce, the Historic Preservation Council, and the Mayor's Advisory Committee. He was a member of the Florida Art Museum Directors Association; the Southeast Art Museum Directors Association; and the Jacksonville Council of the Arts, for which he served as president from 1968 to 1969.[89]

Fig. 13 —Detail: **Joseph Jeffers Dodge and** *Portrait of Jeanne*

Dodge was also an active member in the Delius Association, formed in Jacksonville to celebrate the music of Frederick Delius. The British composer lived in north Florida for about fifteen months after arriving in 1884 to manage his father's citrus grove.[90] Each winter a Delius Festival is held in Jacksonville, Florida, featuring performances of the composer's music and lectures about his life and career. Dodge contributed drawings for the festival programs in 1963 and 1969. In 1963 he did a pen and ink drawing of a bronze mask of Delius by Henry Clews Jr., which was on loan to the Cummer from the Metropolitan Museum of Art in New York City in conjunction with the festival that year. Dodge also made a drawing of the Delius house for the 1969 program.[91]

In anticipation of the centennial celebration of Delius's arrival in Florida at Solano Grove in 1884, and in commemoration of the fiftieth anniversary of the composer's death in France in 1934, Dodge was invited to create a poster for the 1984 Delius Festival.[92] With some hesitation he accepted to paint *Solano Grove, Early Evening* (1984), which was used for the poster image.[93]

Besides Dodge's long involvement with the Delius Association, the artist was also a founding member of and a driving force behind Art Celebration!, a group of Jacksonville's finest professional artists who banded together in 1973. For the next nineteen years they exhibited and sold their works in nine shows, which usually lasted only a few days at a variety of venues. These included sites as diverse as the Dyal-Upchurch building in downtown Jacksonville and the Mussallem Galleries on the city's south side. In a 1981

Fig. 14 —Detail: **Avonel Williams, Joseph Jeffers Dodge, Jeff Dunn, Steve Lotz and Hiram Williams**

article about the upcoming exhibition, the writer referred to it as «one of the most looked-forward-to events of the season.»[94] Margaret Koscielny, another founding member of the group and Dodge's former assistant at the Cummer, explained the mission of Art Celebration! in a statement on the invitation to the 1979 exhibition held at the Le Moyne Art Foundation in Tallahassee, Florida:

> In the original selection of the artists for the group and thereafter, the work for the exhibitions, the stress has been on quality and professionalism. Every artist in Art Celebration! has been recognized by museums, galleries, in competitions: with commissions from corporations throughout the United States and Europe. The biography of every artist reveals years of study and long-standing commitment to his or her profession. And it is this level of devotion to art which sets Art Celebrationists apart from amateurs. The goal ... is to present a high caliber of art that relates visually to the times we live in and [has] a distinct relevancy—spiritually and aesthetically— to contemporary life.[95]

Dodge's paintings and working methods gained broad national exposure in the eighties when his work was included in two publications. Marcia Corbino wrote an article in *American Artist* featuring *Finding* (1971, pl. 58) on the cover.[96] Carole Katchen wrote *Painting Faces and Figures* in 1986 and devoted a chapter to him.[97] Lastly, a painting of his from the Jeanne portrait series, *Portrait of Jeanne: Rear Torso* (1966-1968) was chosen to illustrate the back cover of Katchen's book.

Throughout the thirty-five years Dodge lived in Jacksonville, he maintained an extremely active exhibition schedule. A listing of all known exhibitions during Dodge's lifetime and after his death is included in the appendices to this text. Dodge showed his works almost annually from his arrival in Jacksonville in 1962 to his death in March of 1997. In 1963 he exhibited in Palm Beach, Florida, and in 1964 he was featured in one-man shows at The Group Gallery in Jacksonville and at the Cummer Gallery of Art. The Group Gallery, located at 764 May Street in Riverside near the Cummer, was co-founded by Jacqueline Mullikin, now Jacque

Holmes, and Taylor Hardwick.[98] It was the first commercial gallery in the city dedicated to promoting art of the highest quality. Dodge would have one-man exhibitions there in 1966, 1968, and 1970.

Dodge's first major exhibition in Jacksonville was held at the Cummer Gallery of Art in 1964. The exhibition consisted of eighty-one paintings and twenty-one drawings.[99] Reviews in both Jacksonville newspapers were favorable.[100] It was from this exhibition that the Cummer trustees purchased *No Turning Back*, (1959, pl. 36), which was featured on the cover of the exhibition catalogue, for the museum collection. In 1965 a traveling exhibition of forty-six paintings and twenty drawings titled *Joseph Jeffers Dodge, Retrospective, Paintings and Drawings* was presented by The Columbus Museum of Arts and Crafts in Georgia; the George Thomas Hunter Gallery of Art in Chattanooga; the Georgia Museum of Art in Athens; and the Columbia Museum of Art in South Carolina.

Dodge continued his out-of-state exhibitions at Gallery 31 in Birmingham, Alabama, in 1967; the Mint Museum in Charlotte, North Carolina, in 1968; the Realist Invitational at The Gallery of Contemporary Art in Winston-Salem, North Carolina, in 1969; The Hyde Collection in 1973; and the Gibbes Art Gallery in Charleston, South Carolina, in 1972. Within Florida his works were exhibited in venues all over the state including Rollins College, the University of Florida, Jacksonville University, the Jacksonville Art Museum, and the Cummer in the 1990s. Between 1972 and 1992, Dodge exhibited in Hollywood, Daytona Beach, and Manatee County, and had numerous shows organized by the Foster Harmon Galleries in Sarasota and the Harmon Gallery in Naples. In the last two years of his life, Dodge mounted retrospective exhibitions at Ormond Beach, Florida, and at the University of North Florida in Jacksonville.

During the autumn of 1996, Jerry Dodge's works were paired with those of his old friend and admired colleague Hiram Williams, in a show curated by Steve Lotz at the University of Central Florida. Titled *Two North Florida Master Painters: Jerry Dodge and Hiram Williams*, the exhibition reflected Lotz's respect and admiration for the work of his mentors, these old patriarchs of the profession. A retrospective of Dodge's works from the forties up to his most recent paintings was included.

In 1996 Dodge received a special award from the Cultural Council of Jacksonville in recognition of his many accomplishments and sustained contributions to the Jacksonville community.[101] Writing in support of Dodge's nomination were friends and professional acquaintances. In reviewing the letters, it is evident how highly Dodge was regarded and respected. At the end of his life Dodge was viewed as an elder statesman in the Jacksonville cultural community.[102] The award, presented at a luncheon on April 25, 1996, was immensely gratifying to Dodge.

Dodge the Collector

 Collecting art and *objets d'art* was one of Jerry Dodge's abiding passions. He bought paintings, prints, drawings, small sculptures, prints, fine porcelain, silver, glass, and antiquities. Dodge not only enjoyed collecting, he also enjoyed living with his acquisitions. He surrounded himself with beautiful things and delighted in varying placements of works from his collection, which was comprised of more than 200 pieces. Visitors to Dodge's Jacksonville home could count on seeing rotating exhibitions of his eclectic purchases. Sometimes works by Dodge himself would be featured. He relished organizing works in such a way that thematic or compositional considerations would be enhanced. On one visit a friend noticed Dodge's pewter statuette of the mythological figure Daphne gracing a bathroom counter, standing next to the container of toothbrushes and toothpaste.

Nancy Belote Felton, who with her husband Carle own several outstanding examples of Dodge's paintings, assessed the artist's home as gallery:

> The living room of artist Joseph Jeffers Dodge is an extension of the man. A lifetime immersed in the visual arts, as a museum curator, gallery director and painter, has produced keen sensitivity to his surroundings. The placement of each object in a room is subject to his instinctive sense of proportion and scale. Against a uniformly white background, Dodge has masterfully used limited space to create a setting where each object is allowed to assume its full importance.
>
> A living room visitor is enticed to sink back into plump cushions and feast upon visual delights. Above the sofa, the magnificent canvas by Niels Holm, *Roman Amphitheater at Taormina* (1858) draws the viewer deep into the rocky hillsides, beyond the confines of a living room wall. An actual remnant of Graeco-Roman times, a 4th century B.C. terra cotta head, is delicately poised below the painting. The aura of antiquity is continued along the adjacent wall in both the opaque watercolor, *Classical Ruins* by Clérisseau and the 19th century charcoal drawing by François-Louis Français. A figure of Daphne in pewter by Raoul Larche and Jean-Louis Gérome's bronze doré classical female adorn the 19th century American chest.
>
> Dodge broadens his appeal to the senses through his choice of texture and contour. The silky luxuriance of Tiffany favrile glass, the voluptuous curves of the antique chest and chairs and the bold, muscular legs

of the cocktail table add a sensuous quality to the room. It is fitting that Dodge designed the cocktail table and secured Claude Graham to build it. Centered on the marble table top is a porcelain treasure.... The vibrant blue of the Imari bowl is reiterated in upholstery, pillows, and art glass forming a family of kindred objects throughout the room.

> A library of art books anchors the opposite end of the living room. Crumpled notes and manuscripts amidst the volumes attest to research past and present, for Dodge continues to be a popular lecturer in the community. Familiar blue accents, art nouveau flower vases and a rare Tiffany favrile bowl, assist in unifying the room.

> The fireplace wall is dominated by an intriguing portrait of a shepherd with pipes attributed to the 16th century Venetian master Giorgione. Although identification of the artist's work is continually debated, Dodge's studied opinion is that this is a self-portrait. «Only a half dozen paintings have been positively identified as Giorgione's.» A sprightly Mercury and a Greek terra cotta dancer (both 4th century B.C.) flank the painting. Two landscape paintings visually balance the intensity of the portrait. A Scottish coastal scene, on the left, is by the 19th century English artist John Brett. To the right, William Hart's *Lake George* (1860) is representative of the second generation Hudson River School. On the facing wall, an ink drawing on glass, Palma Giovanni's *Rest on the Flight to Egypt*, c. 1600, completes the journey through cultures and time.[103]

Selections from Dodge's collection were featured in two exhibitions in the nineties. The first, *The Collections of Joseph Jeffers Dodge*, held at the Cummer between September 11 and October 25, 1992, was organized to complement the concurrent exhibition of works by Dodge himself. The second focused on works on paper and was held at the University of North Florida in Jacksonville in 1995.

The brochure accompanying the Cummer exhibition included a «Collector's Statement.» This statement shed light on Dodge's approach to collecting:

> It's been said that collecting is a rare and incurable disease—but obviously not all that rare when one considers the many different kinds of collectors and infinite kinds of things they collect—including people, praise, power, experiences, and other such intangibles.
>
> Collecting is not a biological need, like eating, drinking, sleep, and sex, but it is more spiritual or emotional. As far as I know, it is not fatal, is otherwise relatively harmless, and often has social and practical benefits not only to the collector but, in a different way, to humanity at large in the form of museums, libraries, scientific knowledge, scholarship, and trickle-down economics.

Some collectors are gluttons and some gourmets, and at the time, it's often difficult to tell the difference—only in retrospect. Some acquire out of a hunger or greed that can never be sated. Some acquire competitively, to have the best, or the most expensive, or the greatest number, or the most fashionable, or sometimes just to keep someone else from having it. But to be a real collector, to have the «sickness,» one must have more than can be used or displayed at a given time. A person who chooses not to acquire an admired painting, for instance, because there's no more wall space, is simply not an art collector.

Many collectors are specialists, others generalists. Some limit their efforts to a particular kind of thing. We think gratefully of Ralph Wark's world-class collection of early Meissen useful ware which he so generously gave to the Cummer. I guess I'm a generalist. I love almost all kinds and periods of the visual arts and the only limits are time, opportunity, resources, and my personal decision-making process.

A great lover, but in another area of collecting, once said, «So many women, so little time!» This is a very real problem to all collectors. Even in this day of fax and instant global communications, the realities of space and time impose all sorts of limits. We can't collect, or even consider, regardless of our resources, what we don't know about and haven't seen. As active, as diverse, and as free-flowing as is the art market today, only a small percentage of world art is known and available to each collector at any given time.

Opportunism, therefore, is obviously a very important characteristic of collecting, personally or for a museum. No amount of planning or wishful thinking will conjure up the desired object at the right place and the right time, at the right price. And the more desirable or desired the object, the less likely is this to happen. The market is unpredictable, especially for unique objects. One never knows; one can never plan. If one just happens to be in the right place, at the right time, with the right knowledge and the right resources, and can make the right decision, why then you're a great collector or a great museum director.

Resources are, of course, a limiting factor to every individual and to every institution—only to different degrees. Most of the objects in my collection cost less than $1,000.00, and most were bought from what I received from the sale of my own paintings, which, at the time, seemed like something of an unscheduled disposable income. Thus, in a manner of speaking, my collection represents an exchange, in kind, for my own departed work.

I am very happy with what I have but also regret the things I didn't or couldn't acquire, and almost daily fantasize about what I'd like to have. It has nothing whatsoever to do with value, rarity, price or fashion but with aesthetic love, pure if not so simple. Like my own painting, and perhaps stemming from the same source or the same need, it is endlessly stimulating, endlessly frustrating and also deeply satisfying. They both, the painting and the collecting, which I've been doing somewhat compulsively when I could for half a century, have made my life very rich indeed!

While space is not a limiting factor to the true collector, it was very definitely a factor in selecting what was to be displayed in this gallery. Some painful choices had to be made. Among them was my decision not to include, at this time, works by members of the Art Celebration Group, with whom I show, and other artists of the Jacksonville area. Their work is frequently seen hereabouts, but, more importantly, since I could not show them all, I did not wish to seem to slight those local artists whose work I like and admire but do not have in my collection up to now. I've often had the opportunity but not always the cash and the good sense at the same time.[104]

Dodge's comments make it apparent that the process of pursuit and acquisition of objects brought him great pleasure. By his own admission his collection was a varied one. The range of the seventy-six works featured in the Cummer show represented only one-third of the number of pieces from which the former director Robert Schlageter made his selection in curating the exhibition.

The works chosen for the 1992 Dodge Collections exhibition at the Cummer reflected the collector's diversity of interests and breadth of knowledge. This is evident in the myriad of historical periods represented in the exhibition: a Roman marble fragment, *Head of a Satyr*; Art Nouveau works *Scarf Dancer* or *Loie Fuller*, a bronze figurine by Leonard, and *Lady with Peacocks*, a colored lithograph by Louis Rhead; a pre-Columbian figurine, *Standing Woman*; an untitled lithograph by Fernand Léger; and a sculpture by Dodge's old friend David Smith, *Ring-toothed Woman*.[105] When seen together, a common thread running through the collection joined seemingly disparate works: a commitment to quality and excellence regardless of medium or time period. The artist's profound appreciation for technical virtuosity and exquisite craftsmanship was reflected throughout the exhibition, whether it was seen in the dazzling examples of Tiffany and Steuben glass; or in the works by French artists such as the oil painting *Classical Landscape*, Dodge's favorite by an unknown artist; and the *Wooded Landscape* by François-Louis Français in ink, gouache, and chalk. The aesthetic judgments that manifested themselves in the collection that took Dodge more than fifty years to amass, also inspired and guided the artist in his own creative endeavors.

The works from Dodge's collection paralleled many of the subjects, themes, and compositional considerations the painter used in the construction of his paintings. A love for geometric solids; tight, coherent, and balanced compositions; themes drawn from nature including landscapes and coastal scenes; a pronounced interest in the timeless, picturesque and, at times, romantic view of history; the beauty and mystery of the female form, especially the female nude—all of these preferences informed his choices in collecting as they informed his choices in creating.

The second exhibition to feature works from Dodge's collection was held at the University of North Florida from November 16 to December 13, 1995. *Selections from the Collection of Joseph Jeffers Dodge* was comprised of works on paper. Dodge made available 103 works from which 65 were selected. The works ranged from drawings from the early seventeenth through the late twentieth centuries, to watercolors from the nineteenth and twentieth centuries, to wood engravings, lithographs, etchings, and photographs. The artists included prominent names in the history of art such as Winslow Homer, Pablo Picasso, Stanton MacDonald Wright, and Philip Pearlstein, in addition to regional and national luminaries such as Margaret Koscielny, Mark Howard, Hiram Williams, Steve Lotz, and Jerry Uelsmann. Dodge was delighted to share the works he had created and those he had collected with an audience consisting mostly of students.

Several of the paintings in Dodge's collection received widespread acclaim because of their inclusion in traveling exhibitions. Dodge owned two paintings by American artist Elihu Vedder: *San Gimignano*, and *Street Scene at Capri*. *San Gimignano*, which portrays the central piazza in front of the cathedral in the many-towered Tuscan town, was included in a major retrospective exhibition that was held at the National Collection of Fine Arts, the Smithsonian Institution, and the Brooklyn Museum between October 1978 and February 1979.[106] Dodge later gave the painting to The Hyde Collection to join three other works by Vedder already in the museum.[107] A color reproduction of *San Gimignano* was featured in an invitation to an exhibition at The Hyde Collection, «in celebration of a generous estate bequest, The Hyde Collection proudly announces the exhibition *Joseph Jeffers Dodge: Works from the Curator's Collection*, June 1 through July 31, 1997.»[108]

Another painting from Dodge's collection was included in an exhibition titled *The Lure of Egypt: Land of the Pharaohs Revisited* at the Museum of Fine Arts in St. Petersburg, Florida, from January 10 through June 9, 1996.[109] *The Colossi of Memnon*, a watercolor from 1866 by Carl Werner, shows the famous remains of the temple of Amenhotep III: two seated figures of the king stand eighteen meters high, their massive scale exaggerated by the barren plain around them. Scattered tourists dwarfed by the giant ruins are barely discernible. In the paintings by Vedder and Werner, similarities to Dodge's own pictorial evocations of picturesque vistas can be seen. All three of the nineteenth-century works are marked by an interest in the rendering of stone and references to the intersection of past and present, much like Dodge's paintings of the Yucatán, Greece, Italy, Egypt, and Brittany.

Although Dodge continued to collect late in his life, health issues, including heart surgery and the diagnosis of cancer, slowed his collecting to a more moderate pace. One of the tasks that occupied the last two years of his life was deciding how his collection should be distributed after his death. Dodge gave a large body of his own work to the Cummer in addition to thirty-six works from his collection. He also donated works to Choate, the Fogg Museum at Harvard, The Hyde Collection, and The Museum of Arts and Sciences in Daytona Beach, Florida. In Dodge's gifts to the Cummer and The Hyde, he acknowledged his gratitude to the founders and members of the respective boards of the museums, who had supported his efforts during his tenure at those institutions. He also wished to signal his support for the future growth and prosperity of all of these museums. After Jerry Dodge's death in March, 1997, the artist's close friends were invited to view the remaining works from the collection and to make purchases. In these ways, Dodge's legacy of collecting continues to grace museums and homes throughout the United States.

The Artist's Work

Early Paintings and Photographs from Glens Falls

Jerry Dodge did not really begin painting in earnest until he started teaching art classes in Glens Falls at The Hyde Collection in 1941. He drew constantly as a child and provided numerous illustrations for school and college publications, but hesitated to branch out into a medium that required color, in part because of color blindness. Looking at a sampling of Dodge's works from the early forties, one sees his pronounced interest in experimenting with a variety of styles. He borrows from Picasso's various periods, the Renaissance, and Surrealism, among many other sources. Dodge recalled these early artistic forays:

I was very tentative at first. I depended on other people's work a lot. I could have done this more easily in the «old masters» times. If I had shown a talent for drawing in Florence or Paris, I probably would have been apprenticed to somebody when I was twelve or fourteen and would have gone through all that rigorous studio training, and started out by copying the work of my master and the work of my contemporaries. The whole process would have been a natural, evolutionary one. But we don't do it that way today. If we want to be an artist, we go to art school or a college that features «art» or we are thrown back on art books, art magazines and museums. And now there's this whole world of images and techniques and styles out there. In my case, I liked a lot of it and was drawn to it. So in those early days, when I was about twenty-three and started painting more seriously, my painting vision was, in a sense, born out of art books and art magazines and, of course, my art courses at Harvard. It might be something in a Renaissance painting, a Medieval manuscript, a Picasso, a Bonnard, a Dalí, or an American painter that I would see in a book or magazine or gallery. There were hundreds and thousands of quite varying and quite different influences. When you study art history you learn that, for instance, Raphael came from Perugino, or something like that. You can kind of trace these things like the Old Testament. It's very linear, generally speaking, at least until you get into the 19th century. Like André Malraux wrote in his book *(sic), Museums Without Walls,* today we walk around with our heads stuffed with images from the whole world history of art. We have these «museums without walls» in ourselves and it takes a while to sort these things out.

My paintings for the first several years, and sometimes even after fifty years, have often been inspired by enthusiasm for some work of art that I'd seen. Or conversely, seeing somebody else's painting can be a justification for what I'm doing, so it's an encouragement. I think, at first, my main impulse was to create «Art» or maybe even recreate it, redigest it. I was painting my own pastiches of a lot of people, from a lot of sources.[110]

Pablo Picasso's early paintings influenced several of Dodge's first works. Dodge's *And Then There Were Two* (1942, pl. 4) recalls Picasso's *La Vie,* dating from the Blue Period in about 1901.[111] The works share a sense of lassitude and melancholy, and the posture of Dodge's slumped figure is similar to one in the Picasso painting. Dodge's painting, as he explained it, heralds and anticipates the aftermath of World War II, when the chilling reality that the world's population could be obliterated in minutes crept into the public's psyche.[112] *And Then There Were Two* suggests the possible consequence of the world's advancement in the technology of war, the ultimate reduction of the human race to one man and one woman, an Adam and Eve in reverse.

Also from 1942 is *The Hour of Parting* (pl. 5), reminiscent of a Picasso Rose Period painting, especially because of the pink hues in the work and the inclusion of a harlequin figure.[113] Dodge used oil, pastel, and ink, experimenting not only with style but also with technique. This is one of the few times he used pastel; he found the medium was not to his liking. The title, *The Hour of Parting* was taken from a popular ballad at the time, a practice the artist would use off and on for years. Dodge named the majority of his paintings after they were completed. He rarely sat down with a clearly conceived plan of what he wanted to depict. Dodge once told his old friend Dave Mills that he would have preferred never to have used names or titles at all because he believed each viewer should make up his or her own mind as to the meaning, mood, significance, and subject of each painting.[114]

Dodge's painting titled *Art Student* (1945, pl. 13) presents a wry commentary on Picasso's influence on Dodge.[115] A young man dressed in a red sweater and holding an abstract painting clearly derived from Picasso stands against a blue wall. Tacked on the wall and partially obscured by the art student's head is a more realistic drawing of what appears to be the same young man. The work is a clever quip on the dilemma art students face when choosing an artistic style. It is no coincidence that Dodge signed *Art Student* on the abstract work.

In contrast to the Picasso-influenced paintings, Dodge's painting titled *The Renaissance* (1944, pl. 10) is not only classically inspired but also classically executed. The portrait was derived loosely from *Portrait of a Young Man* by Giorgione in the San Diego Museum of Art.[116] In Dodge's work, the shape of the egg is repeated in the oval shape of the man's face. The egg was often used in the Renaissance to symbolize the promise of eternal life. Dodge saw his arrangement as a kind of trinity and observed:

> ... the two eggs, kind of sitting in the drapery, suggest a nest, the fecundity of male and female and also perhaps the sensuality and nurturing quality of two breasts. In this simple format, multiple allusions of various aspects of the Renaissance were indicated while at the same time I tried to make a painting that really needed no such conscious analysis [for it] to be both provocative and satisfying to the eye.[117]

Major characteristics of Dodge's painting are emerging in this small still life: a preference for carefully executed works; a predilection for still lifes; an interest in suggestions of fecundity, sexuality, and mystery; and a profound knowledge of and appreciation for art history.

The Renaissance brings to mind a photograph taken by Dodge in 1946 titled *Maternity* (pl. 16) in which a napkin has been arranged to hold an egg nestled in a leaf. A print of a Picasso drawing of *Mother and Child* is pinned to the wall in the background.[118] Dodge became interested in experimenting with photography in the 1940s and there are several studio photographs in which he assembled objects in the foreground and contrasted them with a print in the background. One such example is *The Classical Tradition* (1946, pl. 22), in which Dodge assembled a bust, an urn, and a dried leaf, placing them in front of a print of the Temple of Antonius and Faustina in the Roman Forum. In both photographs the leaf is a *memento mori*, a reminder of the transience of life.[119]

Dodge also experimented with photograms in the 1940s, several of which explore the image of the *Crucifixion* (1946, pl. 15). In a juried exhibition, one reviewer singled out *The Classical Tradition* and Dodge's photograms for awards and praise. The reviewer explained:

The photograms which are made by exposing sensitized paper directly to light from an enlarger or other light source by masking and dodging, created considerable discussion among the judges due to the newness of thought and approach in photography. When the present trend among photographers is toward the human interest element the unique and modern aspect presented by the photograms drew one of the judges to term the work «Exciting.»[120]

The «Jazz» Paintings

 Dodge produced another major group of paintings in the 1940s that reflects his fascination with Surrealism, his passion for jazz, and his increasing concern with racism and the «despicable treatment of minorities, particularly Blacks.»[121] Surrealism enjoyed tremendous popularity in the United States after groundbreaking exhibitions of Surrealist works were held at the Wadsworth Atheneum in Hartford in 1931, and at the Museum of Modern Art in New York City in 1936.[122] The Wadsworth Atheneum exhibition, titled *The New Super Realism*, was composed entirely of European paintings and was the first exclusively Surrealist exhibition in America. The 1936 Museum of Modern Art exhibition was more comprehensive and included works of fantastic art, Dada, and Surrealism.

In 1943 an exhibition at MOMA titled *Realists/ Magic Realists* considered another new artistic style:

> ... a widespread but not yet generally recognized trend in contemporary American art has appeared not as a concerted movement but spontaneously in many parts of the country. It is limited to pictures of sharp focus and precise representation whether the subject has been observed in the outer world—realism, or contrived by the imagination—magic realism.»[123]

Magic realism has been defined as «a term sometimes applied to the work of painters who by means of an exact realistic technique try to make plausible and convincing their improbable, dreamlike or fantastic visions.»[124]

The influence of Surrealism and magic realism is readily apparent in Dodge's paintings of the forties that were inspired by the artist's immersion in the jazz scene: *Double Self-Portrait* (1943, pl. 6), *Moon Mist* (also called *Moonlight Madness* and *Mad Moonlight*, 1944, pl. 9), *Black and Tan Fantasy* (1944, pl. 8), *Black and Blue* (1946, pl. 14), *Elegy* (1947, pl. 18), and *Frankie and Johnny* (1947-48, pl. 19). In these paintings, Dodge hoped the viewer's response to the visual imagery would parallel a listener's response to the aural stimulation of jazz.

The *Double Self-Portrait* incorporates obvious elements from the Surrealist movement with the distant horizon, the emphasis on meticulous rendering of seemingly disparate elements, and the sense of mystery. The head of the artist is turned to the viewer. His eyes are obscured by sunglasses in which one sees several figures. The seated elderly lady shown in the right lens is Mrs. Hyde. This rendering anticipates the portrait Dodge painted of her in 1944. In the other lens, Duke Ellington is portrayed playing the piano, and is accompanied by two of his musicians, alto saxophonist Johnny Hodges and trombonist Lawrence Brown. In addition to Ellington, Dodge considered Hodges and Brown to be two of the greatest musicians in jazz. By including all three of them in the lens, he hoped to «suggest the tone of Ellington's music to those familiar with it.»[125] Duke Ellington's music was such a major force in Jerry Dodge's life that Dodge compiled one of the most complete collections of Ellington's recordings in the world. Also depicted in the left lens is blonde bombshell, starlet Veronica Lake; the pose was taken from a photograph in *Life* magazine. To the left Dodge reproduced a Fragonard painting titled *Bathers*, a work he once called «one of those few perfect paintings in art history.»[126]

The *Double Self-Portrait* has a long exhibition history. One of its first venues was the Albany Institute of History and Art in 1944. In 1945 it was included in an exhibition titled *Portraits of Today by Painters of Today* at the Mortimer Brandt Gallery in New York City, where a reviewer in *Art Digest* noted somewhat incorrectly:

> Perhaps, the most felicitous fusing of objective and subjective statement is the portrait by J. J. Dodge, in which the mirroring lenses of the sitter's glasses reflect the world about him or his reaction to it. In either case, it proves a challenging canvas and, one instinctively feels, an excellent likeness.»[127]

This reviewer made a common mistake in interpreting the role of the glasses and the images seen in them. At first glance the viewer may think that the subject in the *Double Self-Portrait* wears sunglasses that show reflections. It was Dodge's goal, however, to show images that are behind the glasses, not reflections, thereby making the head into kind of a mask. His aim to challenge the viewer's first impressions while underscoring initial misconceptions links the painting even more compellingly to the Surrealist movement.

Double Self-Portrait was followed by *Moon Mist* and *Black and Tan Fantasy* in 1944.[128] Both paintings have cloudy, dark, and brooding backgrounds with figures and objects placed against a very low horizon line, resulting in the suggestion of a vast and flat infinite space, a device often used by Surrealist painters such as Dalí, Max Ernst, and Yves Tanguy.[129]

In *Moon Mist* two figures dance on a rickety stage. Three musicians are emerging from and contained within the shadows of the centrally placed trees: a bass player; a trombonist; and most clearly seen in a white shirt, a seated guitarist who sings. An upholstered chair is placed near the largest of the trees while a nude blonde woman sits on a fence. Her hair covers her face and she is slumped over in a posture that conveys grief and misery. A woman in an elegant dress peers around the fence where two men on horseback ride into the distance. The painting is enigmatic. Its combination and contrast of races and social classes adds to the mystery and tension of the work.

Moon Mist was exhibited in the Annual Exhibition for Michigan Artists at The Detroit Institute of Arts from November 12 to December 15, 1946. Below a photograph of the painting in an unidentified newspaper clipping the caption read, «Importance of the exhibition is registered by the fact that native Michigan artists no longer living here send show entries. *Moon Mist*, canvas striking for its rich, deep color and composition, was sent by Joseph Jeffers Dodge, art curator, and son of a Detroit banker.»[130] The painting was also noted in the *Christian Science Monitor*, «At the DIA runs the annual for Michigan artists, which includes 263 works in painting and sculpture chosen.... Greens and violets intensify the symbolism in Joseph J. Dodge's *Moon Mist*, in which Negro and white folk dance near a 'lynching tree.'»[131] Dodge also exhibited the painting at the Pennsylvania Academy of the Fine Arts in 1945 along with works by Joseph Albers, Ben Shahn, John Marin, Joseph Stella, Eugene Berman, Milton Avery, Georgia O'Keeffe, Charles Burchfield, and Abraham Rattner, among many others. Dodge's painting received passing notice in this huge exhibition with a remark by C.H. Bonte who acknowledged «J.J. Dodge's strange Negro dance, *Mad Moonlight...*»[132]

In *Black and Tan Fantasy* titled after a Duke Ellington composition, wooden constructions dominate.[133] The implicit skeletal framework of a building occupies the center of the painting, while at the left, references to scaffolding, lynching, and the crucifixion are much more explicit. Various draperies twirl, flutter, or hang. Four musicians are included in this work: a trombonist, Duke Ellington at the piano, a seated trumpet player, and a bass player. To the right in the far distance on a disintegrating pedestal is a partial, crumbling bust of Abraham Lincoln rendered in a Dalí-esque way. The full promise of Lincoln's Emancipation Proclamation was not realized and the disintegrating bust is an indictment of the treatment of many African Americans in the first half of the twentieth century.

At the Annual Exhibition for Michigan Artists held in 1944 at The Detroit Institute of Arts, *Black and Tan Fantasy* was mentioned by Florence Davies who noted, «Joseph Dodge deals with space in a particularly interesting way in his Dalí-like imagery with its phantom figures and its lovely paint quality.»[134] Brief remarks made by reviewers of both paintings show that the Surrealist influence in both of these works did not go unnoticed.

Dodge's commentary on his early canvases of jazz-related themes also offers the viewer a symbolic framework for understanding them. As has been mentioned, the music of Duke Ellington in particular, and jazz in general, had been major loves in Dodge's life since about 1931. He described jazz as «a major source of inspiration and joy, of consolation and release.»[135] Of his works inspired by jazz Dodge explained, «some people have tried to express jazz one way or another in paint, usually abstractly—like Stuart Davis, for example. Mine is a somewhat different approach, in most cases using elements of jazz as part of a pictorial vocabulary of images.»[136]

In relation to several of these works Dodge also remarked that he was «very concerned about [racism], sometimes very emotionally.»[137] One of the signature pieces of famed jazz vocalist Billie Holiday, *Strange Fruit*, was a deceptively simple poem set to music about a lynching.[138] The lyrics contain graphic imagery and «the picture it painted—of innocent victims of southern mob violence hanging from poplar trees, faces distorted in death, blood splattered on roots—was brutal in its candor: 'Scent of magnolias, sweet and fresh. Then the sudden smell of burning flesh.'»[139] The strange fruit hanging from the southern tree is the body of a Black man. Columbia Records rejected the song because of its controversial content. Dodge recalled his reaction to hearing Billie Holiday's *Strange Fruit* for the first time: «It was very moving and affecting ... it was emotionally shattering. It was one of the most effective things of its kind that I've heard, read or seen anyplace.[140]

The title for Dodge's *Black and Blue* was inspired by the last lines of a famous blues song by Fats Waller, which were «My only sin is the color of my skin. That's why I'm so black and blue.»[141] Dodge would have known a 1929 recording of the melody made by Duke Ellington and his orchestra and that it was once described as «a triumph of composition in its balance of the sweet and the bitter, with an undertone of anger of being born.»[142]

The elements that compose *Black and Blue* were chosen for their socio-historic meaning and to suggest the roots of jazz and the blues.[143] The cemetery, for example, is a reminder that much of New Orleans jazz originated from the funeral celebration. The church and statue of Jesus in *Black and Blue* are related to the role spirituals played in the inception of the blues. The rake symbolizes physical labor and the work song. The urban background is a reminder that jazz was a product of the city and a momentary release from poverty. Another wellspring of jazz is sex, about which Dodge included several unmistakable masculine and feminine references. Other symbols are the rope, representing the fear of lynching, and bottle, a reference to escape through inebriation.

In a review of a Dodge exhibit held at the Albany Institute of History and Art in 1949, a perceptive Robert Wheeler made the following observations:

> Dodge works chiefly through symbols and certain of his symbolic forms carry unchanged through more than one of his works. The cemetery motif, for example, appeared in *Elegy*, in *Black and Blue*, and in *Fugue*. In each of these ... appeared musicians. Musicians and musical instruments were shown also in *Trio*, *How High the Moon*, *I Have Immortal Longings in Me* and in *Young Man with a Horn*. A violently green church spire pointed upwards in *Black and Blue*, in *Trio*, and in *How High the Moon*. What the meaning of these most obvious symbols are, this writer will not now venture to say. Obviously Mr. Dodge is working in his own vocabulary. For enjoyment of his paintings such symbols need not necessarily be understood as Dodge meant them. They do add greatly to the design strength of each work. They are certain to speak to each viewer in light of the viewer's own experience.

> It could be easy to say that Mr. Dodge has leanings towards the surrealistic but this would be too easy, and would also probably be an untruth. True, strange and wonderful objects are placed in juxtaposition. Wonderfully detached humans ignore their fellows on the canvases. Yet the impression comes that this was not done to startle. Rather Mr. Dodge is making a definite statement in each of his works. To him symbols, construction and color are merely devices to express more firmly his own thoughts or feelings.

> Through use of these devices, Dodge has created haunting and sensitive works. The observer is struck with a sense of loneliness, a sense of the poetic. Almost all of the pieces have an enigmatic quality. Titles, of course, are somewhat explanatory. They point up the artist's ideas. Yet, even without titles for guides the observer would not be at too great a disadvantage. He would merely find himself in the role of creator, building up his own story or experience for each work viewed.

> Color is handled in a most sensitive manner. In other hands this could mean a weakness. Dodge, however, keeps color always crisp and vibrant.

> All in all, this was a most satisfying show. It was perhaps the most provocative in the series of exhibitions by regional artists held at the Institute in recent years.[144]

Wheeler's sensitive appraisal of Dodge's goals and stylistic characteristics must have been enormously satisfying to the thirty-two-year-old artist. Combinations of the qualities Wheeler identified in Dodge's paintings, those «wonderfully detached humans [who] ignore their fellows» in enigmatic, haunting, lonely, and poetic compositions, would repeatedly show up throughout the remainder of the artist's œuvre.

In *Elegy* (1947), a redheaded female plays a harp and a young man holds a trombone and reclines on a fallen tree. Several elements are similar to those found in *Black and Blue*. The couple is seated before a graveyard and marked by a variety of funeral monuments including a cross, statuary, and an obelisk. The impression created by placing the guitar-playing statue in front of a leafless tree suggests an angel. Dark red drapery hangs over the low white wall of the cemetery and cascades over the tree trunk. Two pages of music lay on the ground by the tree trunk; one is titled *Elegy*.

The woman featured in *Elegy* is Susan Reed.[145] Dodge met her when he and Douglass Crockwell, a renowned illustrator and a good friend, visited New York City's better jazz venues in search of an entertainer who would perform in Glens Falls. Reed, a young musician from Columbia, South Carolina, had become a sensation for her renditions of folk music. Major magazines including *TIME* and *Life* had published articles about her.[146] Incidentally, Dodge met Billie Holiday when Reed was performing at the Cafe Society, the first racially integrated nightclub in New York City. Reed and Dodge were romantically involved until their largely incompatible schedules led to their break-up. He recalled the passionate interlude as being «exciting and poetic» but also «educational.»[147] Dodge remembered that Reed, «like all performers ... was very centered on herself, almost narcissistic. I learned much about myself and, not in the least, to avoid performers.»[148] This painting, in addition to evoking associations with mournful melodies, serves as a visual farewell to Reed whom Dodge still remembered some fifty years later as «an enchanting, magical person, not only in her performances, but at times in real life.»[149]

Dodge paid a tribute of another sort in *Frankie and Johnny (In Memory of «Tricky Sam» Nanton.* In 1945 Ellington invited Dodge to attend a recording session for overseas broadcasts to American Armed Forces. In a rhapsodic arrangement of *Frankie and Johnny*, «Tricky Sam» Nanton, recognized as the greatest of the Plunger Mute artists on trombone, played a long solo that moved Dodge to tears.[150] Nanton was a member of «Ellington's unmatched trombone section» and along with Juan Tizol and Lawrence Brown, he had been dubbed a member of «God's Trombones.»[151] Nanton died just

Fig.15 —**Susan Reed**, c. 1945

a few weeks after the recording session, on July 21, 1945. In homage to Nanton, Dodge included «To July 21» in the painting.

Symbolic motifs in *Frankie and Johnny* parallel those seen in *Black and Blue* and in *Elegy*. Dodge discussed the painting in the two major lectures he gave about his work in 1969 and in 1990.[152] Nanton is at the left in front of a graveyard and the statue of Christ. The rope appears again as does the fence. In the foreground, in sunlight, life goes on. According to the artist, the boy drawing abstract designs in the dust implies that art styles come and go. The girl symbolizes youth and innocence, both of which will fade, and skipping rope represents rhythm. Another boy offers an apple, which can also be read as a nipple, to a large poster of a voluptuous blonde. The gesture recalls a variety of associations ranging from the Judgment of Paris to the Temptation in the Garden of Eden. The symbolic apple recurs in a variety of Dodge's later paintings. Dodge conceived the beauty in the poster as an older version of the girl skipping rope. Again, the never-ending pageant between the sexes is a major subject of jazz. Dodge also said, «Curiously enough, the image of the blonde love goddess which, like most of the things in my pictures in those days was completely made up, anticipates Marilyn Monroe by a couple of years.»[153]

In addition to intertwining his disgust for racism and his profound reverence for jazz in paintings such as *Black and Blue*, *Elegy* and *Frankie and Johnny*, Dodge also interwove the thematic strand of religious symbolism in these works.

Dodge remembered:

> There was a period in Glens Falls during my mid twenties
> when I was much more interested in religion. This was
> after Jane departed (his first wife); but that didn't have
> much to do with it. I think it was in the air after the war.
> There was kind of a religious revival. There was a young
> woman ... named Felicia Cunningham. I developed very
> strong feelings for her at that time. She was a rather reli-
> gious Episcopalian. She got Hodgkin's disease and died
> during that period. She was great gal, very bright and full
> of life. It was a short but very uplifting episode in my
> life.... Anyway, these things, I'm sure, affected some of
> my paintings and photographs.[154]

Two paintings that are less reliant on the Surrealist
mode of representation and are more straightforward
and celebratory of the brilliance of Duke Ellington's
performances are *Jazz Quintet* (or *Black and Tan
Fantasy*, 1943, pl. 7) and *Rockin' in Rhythm* (or *The
Ellington Rhythm Section*).[155] Jerry Dodge began *Jazz
Quintet* in the summer of 1943 when he was studying
with Yasuo Kuniyoshi in Woodstock, New York.
Dodge started *Rockin' in Rhythm* in Woodstock
but completed it around 1945. [156] The first of these
was painted in a horizontal format and shows what
Dodge referred to as the Ellington «genius» section
with the Duke at the piano, Rex Stewart on cornet,
Lawrence Brown on trombone, Johnny Hodges
on saxophone and Ray Nance on violin.[157]
The second work was painted in a vertical format.
Rockin' in Rhythm shows Duke at the piano, Sunny
Greer on drums, Freddie Guy on guitar and Wellman
Braud on bass.[158]

In *Jazz Quintet* Ellington is at the piano in an open
necked white shirt; the viewer sees him over
the top of the piano from about elbows up looking
down at a musical score. Two glasses and a bottle are
at his right. His musicians are arranged in a clockwise
composition that fans out behind him. The paint is
applied in a loose and thick manner, a working
method rather unusual for Dodge. The splashes of red
and emphasis on diagonals reinforce the suggestion
of energy, tempo, and rhythm that the artist so
admired in Ellington and his orchestra.

Dodge traveled at every opportunity to see Ellington
perform. After completing *Black and Tan*, Dodge took
it to Mrs. Hyde's apartment on Park Avenue in New
York City. He was allowed to use the residence in the
summers when Mrs. Hyde remained in Glens Falls.
One evening in the mid-1940s when the Ellington
Orchestra was performing at the Hurricane Club near
Times Square, Dodge and the Duke were talking and
Dodge told him about the painting. During intermis-
sion they took a cab to the apartment at Park Avenue
and 58th Street. Dodge remembered that the furniture
was covered with sheets and the cupboard was bare
but that Ellington admired the painting enormously

and «seemed to be very impressed.»[159] Dodge became
nervous because their conversation went on for some
time and he remembered, «when we got back, the
band was playing without him. He just strolled on
stage and took his place at the piano as if this sort of
thing happened every day.»[160] Ellington called Dodge
«the Park Avenue Kid» thereafter.

Some twenty-five years later in 1971, Dodge was
visiting Mexico when he discovered Ellington would
be performing in Mexico City with The National
Symphony of Mexico.[161] Dodge managed to secure
a second row seat. He remembered:

> A couple of guys in the sax section recognized me and
> waved at me at one point. That night in his dressing
> room backstage, the Duke mentioned that he had seen
> one of my paintings in St. Louis when he had given a
> concert there a year or so before. I said I thought he was
> just making sweet talk; but he said no, it was the one you
> showed me in your 'Park Avenue apartment.' I said I
> don't have any pictures in St. Louis, as far as I know.
> He had given a concert at the symphony hall and it was
> in the lobby. Someone asked him to autograph it, which
> he did. I thought he was pulling my leg. Subsequently I
> found out that the doctor in Glens Falls who had bought
> it from me had died and left it to his son. His son had
> moved it to St. Louis and that's where it was—which is
> weird to say the least.[162]

During the Jacksonville years Dodge maintained
contact with Duke Ellington. In a conversation with
Ellington after the concert in Mexico City, Dodge
mentioned that Jacksonville was planning a special
sesquicentennial celebration of its 1822 founding and
that the symphony orchestra was considering the
commissioning of a composition to commemorate the
event.[163] Duke later called Jerry and said he was working on a piece called *Centennial*. He also asked Dodge
about the wind musicians in the Jacksonville
orchestra because Ellington felt a particular passage
was crucial to the composition. Dodge immediately
recommended Dr. Bernard Kaye, a prominent plastic
surgeon and a musician in the orchestra. Ellington
called Kaye at two in the morning and asked if Kaye
would play the saxophone for him. Reportedly, Duke
replied after hearing Kaye, «That's fine. Now I know
what to write.» The symphony played Ellington's
composition to great acclaim.[164]

In a curious twist of fate, Dodge happened to be in
New York City when Duke Ellington died on May 24,
1974.[165] Dodge was shopping in Saks Fifth Avenue
when he noticed that Ellington's *Mood Indigo* was
playing on the store's sound system. Knowing that
the great composer had been hospitalized since
March, he immediately concluded that the Duke had
died. After confirming his suspicion he visited the
funeral home in Harlem to give his condolences to
the composer's mistress. On May 27, Dodge joined

ten thousand mourners in attending the funeral at the Episcopal Cathedral of St. John the Divine on Manhattan's Upper West Side. Many of the members of Ellington's orchestra served as ushers. Dodge was recognized when he entered the church and was escorted to sit at the front of the sanctuary near family members. The memorial service was a stunning tribute to one of America's great talents.[166]

The body of works created by Dodge in the forties is not only a testament to his musical lifelong love affair with jazz and the music of Duke Ellington and his orchestra, it also reflects his increasing awareness of racism and his exploration of religious meaning. Dodge's interest in music would continue to influence his works during the fifties but the representation of racial themes would lessen considerably.

The «Rooftop» Paintings

During the forties and fifties, Dodge incorporated a new motif into his work—figures on rooftops. *Trio*(1947, pl. 20), *The Key is Lost*(1950-51, pl. 24), and *A Place in the Sun* (1951) are representative of this series of paintings.[167] Dodge explained that this choice of settings «appealed to me because it was contemporary, natural, compositionally flexible, full of interesting shapes and textures, and suggested the same sort of carefree remoteness as the Arcadian landscapes of Giorgione or Poussin—only in modern urban terms.»[168] The young Dodge also knew of romance on rooftops. At a party at Douglass Crockwell's studio in Glens Falls, Dodge and Susan Reed snuck away to the roof; he recalled, «that was the first time I kissed her and the romance started.»[169]

Trio was the first of Dodge's rooftop pictures. In his 1969 lecture Dodge explained:

I was doing a kind of modern version of Giorgione's famous *Pastoral Symphony*. The title *Trio* not only describes the musical combo of cello, guitar and trombone (which might make a pretty wild sound) but suggests an emotional triangle as well.

The woman in the middle, oblivious to both the joy and misery her beauty is arousing, is in her own secret dream world. The cellist on the left is playing on the very feminine shaped instrument with his very masculine shaped bow, which is pointing to the girl. Is he the successful lover? Or is he playing by/or to/or with himself, so to speak—expressing his fantasies through his art, his music? Is the trombonist on the right who is playing into the empty trap door the dejected loser of this triangle and playing the blues, or is he musically reminiscing? Or is he simply exhausted, after making love with his trombone?

These are deliberate ambiguities and I still don't know the story myself. And, if I did, I wouldn't tell. And, as in any good musical arrangement, the background is in harmony with the main theme; and so here, the trio is surrounded by sex symbols, of both genders, to reinforce the mood and the meaning.»[170]

In *The Key is Lost* four figures, two male and two female, are shown on a rooftop. The two men, one nude, the other dressed, play horns. One man points his horn into the dark space of the stairwell. One woman faces away from us; she stands on tip-toe, her hands placed on a chimney stack as she tries to peer over it. The other woman sits almost back to back with the nude man, looking out of the picture to the viewer's left. A guitar rests on the ground. It leans toward her and she holds it in between her legs. The painting is composed of predominantly red, yellow, and brown hues. The sky is a fantastic orange and pink. One wonders if the sky is supposed to indicate sunrise or sunset, although one might also surmise from the way the sky is presented that it underscores a mood rather than suggests a specific time of day.

Dodge did not specifically discuss *The Key is Lost* in his two major lectures about his work. He implied in the lecture given at the University of Florida in 1969, that his comments about *Trio* would provide adequate context, noting, «since it's (*The Key is Lost*) in this present exhibit, I'll let you all enjoy it in your own way. I think I've probably given you enough hints, enough 'keys,' so that the picture doesn't have to be explained in detail; and, anyway—in all these compositions—a little ambiguity is deliberately built in, so to speak.» [171]

Three of the rooftop tableaux, *The Key is Lost*, *Trio* and *A Place in the Sun* were exhibited along with fifteen other paintings in a major show at the prestigious

Fig. 16 —**Alan Jay Lerner and Joseph Jeffers Dodge in Doug Crockwell's studio**, 1956

36

Wildenstein Gallery in New York City in 1952. The exhibition program contained remarks by Dodge's close friend Alan Jay Lerner, the author of Broadway musicals *Paint Your Wagon*, *Royal Wedding*, and the film *An American in Paris*.[172] Lerner's preface read:

The world of Joseph Jeffers Dodge has only two Seasons: Spring and Autumn. It is a world of longing and promise, of loneliness and despair. His men and women are beautiful and young but they never quite touch. At times their physical proximity makes their emotional distance almost unbearable to watch. Why don't they discover each other? Does the pre-occupation with the search prevent the finding? Are the men making music and dreaming dreams because they can't find that for which they seek? Or are they making too much music and dreaming too many dreams to find that for which they seek? And what of the women? Are they truly waiting to be made women? If so, why don't they take the lead and reach out? Or does the anticipated rejection prevent them from doing so until their longing is so great that all possible reality becomes inadequate? Whatever the reason, these people are isolated, hermits living under one roof.

In this world God is remote. Even the security of faith is somehow beyond reach. Perhaps too many scientific questions were asked of things for which there are no scientific answers. Perhaps these people are victims of freedom, of freedom to think what they will and freedom to believe what they will, until there is too much to think about and nothing to believe in. Perhaps these people are lost in enlightenment. Whatever the reason may be, God is remote but the need for Him is cruelly immediate.

All this is painted with the beauty of compassion. The artist is not viewing his world from the Olympian heights of detachment. The colors are warm and rich. The people are bursting with a kind of sensuality born of love for them. For all their sadness and confusion the artist sees them as beautiful people.

I think this is the world of Joseph Jeffers Dodge. I think it is very much the world of us all.[173]

David Mills recalled that Dodge was very disappointed in the public reaction to the Wildenstein exhibition, especially since it resulted in very few sales. The reviews were decidedly mixed. Dodge's files contain several clippings that do not indicate their sources. In one clipping bearing the heading «In Brief: Exhibitions, Joseph Jeffers Dodge at Wildenstein,» a reviewer noted that Dodge's « ... luminous realist paintings treat disquietingly romantic subjects.»

Another review with the caption «Dodge at Wildenstein» contained a fuller assessment:

The line between poetry and vulgarity in Joseph Jeffers Dodge's paintings at the Wildenstein Gallery is very thin. Sometimes his empty-faced nudes standing around at picnics, reclining on roof tops, or just blandly posing for the spectator, are as banal as the figures in a poster, and as slickly painted. In just a few, however, a sense of enigmatic melancholy, of mysterious silence, of unhappy isolation, comes through. Conceptions are frequently as banal as execution.[174]

A review torn from a magazine or journal stated:

Joseph Jeffers Dodge (Wildenstein; to May 14), who majored in art at Harvard under Arthur Pope and is now curator of the Hyde Collection in Glens Falls, New York, is having his first one man show of oils.

In a vein of almost photographic realism, Dodge pursues idyllic allegories of adolescence in settings of backyard gardens and rooftops. Although some of these compositions, especially the larger ones, seem somewhat contrived and artificial, he achieves in many of them a feeling of Arcadian remoteness with the evocation of moods bordering on Surrealism. The paradoxical isolation of his figures, standing or moving as if in a trance, distills an air of mystery and melancholy which is enhanced by sensuous, romantic color with fully developed light and shade. Sometimes this seems a trifle too derivative, but there are some fluently glowing passages, as in the foreground of *Play Time* and in the intricate geometry of walls and parapets of *The Key is Lost*. [175]

In «Gallery Previews in New York,» published in *Pictures on Exhibit*, May, 1952, the unidentified reviewer recorded:

Adolescent libidos get complicatedly mixed up with otherwise innocent rooftop and picnic ground revels in a series of very expertly but too earnestly painted canvases. Mr. Dodge has seemingly learned a great deal from the old masters; and in the simpler of his conceptions such [as] *I Have Immortal Longings in Me* and *Palpable and Mute*, he attains a poetic synthesis of color and design.[176]

A critic in an *Art Digest* review commented:

Luscious nudes people Dodge's world of roof-tops, of forest streams, or of wrecked buildings. Warm sunshine bathes them as they practice on musical instruments.... It is a world of youth in which impersonal figures are impersonally described—a world of texture and detail. Here comparative simplicity allows for a romantic quality that a wealth of accuracy and detail overshadows in Dodge's elaborate compositions.[177]

This body of contemporary criticism and reaction to Dodge's work is valuable, for it documents his increasing exposure as an artist and reflects the development and expansion of his subject matter.

It is interesting to note that in relation to the rooftop pictures, Dodge once admitted:

> I've always been kind of frustrated that I wasn't a musician. Perhaps I could have been a wind player and played the saxophone, trombone, or trumpet. I could do a single line, I think, but I can't imagine doing something that involves more than one note at a time. Harmony and counterpoint, it seems inconceivable to me. In some of my paintings the trombonist or trumpeter is, in a sense me, a fantasy me, or a wannabe character. It's something I often dreamt about.[178]

What Struggle to Escape, No Turning Back, and Related Works

Dodge's interest in nubile, pubescent young women is evident in several paintings completed in the late 1940s and 1950s, including *Another Autumn* (1947, pl. 17), *The Nest* (1951, pl. 27), *Spring* (1953), *What Struggle to Escape* (1953-55, pl. 28), and *No Turning Back* (1959, pl. 36). *What Struggle to Escape* and *No Turning Back* share compositional and thematic similarities, as both explore the imminent transformation of an adolescent girl into a young woman.[179] In *What Struggle to Escape*, a young red-haired woman sits on a board that appears to be part of a bleacher or shelf display. The light pours in from the viewer's left and its shadows are carefully and consistently rendered. In his 1969 lecture Dodge discussed the work:

> The girl-woman is tightly confined by her dress and all the other forms are likewise encased. She holds a butterfly in her hand which is also struggling to escape. The various still life elements kind of developed while I was working on it, as I thought of things which echoed the basic idea—such as the spring tulips in the flower pot, still tied to the stakes by a web of strings, or the rope, like a live snake, half in and half out of the iron cauldron.[180]

No Turning Back is also brimming over with symbolic allusions. Both paintings have dark backgrounds but in the later painting the negative space is almost black. Here the figure is positioned at the viewer's right. Rather than sit «side-saddle» as the young woman did in *Struggle*, she straddles the bench and holds it with both hands in a much more provocative pose. In discussing *No Turning Back* Dodge explained that the young woman:

> ... is looking backward with regret and forward with apprehension, or perhaps with eagerness, depending on the girl. She is in a child-like pose astraddle a bench on which are mementos and symbols of her childhood—including a doll struggling with the symbolic, umbilical cord—and the sheltered violets just coming into bloom. The upper half represents maturity and things to come:

> just as the upper part of her body is more that of a woman. The cut roses symbolize love, or the full bloom of life, and finally death, in contrast to the early spring of the violets growing below. The apples, of course, refer to Eve, The Garden of Eden, and the Temptation. On the lower shelf [the apple] is whole ... while above, it's been cut and one slice is missing—presumably eaten. There's a certain ominous finality about this section which is very effective, I think in this context—and by itself, for that matter.[181]

Dodge was always very proud of *No Turning Back* noting that, «if I had to, this is one I'd surely consider as among my very best.»[182]

The model in *No Turning Back* was Derinda Duross, one of Dodge's favorites. There are several photographs of the nude Derinda taken by Dodge for studies. The figure in the painting is not an exaggeration, but rather an accurate reflection of the model's proportions. This woman with large breasts is Dodge's ideal of beauty. Dodge remembered how he first met the young Derinda. He and his wife, Dorothy, were shopping when they encountered her in her grandparents' store in Glens Falls. Dodge remembered:

> ... she was sitting on a pile of rugs in the corner. She was striking, not beautiful but striking. Her body arranged itself naturally in good ways. I asked her grandparents if their granddaughter would like to pose for my class sometime and they were agreeable. That was one of the nice things about a small town, almost everybody knew who you were. It was also kind of inhibiting in a way because you knew you couldn't get by with anything.[183]

Dodge indulged his fascination for the blossoming fecundity of young women in his works *Another Autumn, Day Before Spring* (c. 1945), *The Garden Wall* (c. 1951), and *Spring* (1953).[184] Incidentally, *Another Autumn* is the title of a song from Lerner's musical *Paint Your Wagon*. Dodge gave *Another Autumn* to Professor Sydney Freedberg, his tutor and friend at Harvard, as a wedding present.[185] In the painting, a woman who is nude down to her draped hips faces the viewer. With both hands just below her navel she holds a terracotta pot from which falls a vine. It should be noted, however, that the artist described the plant as dead on an index card in his files.[186] Centered in the composition, the woman stands before a blue wall on which hang two representations from the art history canon, the *Madonna del Granduca* by Raphael and van Gogh's *Sunflowers*. The *Sunflowers* painting hangs from a string on a nail in the wall above the woman's right shoulder; below it and contained within the same frame is a white sheet of paper against which is propped the handle of a mop. Is the paper for notes? Is it possibly a calendar? The glass covering the Raphael is cracked and shattered. Beneath the Renaissance Madonna and child is a pail, its bottom placed next to the white baseboard with its curved handle casting a shadow on the wood floor.

In Raphael's painting the viewer recognizes Dodge's reference to the concept of the ideal mother and virgin. Dodge also may have selected the painting as a veiled tribute to Freedberg who was an eminent scholar of the Italian Renaissance.[187] The cracked glass may refer to the loss of tradition in art and culture, a theme the artist explored in the *Gods of Our Fathers: The Classical Tradition* and *The Christian Tradition*, (1949-50, pls. 21, 22). The sunflowers in *Another Autumn* refer to nature and reproduction and seem more alive than the contents of the flowerpot. The painting appears to present opposites or at least contrasts between the traditional and the modern. It can also allude to the nature of woman's transformation from virgin to mother.

Dodge seems to have reveled in the sinuous curves of the van Gogh composition, repeating its undulating contours in those of his female model. Even the placement of the woman's curls and tresses relates to the oppositional elements in the paintings above her shoulders. Is the inclusion of mop and pail a reference to domesticity? A sexual innuendo? Both? Dodge has clearly stated in his many writings and lectures that he delighted in ambiguity.

In the works considered above Dodge brought together the two subjects that had figured prominently, and would continue to figure prominently, in his artistic production: the beautiful nude and the still life. Throughout the forties and fifties, Dodge would paint young, voluptuous women. Dodge was intrigued, some would say obsessed, by the incipient sexuality and latent eroticism of young women on the brink of self realization.

Dodge exploits his awareness of the symbolic significance of the nude Aphrodite or Venus in the history of art and culture in the small pendants *Gods of Our Fathers: The Classical Tradition* and *The Christian Tradition* painted between 1949 and 1950. The general theme of the pair of works is that both the classical and the Christian doctrines have deteriorated in modern society; Christian and pagan images have been discarded.[188] A fallen and broken statue of a beautiful Venus symbolizes the classical tradition that has, in a sense, been junked by the Christian tradition. Venus represents the love of life and the life of love. There is also a reference to the discovery of sex by the three adolescents who examine the damaged statue; appropriately Venus is equipped with the attributes of love, a bow and arrow, usually given to her son, Cupid.

In the second painting, another broken sculpture, in this case a male angel that the boys are trying to reassemble, represents the Christian tradition. One holds a chunk of the wing. Another holds the

Fig. 17 —Detail: **Derinda Duross**, Model

head, which looks very much like an older version of the youngster's, next to his own, repeating the curious juxtaposition seen in *The Art Student*. As the angel has fallen, a kite, representing heavenly aspirations, is also grounded. The placement of the narrative in a cemetery recalls the slightly earlier works *Black and Blue*, *Elegy* and *Frankie and Johnny*, where the tombstones and monuments referred to the origins of jazz and the blues. Dodge used the cemetery setting here to represent Christianity's central tenet, belief in life after death.[189]

Another related work from this early period is *The Nest*. A young man playing a guitar leans against the base of a fallen tree. Engulfed in its roots, he seems lost in his own thoughts and oblivious to the nude woman behind him who straddles the tree in a provocative pose as she reaches upward, arm silhouetted by the sky, for a nest. When asked about this work, Dodge responded that women are often the nest makers and the nurturers, while men are often the dreamers and the planners. He also explained that:

> It's ... full of symbols of the relation between Man and Woman, sexual and otherwise. Like in ... *The Key is Lost* where the girl presses her bare body against the rough bricks of the chimney, the girl here, astraddle the tree trunk, is, I'm afraid, a slightly sadistic attempt to create a physical reaction on the part of the viewer.[190]

Fig. 18 —Detail: **Lisa, Tia, Jamie, Jeff, and Julie**, 1959

Toward the middle of the fifties and into the early sixties, Dodge increasingly presented the nude as a subject in her own right. Kenneth Clark noted, «the nude is not the subject of art, but a form of art.»[191] Clark contrasts the meanings of the words naked and nude noting that the former means:

> ... to be deprived of our clothes, and the word implies some of the embarrassment most of us feel in that condition. The word «nude,» on the other hand, carries, in educated usage, no uncomfortable overtone. The vague image it projects ... is ... of a balanced, prosperous and confident body: the body reformed.»[192]

The Awakening (1955, pl. 30), shows a young woman sitting at the edge of a bed that is covered with white sheets in disarray. Nude to the waist, she stares out at the viewer and holds a mirror. As the title suggests, she seems at the edge of self realization in the process of her own development and maturation, much like the clothed but also voluptuous figures in *No Turning Back* and *What Struggle to Escape*. Dodge noted that he was «trying a different color range here» and «the drapery held equal fascination and its busy form served to balance the girl, who is awakening both from sleep and symbolically into womanhood.»[193]

Other nudes from this time show not the explicit symbolism of *The Awakening*, but women partially clad and partially exposed.[194] Of *Nude Girl Seated on a Bed* (1961), Dodge observed that his paintings of adolescent girls in the early sixties «were running somewhat parallel to those of Balthus in France; and, in some respects, I definitely was influenced— even though I had been doing quite similar themes some years before I heard of him.»[195]

The models Dodge used for his own paintings were often those used in his classes taught at The Hyde Collection. In his autobiographical musings Dodge confided:

> I never, absolutely never, made a pass at any of the models that I had, either for the class or myself. There were times when it was tempting, I must say. I think in some cases some of the models expected it, or thought that it was part of the adventure of being a model.... But I never did, and partly it was my own reserve, shyness, and to some extent fastidiousness, and partly because I wanted to avoid bad consequences, and partly because I didn't want to lose a good model by making unwanted advances. These outweighed the momentary lure or lustful gratification, or even the possibility of true romance.[196]

When Dodge mused about his preference for painting nudes he recalled an episode from his youth in Detroit involving the mother of a friend next door, who was, as he remembered, «quite a voluptuous woman, very busty, beautiful skin, and reddish blond hair.»[197] Tadé Styka, a well-known portrait painter at that time, was painting her and the young Dodge was allowed to observe the artist at work a few times when he was over playing with his friend. Up until this point in Dodge's young life he had thought «that what was under a girl's dress was a mystery.»[198] One day when Dodge and the boy were playing with pop guns, Dodge was on the balcony and became aware that the mother was stepping out of the bath. He remembered:

> I'm pretty sure now that she must have heard or seen me out on the porch. I think she deliberately let me get a look. It was quite something; but it was from a sunny outdoors into a dark bathroom with a half opened

window. I just saw glimpses, not much more than that. But it was a pretty exciting event in my young life for a while. I guess that's the only real woman I saw naked until I got married in my twenties, although when I was in my late teens, I had managed to discover the mysteries of the brassiere, but not much beyond that. Maybe therein lies the reason why I like to paint nudes.[199]

Dodge would continue to paint nudes throughout his life. During the latter half of his career in Florida he occasionally drew from photographs he had taken of models in Glens Falls. Much of his inspiration, however, would be drawn from a beautiful woman he met in Jacksonville: Laura Jeanne Klempf would serve as his primary and central source for the depiction of the female nude after his move from Glens Falls.

Portraits of the Artist's Children

Dodge also painted portraits, although portraiture was not a major category in his work. In addition to self-portraits he painted several commissioned portraits, among them: Sandy Beeman in Glens Falls; Mary Whitney Renz, the granddaughter of Mrs. Hyde, painted as a girl and as an adult; her husband Franklin Renz; and Harold Colee, the president of the Florida Chamber of Commerce. Dodge painted portraits of all of his children, including a portrait of his first son, Joseph Morrell Dodge II, (c. 1949-50), and later portraits of Tia as an adult, the Dodges' eldest daughter, which he realized in 1985 before her death from cancer in 1993.

In Glens Falls between 1958 and 1959, Dodge painted two depictions of his children from his marriage to Dorothy MacArthur Dodge. Both paintings show young children on an oriental rug. In the first and smaller of the two, *The Artist's Children: Tia, Jeff, Lisa, and Julie* (1958, pl. 33), all four are shown.[200] Tia and Jeff recline at the viewer's left. Jeff's head rests on a small pillow and he holds a toy helicopter, its red body and yellow blades echoing the colors of the boy's outfit and the carpet beneath. Tia, dressed in an orange jumper, a white tee-shirt, black Mary Jane shoes and white socks, rests her head on her right hand; her blonde tresses spill over her forearm. She looks out of the picture and her gaze is dreamy but alert. Beneath Tia's elbow and under Jeff's pillow are children's drawings. Behind Tia's head is a book.

Lisa and Julie are at the right in the painting.[201] Julie sits primly in a blue dress with a lace-trimmed collar, her hands clasped in her lap. Lisa sits facing the viewer; her right arm is extended and in her hand she holds an apple with green leaves and a long stem. In the corner of the work there is a white plate that holds three apples. Dodge has provided an apple of innocence, of knowledge, of life, for each of the four children.

For all the references to childhood in the dress, the drawings, and the toy, the painting is subdued in a kind of arrested moment. One writer found the work to be puzzling, remarking:

> Dodge charges his children's portrayal by the enigmatic presentation of each. Grouped on an oriental rug, the youngest of the two girls seated at right holds up a green leafed red apple; lying on the contrastingly patterned carpet, the 8 year old boy holds a toy helicopter as his oldest sister gazes into an unseen distance through the right edge of the canvas. Psychologically we are pulled into this group portrait by the atypical stilled action of the four young kids, by the expressionless mouths and the staring eyes of the three that look directly at the painter, father, observer and you. What *is* each thinking, feeling?[202]

Of the second painting of the two older daughters, *Tia and Julie* (1959, pl. 38), Dodge observed:

> ... the composition as a whole is interesting, I think, and the colors more decorative than usual.... Julie ... really did sit in cardboard boxes when she was 5. She's still a loner but as she's grown older, she's found other kinds of boxes in which to take refuge from time to time—psychological and intellectual ones.[203]

Compositionally *Tia and Julie* is an interesting study of interrelationships of lines, shapes, and forms. There is a geometrical quality to the interplay of the box, the carpet, and the room itself. In the earlier painting of the four children, the bodies are either largely parallel or perpendicular to the picture plane, whereas everything is placed at an angle in the later portrait.

As in the earlier portrait, an apple and a book appear in *Tia and Julie*. The doll in the chair at the viewer's right is positioned much like the doll, obviously the same prop in *No Turning Back*. Clearly the artist's daughters are preadolescents here and the symbolism in *No Turning Back* painted in the same year is neither necessary nor appropriate. Yet the innocent plaything foreshadows womanhood and serves as a reminder of the transitory and illusory qualities of childhood. Again Tia looks out of the picture smiling sweetly, while Julie, engulfed by the box and her green dress, tilts her head and meets the gaze of the onlooker. In presenting his children in positions of quiet repose, Dodge allows for analytical introspection about the nature of childhood. Both portraits are bittersweet records of evanescent youth.

The Still Life

In reminiscing about the development of his early work Dodge pinpointed three areas of major importance. The first was his excitement about Modern art:

I think that enthusiasm was an element that permeated these various excursions into the styles of Picasso, Bonnard, Dalí, Soutine (of all people), Eugene Berman (I still love his work), Hopper, Alexander Brook (who seems pretty weak to me now), whatever was in *Art News*, *Art Digest* or whatever book or magazine I'd seen last. It took me a long time working through that, partly because I liked so much of it. In the paintings I was doing then, I was trying to make «Art» in the form of, or in the costume of, those artists I mentioned.... I began to work out of that, I think, when I started trying to paint my feelings about Jazz.[204]

Another breakthrough occurred when:

I started painting romantic ... mildly erotic images, kind of like late Bellini, Giorgione, Watteau, Fragonard.... I wasn't really trying to paint in the style of those artists. I just realized that they were kindred spirits and felt justified that, if they could do it, I could too. If they could paint men and women in romantic or erotic relationships with people playing musical instruments in a landscape, well, so could I in my own terms and with my own experiences.[205]

A third area Dodge saw as a significant milestone in his artistic maturity was his personal discovery of the expressive possibilities of the still life:

Painting still lifes for me became quite unlike the Cézanne thing, which was the accepted touchstone of still life painting at the time. It was something that had other overtones. It had a certain mystery about it or a kind of symbolic value. These objects weren't just apples put in the composition as spots of color, but it was an apple because of a reference to Adam and Eve, let's say, or something else.... It wasn't just a matter of a spot of color or an arrangement of shapes, but an arrangement of suggestions, resonances, surprises, mysteries.[206]

Dodge's treatment and presentation of the various symbolic objects in *What Struggle to Escape* and *No Turning Back* reflect his growing interest in the still-life genre.[207] In fact, his style is one of such insistent precision and meticulous execution that many of his subjects, whether landscapes or figure studies, share a still-life quality.

An early still life, *The Fruit of Knowledge* (pl. 26) completed in 1951, was included in the artist's Wildenstein exhibition of 1952.[208]

Dodge discussed the work in his 1969 lecture:

The title and subject, of course, allude to the apple of the Garden of Eden, and [suggest] that knowledge, by itself, is a rotten fruit. Here you see, I've emphasized the geometry of the stark, simple forms in contrast to the natural form of the apple, and, as part of this, made carefully planned use of shadows as positive elements in the design, creating in this way a certain feeling of distillation, let's say, and a kind of visual drama that would be in the tradition of Caravaggio and Georges de la Tour.

I was also interested in the repetitions and variations of certain shapes and a kind of rhythmical «phrasing» of these shapes—such as you'd find in the spacing of figures in the frescoes of Piero della Francesca, or in the *fêtes galantes* of Watteau, or the ballet dancers of Degas.

If I compare my works with these great masters, please believe me, it's not out of conceit. I have learned a lot from them, but any references are to particular characteristics and are not in any way an attempt to equate my work with theirs on the level of either quality or achievement.[209]

The Fruit of Knowledge shows the artist's interest in presenting the objects close to the picture plane and setting them off by a black negative space. This practice will be seen in numerous works throughout the artist's career. The apple also recurs as a major symbol for Dodge. It was present in *Frankie and Johnny* in *Trio* in the portraits of his children, and in *No Turning Back*.

Mr. and Mrs. Lyman Beeman Senior originally purchased the *Fruit of Knowledge*. Beeman was president of Finch, Pruyn and Company, Inc. in Glens Falls, and the painting hung in Beeman's office there. When Governor Nelson Rockefeller visited the paper mill on August 7, 1962, he admired Dodge's work and quipped that the rotting apple couldn't possibly be a New York variety. Beeman replied, «that the books [in the painting] were of high quality, though, because they were printed on Finch Textbook, one of Finch, Pruyn's latest product developments.»[210] A photograph of the smiling Governor in front of Dodge's painting was included in the company publication, *The Scout*.[211]

In 1954 Dodge painted *The Chinese Puzzle (Still Life with Wooden Chinese Puzzles*, pl. 29*)* in response to the Quemoy-Matsu crisis. Quemoy and Matsu are two small islands less than two miles off the coast of China. They had been claimed and garrisoned by Chiang Kai-shek, the leader of the Chinese Nationalists, whose troops used them to observe the mainland, stage raids against the Chinese Communists, and to disrupt Chinese coastal shipping.[212] The People's Republic of China retaliated by shelling Quemoy, now called Jinmen, in September, 1954. President Dwight D. Eisenhower's advisers urged him to defend the islands even to the point of «including the use of atomic weapons.»[213] The defense of Quemoy and Matsu was tied to the security of Formosa, now Taiwan, and the actions of the United States were seen throughout the world as potent commentary against the spread of communism. Secretary of State John Foster Dulles predicted «at least an even chance of war» and warned of a «quite serious showdown.»[214] The crisis did not end until April, 1955, when the Chinese Communists initiated a conciliatory line of communication.[215]

The Chinese Puzzle contains two puzzles, one is partially reconstructed while the other is complete and forms a globe. The globe rests in a nest of twine atop a lidless box. The twine hangs down and looks convincingly like a fuse for dynamite, which would be very appropriate in this case. Painted in a convincing *trompe l'œil* is a sheet of directions for the puzzle tacked to the wall; at the bottom right is «Made in Japan.» One wonders if this is a subtle commentary on the political crisis because Japan had occupied Taiwan for fifty years before the Nationalist Chinese invasion. On one level *The Chinese Puzzle* is a characteristic still life for Dodge. The light streams in from the left. The objects are presented on a tabletop close to the viewer. The geometrical interplay of the pieces of the puzzle probably delighted the artist. On another level, Dodge deftly alludes to the political complexity of the Quemoy-Matsu situation. Dodge gave the painting to his father who, in turn, presented it to President Eisenhower. The work is now part of the collection of the Eisenhower Library in Abilene, Kansas.[216]

Other still lifes painted during the decade of the fifties include *Still Life with Coffee Grinder* and *Sewing Basket* or *Work Basket* (pl. 32, both 1955). Dodge recalled:

> During the 50's, a variety of subjects occupied my atten-tion. I did a number of still lifes, for instance. This small *Sewing Basket* is one that's very detailed, and I really knocked myself out on the lace, the thread, and so forth. Every once in a while, for some unknown reason, I feel compelled to do this kind of thing. I don't know whether it's a purge or a penance, or a subconscious need to prove myself, or the need for self-discipline. Who knows?[217]

Still Life with Coffee Grinder shows a coffee grinder wrapped in burlap with an apple in a blue and white bowl and a tin cup .[218] The objects are placed on a tabletop in front of a black background, decidedly reminiscent of Baroque works from the seventeenth century by artists such as Caravaggio and Zurbarán. Dodge observed:

> For some reason or other, I work more naturally in this technique than any other—that is, working out from a dark background. Maybe I should have been a Baroque artist like one of the followers of Caravaggio or Zurbarán. I admire their work immensely; but I didn't

Fig. 19 —**Governor Nelson Rockefeller and** *The Fruit of Knowledge*, 1962

get this idea from them—at least not consciously and directly. As best I remember, it was a small, black and white reproduction of a still life by André Derain that began this train of thought and prompted *Girl With a Blue Cloak*. But I suppose a general familiarity with the Caravaggesque school was behind both Derain's painting and my own sudden discovery of Zurbarán.[219]

The Girl with a Blue Cloak (1955, pl. 31) mentioned above was the first of the black background paintings Dodge would paint.[220] As has been seen already in *What Struggle to Escape* and *No Turning Back,* the black acts as an effective foil for the objects, throwing them into prominent relief. The importance and masterful use of negative space continued to be a distinctive characteristic of future works by Dodge up through his last paintings. For examples see *Dancing Pears I and II: Fandango* (1992, pls. 95, 96) and *Still Life: Bundle and String* (1996).

The black background dominates Dodge's still-life paintings of the sixties. From 1960 is *Pavane*, titled after its completion. The juxtaposition of the two apples with their flowing, skirt-like leaves reminded him of the stately court dance by couples contained in the meaning of the title, which implies courtliness and courting.[221] This idea of «dancing» fruit would be revived thirty-five years later also in *Dancing Pears I and II: Fandango.*

Dodge painted numerous other still lifes against dark backgrounds in the sixties, and his works show the tremendous variety that is possible within the confines of this genre. The saturated intensity of the red in the *Bell Peppers* (1960, pl. 39), coupled with the shiny surface of the waxy peels, glows against the white bowl rimmed with a blue pattern. The tablecloth is rumpled and exposes a portion of the table, which is placed at an angle to the picture plane. The corner juts out in what recalls a standard Baroque device.

Still Life with Lemons and Yellow Tulips (1960, pl. 40) presents more objects with which the viewer must contend. One lemon is placed on the table.

43

Three lemons rest in a bowl; behind the bowl a knife rests on another. A napkin is draped over the edge of the table. To the right are three vessels, a white pitcher, a blue vase holding seven tulips, and a glass goblet. In this work there appears to be an interest in asymmetrical balance with the visual weight of the three cylindrical containers answered by the compelling and defining foil of the negative space.

Of these selections one notes that in *Still Life with Three Persimmons* (1964, pl. 43) three objects are again nestled in a bowl. Obviously this was a highly satisfying compositional motif for Dodge. Again the crumpled napkin is present. The rich orange of the fruit contrasts effectively with its complementary color, the blue in the rim of the bowl. Again a knife rests on an empty bowl. A tin pitcher, its handle placed toward the viewer, catches the play of reflected light and colors from the napkin, the plate, and the fruit. Of this painting Dodge observed, «The more massive group of forms on the right is easily balanced, in my opinion, by the single napkin on the left. When isolated, this napkin seems to have a kind of life and mystery and visual interest of its own.»[222]

In all three of these works with fruit, bowls, and napkins, Dodge has considered the light with great care; the reflected shadows painstakingly acknowledge the red, yellow, and orange, respectively. As is true in all of Dodge's works there is a delight in details, in accuracy, and in a compositional poetry that stems from the interplay of shapes, forms, and volumes.

With its dramatic *chiaroscuro* and its black background, *Easter Still Life* (1965, pl. 44) is the largest of Dodge's «black background» paintings. In a very symmetrical composition objects are arranged to evoke Eucharistic allusions of communion, sacrifice, and rebirth.[223] The selection comes from the increasingly recognizable repertoire of Dodge's favored images. From the left is a white plate, in front of which stands a lone artichoke; between those are a crumpled napkin and a red rose, its bloom facing out. A pomegranate is close to the edge of the dark tabletop, its vine trailing off the edge and out of the picture. In the center is a potted daffodil with three flowers. The clay pot is partially visible under a material or foil wrapping. To the right is a loaf of bread, its end is already cut. A knife's handle rests on the tabletop, its blade is poised in an arrested slice in the bread. A goblet of wine is placed in front of and to the right of the loaf. There are two eggs near the knife's handle. To the right of the bread and wine are the remaining eggshells of another egg. Although the still lifes following *Easter Still Life* would never be quite as ambitious in either the sheer number of objects included or in the Christian symbolism intended, there were still outstanding and highly original treatments of the genre to come.

Two noteworthy still lifes from the late sixties are *Apples and Knife* (*Five Apples with Knife*, 1967), and *Mushrooms* (1969, pl. 53). The precisely rendered mushrooms are arranged in a variety of positions almost as if Dodge were presenting figures to illustrate frontal, profile, and three-quarter views. The light pours in from the right, and the shadows create a pattern of shapes in response to the forms above them. The curvilinear lines and edges suggest movement and create a rhythmic cadence, calling to mind a piece of music.

Dodge described *Apples and Knife* (*Five Apples with Knife*) in his 1969 lecture at the University of Florida:

> The knife slicing into one apple is not only a compositional device but, even more, an emotional one. But the real visual pleasure, to me, is in the drapery, which is kind of a landscape, or perhaps a pure abstraction—depending on how you're esthetically oriented.[224]

This slicing knife would become a motif, occasionally reappearing in later works. More importantly, Dodge's statement presages his later renderings of rocks, drapery, and paper.

Dodge moved with his wife and four children to Jacksonville, Florida, in 1962 to assume the position of director of the newly opened Cummer Gallery of Art. *Florida Bouquet* (1968) is a whimsical reference to his newly adopted state. An empty container for Minute Maid™ orange juice concentrate holds an arrangement consisting primarily of azaleas and oleander that came from the family yard. The casual, clever work brings an instant smile of recognition at Dodge's intended humor.

Another bouquet, magisterial in contrast, is *Crinum Lily and Shells* (1969, pl. 51). Set in a white vase, one long stem supports cascading white flowers in full bloom, tight buds, and half-opened blossoms. The flowers cascade and undulate as if they were pouring forth from a fountain. At the base of the vase are three shells—another nod to Florida, perhaps? The shell on the right projects from the tabletop at an angle. The shell closest to the container on the left is reflected in the pearly surface. The shells are painted with Dodge's characteristic attention to texture. Taken singly each has its own topography. The contrast between the hardened shells placed on the firm horizontal of the table, and the luxuriant and sinuous lilies that emerge and dangle from the pale green vertical is arresting. Yet the formal similarities of curves and crevices link and unite the disparate objects.

The last of this selection from the group of still lifes set against dark backgrounds to be discussed is *Dixie Eggs: Portrait of Edward Klempf and his Father* (1969, pl. 52). Dodge met Edward and Laura Jeanne Klempf shortly after his arrival in Jacksonville, Florida.

They would become close friends, and Jeanne would be his primary model, confidante, and adviser. In fact, Dodge often referred to Jeanne as his muse.[225] It was Jeanne who asked Dodge to paint a portrait of her husband's father as a surprise birthday gift for her husband. The portrait is inventive. The family business, Dixie Egg, is one of the largest distributors of eggs in the Southeast. The elder Klempf had died in 1966, and all Dodge had to work from was an old photograph. The artist recalled that the idea of using a prism paperweight to reflect and refract images of father and son came out of the blue. Here the fractions of the father's image are mirrored in his son's and vice versa. Three whole eggs are joined by the cracked shell of another recalling a similar treatment in *Easter Still Life*. On one level the eggs can be seen as heraldic family emblems. Symbolically they retain their suggestions of the promise of life and continuity as the cracked and empty pieces of shell memorialize the dead patriarch.

Abandoning the still life in the seventies, Dodge decided to embark on a major project to depict Jeanne Klempf. He was also stimulated by his new environment and painted and drew images drawn from the immediate vicinity, including Fort Clinch and the coquina rock formations at Washington Oaks Park south of St. Augustine. Lastly, he began to travel frequently, especially after his retirement from the Cummer in 1972. Trips to the Yucatán, Greece and the Greek islands, Italy, and Egypt inspired Dodge and influenced his work with increasing regularity. The artist resumed his interest in the still life around 1979. Rare, however, would be the black background of the still-life paintings of the fifties and sixties. Instead, the artist changed the repertoire of images in his later still lifes to include new elements, which included crumpled paper and «dancing» pears.

The Later Paintings

Paintings of Jeanne

Laura Jeanne, Mrs. Edward Klempf, was one of Dodge's closest friends in Jacksonville. The artist met the Klempfs not long after moving to northeast Florida. They have one of the finest and largest private collections of his paintings and drawings. Dodge referred to Jeanne as his friend, model, and muse. They spoke almost every day, sharing life's triumphs, tribulations, and above all, an abundance of laughter.

In a 1994 newspaper article titled «Chosen to become an artist's muse,» Klempf explained that she first became acquainted with Dodge's work at a Jacksonville University exhibition; she would come to her class early so she would have time to view his creations.[226] When they first met she found Dodge to be «gruff» and she was suspicious when he said to her, «I've been painting you my whole life.»[227] In fact, Jeanne Klempf was the ideal beauty for Dodge.

In Dodge's 1969 lecture at the University of Florida, he addressed the genesis of an idea involving the representation of Jeanne that would inform his artistic production for the next twenty-five years:

> I've been saving the best for last—not only because it fits here chronologically, and because it's still incomplete—but because I think of it, so far, as my unfinished masterpiece. About two and a half years ago, I started to do a portrait of a very good friend—a young matron, with three children—who was interested in the arts and who was willing to sit from time to time. She and her husband were collectors and had bought a couple of my things—and, although the portrait wasn't a commission, it was something they were both interested in. As I got thinking about it, the primary problem of portraiture seemed more and more insurmountable, and that's the problem of selecting that <u>one</u> pose, that <u>one</u> angle of the head, that <u>one</u> expression, that <u>one</u> gesture of the hand, that <u>one</u> light and costume, and so forth that effectively sums up the subject.

> The problem was compounded by the fact that she's a very beautiful person—in every way, and, as any painter knows who's tried it, a beautiful woman is much more difficult to paint (although certainly more fun) than an ugly one—or even a plain one. In fact, this became something of a challenge after one of her less tactful friends made an issue of it one night, saying that she didn't have enough «character lines» in her face to make an interesting portrait.

> Anyway, the more I thought about it, and the more I wrestled with it; the more absurd it became. Nobody is just one thing; everyone has different facets to [his or her] personality—and even to [one's] appearance—especially a woman. No one image therefore, can express the whole person—or come even close to it.

> And then, suddenly with bulbs flashing on and off, the obvious occurred to me, one night. Why not try to express these different facets of personality and so forth, in a series of images. Why be satisfied with just one? But how? On one canvas? Fifty years ago, the Cubists had expressed multiple facets of the subject on one canvas, but those could hardly be called portraits. Motion pictures could do it; but to my knowledge even that approach to portraiture hasn't been attempted as yet. And in any case, I'm a painter not a cinematographer, so I had to solve it in terms of the painted surface.

> Well, anyway, once I'd discovered what the obvious problem was, the solution, or at least, a solution became equally obvious, and strangely enough, the answer was to be found back in my own career, where I'd painted

several subjects (like the quarry), in a series because just one canvas didn't exhaust its possibilities. So with this portrait, where the subject was infinitely more complex—and interesting, why not simply paint a series of images of her, rather than try to compress all into one?

The next observation stemmed from the first one and helped determine the format, so to speak; and this was the fact that one rarely looks at the whole person. We tend to focus on parts—usually the face, but occasionally such details as an ear, or a hand, or a knee, or whatever—and these fragments can also be expressive of the subject, can add up to a total picture.

So then, when I got those two ideas, I felt something like Columbus must have felt. Here was this round world and this great continent sitting there all this time and nobody had noticed it before. I can't tell you how elated I felt.

But it also presented a few problems of its own. In the first place, I felt that each of these facets should be independently a work of art, esthetically complete in itself, and not just a part of some large puzzle. I don't know whether or not I've succeeded in this, but I've certainly tried.

Secondly, it has turned out to be an open-ended project. The better I got to know the subject, the more facets were revealed; and each new facet seemed to suggest still others; and about the only limits are those of time, and the good will of the subject (and her family), and my own abilities. Again, I've been lucky. I haven't tried to flatter her. In fact, I don't see how I could have made many improvements with this subject. Nor has she (or her husband) demanded them—as so many portrait subjects (and their loved ones) usually do. I shudder when I think of what might have happened had I gotten this idea with someone less understanding or less tolerant—probably what happened to that great realist, Thomas Eakins, who complained that every time he painted a portrait, he lost a friend.

I've simply painted what I saw—told it like it is, so to speak, have tried to make the art 'The Mirror of Nature,' as Leonardo said, and they've turned out to be my most realistic paintings to date and taken as a whole, I think my very best.[228]

For the next few decades Dodge regularly exhibited a selection of the canvases that examined the many aspects of Jeanne. Reaction to the portrait was highly favorable. Twenty of the paintings were shown in his 1968 exhibition at The Group Gallery. A reviewer found «the series itself to be a remarkable achievement—certainly one of the most outstanding by a Jacksonville artist in recent years. In sum, Dodge has given us a composite portrait of one woman, and has done so with candor, taste, and skill.»[229]

At the Realist Invitational in October, 1969, at The Gallery of Contemporary Art in Winston-Salem, North Carolina, Dodge was one of ten southeastern artists

who were featured with five artists of international reputation. Dodge shared the billing with Andrew Wyeth and John Koch among others. In addition to *Sunday Afternoon at Fort Clinch* (1964, pl. 42), *Lush Life (The Good Life,* 1966, pl. 45*)* and *Easter Still Life* he exhibited twenty-nine panels of the *Portrait of Jeanne.* The response to Dodge's project was glowing:

> Ted Potter, director of the Gallery of Contemporary Art ... has hung a show in his gallery that may restore faith in contemporary art to a confused and frequently disgusted public. It is the Realist Invitational and it would be difficult to find an exhibition ... more distinguished and more pleasing.

> Dodge, with 33 canvases, outscores all others, who are represented by three or four paintings. This was achieved by covering one gallery wall with 29 canvases hung as a unit and titled *Portrait of Jeanne.* Dodge, who was an art history major at Harvard, took up painting without a lesson. He has fragmented Jeanne in what he labels his «multi canvas» portrait, a miscellany of an ear, a hand, an eye, a selection of chaste nude sections. All done with skill and impact. And there, her superb form completely intact and delivering plenty of impact in her own right, was the model herself, Jeanne Klempfh (*sic*) of Jacksonville, Fla.[230]

Dodge painted between eighty-five and one hundred paintings in the *Portrait of Jeanne* (Fig. 22) series. They include studies of facial expressions that range from contemplative introspection, mirthful grins, pleasant smiles, pained anguish, an assessing stare, to dreamy slumber. One particularly effective treatment shows the reflection of a troubled visage in a round mirror surrounded by black. There are also fragments of the model's body and close-up details including a palm, an ear, knees, and legs. Dodge does more than objectively render anatomical parts; he also explores formal and compositional possibilities on realistic and abstract levels. In these various panels there is also a frank celebration of the voluptuous sensuality of the female form. The torsos, draped and nude, are beautiful female topographies.

In one panel *Draped Torso* (1966-68), the subject holds drapery in front of her bare torso. The effect is reminiscent of Greek sculptures of women in the fifth century b.c. who are draped in «wet» cloth, which seems to conceal as it reveals. It is clear that Dodge delighted in the fullness of the female form in addition to the cascading folds and pleats of the white material. Set close to the picture plane and against a black background, the painting is contemporary with still lifes *Apples and Knife (Five Apples with Knife)* and *Mushrooms.*

Hand Holding Apple (pl. 46) also painted between 1966 and 1968, shows only a bare midriff. The left hand offering an apple with a bite taken out of it, reminding the viewer of Dodge's earlier symbolic uses of *The Fruit of Knowledge, Frankie and Johnny* and the portraits of the artist's children. To the viewer's right, the curves and lines of the leaves of a sellum palm echo the contours of this evocation of Eve. In another canvas from this period, *Hand Holding Rose* (1966-68), a right hand silhouetted against a blue background grasps the flower that is past its prime. There is a carefully observed balance at work in this simple image.

Over the decades, Dodge stayed true to his original idea of fragmenting the figure. In *Bust* (1968, pl. 49) from early in the series, one does see Jeanne's face but it is cropped at the head's edges. In this narrow vertical panel the curves of the breasts answer the diagonals of throat and chin. An hourglass figure predominates in *Back* (1979, pl. 48) where only slivers of the distant beach can be seen between Jeanne's elbows and waist. In an untitled panel (1979), Dodge shows her again from about mid-forehead down to her waist. One sees a profile and a portion of her back as she turns. Her left arm rests on her breast, which is accentuated by the protrusion of a firm nipple. About ten years later in another untitled work (1988), there is a frontal torso that extends from below the navel to just above a smile. Here, too, the figure is set in front of beach and sky. In this painting, Jeanne holds her hands above her breasts resting her fingertips against the collarbone.

When interviewed by Sharon Weightman in 1994 regarding modeling nude, Jeanne noted, «twenty-five years ago it wasn't something you did. But I discussed it with my husband, who thought Jerry was such a wonderful artist. And he said, as long as it's in good taste. And it always has been.»[231] The paintings did raise eyebrows among the conservative sector of Jacksonville. Jeanne was actually asked directly by a woman if she were having an affair with Jerry Dodge. She replied «Oh, yes! An affair of the eyes, the mind and the heart.»[232] Jerry Dodge was very much part of the Klempf family. He convalesced in the Klempf home after major surgeries; he shared holiday dinners and he celebrated birthdays there. Jeanne Klempf was indeed Dodge's muse, his soul mate, his model, but above all, she was his dearest friend.

As Dodge noted in his 1969 lecture, he always thought of the paintings of Jeanne project as open-ended. Although Dodge created fewer works for the *Portrait of Jeanne* series in the late 1980s, he used Jeanne as a model for numerous other works including *Lady of the Rocks* (1967) and *Interlude on the Rocks #4* (1976, pl. 71) among many others. Regardless of how or why he painted Jeanne Klempf, he always painted her «lovingly, lavishly, luminously.»[233]

Throughout much of the sixties, in addition to being absorbed by his project of painting Jeanne, Dodge was also painting the still lifes with black back-grounds; scenes of Fort Clinch, the Yucatán, and Greece; and numerous beach and coastal subjects. In the seventies Jeanne appears in paintings, but less as part of the portrait endeavor and more as an ideal nude in the sense alluded to above in Kenneth Clark's characterization «of a balanced, prosperous and con-fident body: the body reformed.»[234] Dodge's refined technical abilities in rendering space and anatomical details is demonstrated in such works as *Model Adjusting Drapery* (1974), where Jeanne is clearly recognizable as she sits and arranges a white sheet. Her left hand holds the sheet in between white breasts. The resulting triangular area is subtly echoed throughout the composition from the head and shoul-ders of the figure to the slanting arms of the chair. This blue chair was a prop Dodge used again in *Nude in Blue Victorian Chair* (1974, pl. 64), where Jeanne has thrown her head back and is holding it with her hands. This results in long lines of hips to arms and upraised elbows, answered by a soft and vulnerable throat. The chair is also seen in *After The Bath #2* (1981, pl. 78) where Jeanne's elbows are also raised with hands behind the back of her head, but here her face is clearly visible. She gazes into the distance and the yellow is an effective foil for the model's red hair. In all three of these paintings, the carved circular design at the ends of the chair arms seems to repeat the breasts' adornment, the nipple. As in the majority of Dodge's nudes, the figures are presented in front of a negative space defined by one color. Little if any-thing competes with the contemplative admiration of the contours of the body. An appreciative critic once remarked about a Dodge nude that the artist «has managed to maintain a delicate balance between cool detachment which goes with classicism and the implicit eroticism of both concept and treatment.»[235]

There are paintings of the nude Jeanne sitting; reclining on a bed in a variety of poses, some more provocative than others; and walking on the beach. Dodge worked from photographs, and in comparing the nudes one can see that related poses were proba-bly captured at one sitting on a roll of film. Examples would be the small *Study for Laura in a Deck Chair* (1980) where the model is set against a blue wall, and *Laura Jeanne in a Deck Chair* (1980) in which she is on the beach, and *Laura Jeanne in a Bentwood Chair* (1976, pl. 72).[236] *A Time in the Sun* (1972) is also related to this series. The vantage points differ, but from the robe, the pose, and gesture, it is clear the images are from the same photographic session.

Typically, Dodge's nudes are shown in various positions in beds. The drawing technique and the use of black and red pencil in *Nude* from the seventies are reminiscent of Fragonard or Boucher as is the erotic abandon. In *Summer Siesta* (1976), a work in ink, the figure's legs are drawn up and one breast is exposed. In reference to *Summer Siesta*, a reviewer commented on the « idealized view of the nude.

Here she is self-enclosed, satisfied, connected with herself. The viewer—and the artist—look on her beauty.»[237] In *Summer Slumber*, a pastel from 1984, the sleeping beauty is close to the picture plane, and the artist's delight in rendering the folds of the sheets and the pleats of the bed skirt are obvious. Jeanne is also seen from the rear seated on a bed in *Reminiscing* (1981). The green wall is another effective complement to the model's red hair. The contour of her back calls for a comparison to the works of the French painter Ingres. The contemplative introspection of the model in this serene moment is given life by her loose curls, one of which dips down onto her smooth, sculptured back.

Dodge realized that his nudes were problematic for some viewers. He once observed that the American public was uneasy with paintings of nudes and erotic themes, but that from the late Middle Ages through the eighteenth century almost all music, literature, poetry, theater, ballet, and now TV and movies dealt and deal with love and the male and female relationship.[238] He was also very much aware of feminist scholarship about the nude and several books addressing feminist issues were included in the artist's library.[239]

In several canvases painted between 1991 and 1992, Dodge paid tribute to the profound importance of the nude and what it represented in the long tradition of idealizing classicism. Jeanne is featured as the artist's model and inspiration. As if to confirm Dodge's observations, *The Artist and Muse* (1992, pl. 94) was exhibited in the Jacksonville International Airport where, within hours of its hanging, it was taken down for fear it would offend the public. From his earliest works to among his latest, paintings and drawings of the female nude occupied a major place in the artist's œuvre. After the middle of the sixties, Jeanne Klempf occupied a major place in Dodge's depiction of the ideal beauty.

Rock Transformed

 In addition to still lifes, nudes, and the early «situation» narratives loosely based on the *fête champêtre* tradition and the artist's exploration of jazz, Dodge was drawn to paint rock formations. His fascination with rocks manifests itself in numerous works including modern pastoral settings; depictions of the desert of the American Southwest; works inspired by his travels to the Yucatán Peninsula, Greece, Italy, Egypt, Spain, Brittany, and other locales; and especially in the paintings and drawings of the sea and coastline. The aesthetic potential of rock formations even influenced his paintings and drawings of crumpled paper.

In his 1969 lecture Dodge noted:

> In trying to analyze my preferences for subjects, I've come to the conclusion that I feel more at home painting things with more or less continuous surfaces (like people, drapery, sand, rocks, fruit, and architecture), rather than subjects with open or disconnected surfaces, like foliage, which are better done impressionistically.
>
> I enjoy creating solid form, modeling the ins and outs.... [240]

Dodge also explained:

> I love rocks. I like the continuous geometrics of forms like rocks and buildings, body, and drapery. I still like to paint people in either natural surroundings or architectural settings. I like beaches or some aspect of the shoreline as a subject or setting because it is a natural place for people to be at their leisure, dressed or undressed, in interesting groups and poses with or without the opposite sex and with almost infinite pictorial variety and mood.[241]

Early examples of Dodge's sustained interest in painting rocks can be seen in his series of about thirty works in which the subject is an abandoned quarry he discovered near Glens Falls in 1954. Several of these were painted on the spot, which was unusual for Dodge's working methods. Dodge was particularly attracted to the «pattern of the rocks,» striving in his paintings for a «simplicity of ... treatment of the forms.»[242] *Quarry #1* (1954), contains no figures but many of the later quarry paintings do. Of *Quarry with Swimmers* (1955), a reviewer observed that Dodge:

> ... shows what a serious and independent painter he is. While he works within the limits of naturalism, Mr. Dodge does not merely transliterate factually what he sees. He has painted the details of the quarry in a manner that approximates abstraction. He has maintained a poise, a balance, which suggests the disciplined approach of a classically disposed artist.[243]

Even before his paintings of the quarry, Dodge had completed *Lake George Picnic* (1949, pl. 23).[244] Inspired by past masters Dodge often evoked the ambience of traditional subjects and grouped figures in modernized pastoral settings and *fêtes champêtres*. Dodge cited Bellini's *Feast of the Gods* as the inspiration for *Lake George Picnic*.[245] Dodge's painting was prompted by a real-life outing when a group of friends boated out to Dollar Island to celebrate a couple's engagement. In this up-state New York Arcadia, a style that was becoming particularly Dodge's own emerged. It is balanced and carefully composed. The trees divide and anchor the figural groupings. The viewer sees a couple arriving; young men cooking, playing, and listening to music; and young women changing their clothes and eating. The figures are drawn clearly and all of the objects are clearly rendered. The light is painstakingly modeled and the luminosity of the reflections off the leaves on the central tree recalls the pastoral Venetian painting style. The figures pose in a variety of styles, some reminiscent of those found in Greek pedimental sculpture, but there is no sustained inter-action. For all the physical proximity of the men and women on this gay and carefree outing, there is little obvious camaraderie. The precision in rendering and the careful organization of the composition would become hallmarks of Dodge's mature style. The firm horizontal zone of rocks, hugged sinuously in places by roots, would appear in numerous works by the artist. Of the pastoral tradition in Venetian painting, noted critic John Russell observed:

> Of high drama, there is never a trace. It is a world at one with itself, in which nothing untoward ever seems to occur. Well-favored people sit around, talking, singing, playing unamplified musical instruments, ... minding their own business and giving no trouble to others.... The sky is clear and blue, all trees are in good health and protective, and every passing animal is in sympathy with the ideal harmonies set up....[246]

Russell aptly described Dodge's twentieth-century versions of the pastoral tradition. The *fête champêtre*, or the pastoral symphony, is seen repeatedly in the artist's œuvre, whether in the early decades in figures gathered on rooftops—an urban respite offering fresh air, sunlight, and some privacy—or later in his career where individuals, couples, or groups engage in a variety of leisurely activities on beaches or at the coast.

Dodge's approach to «pastoral inaction» can be seen in *By the Old Mill Stream* (1951, pl. 25), *On the Edge* (1959, pl. 37), and *Lush Life (The Good Life)*. *By the Old Mill Stream* shows eight figures in various poses. The composition is carefully studied and arranged in a highly academic manner. The figures serve as compositional building blocks. The solid, massive forms of the stones and boulders are emphasized. A sense of detachment and mystery pervades the work. Of this work Dodge noted:

> Not all my pictures were so thematic or so highly charged with symbolism. Some, like *By the Old Mill Stream*, are more simply arrangements of people in a certain setting interrelating (or not relating) to create a certain mood perhaps or situation, interesting to the eye and provocative to the imagination.[247]

In *On the Edge* the treatment of space and mass is similar, although here the figures are positioned against a sea wall, an indication of the many works of figures and rocky shore-lines to come. Dodge discussed *On the Edge* in his 1969 lecture:

> Here is one of those purely improvised pictures that I mentioned earlier ... it began with a sort of cubist arrangement, completely abstract, which gradually developed into the rocks, the houses, the masonry, the dock, etc. Once the idea, or the setting began to materialize, my imagination then began to people it. There was no specific meaning or symbolism intended. It was simply a situation, with a vague mood and emotional overtones, a poetic visual fancy in which your imagination could roam. [248]

Related to *On the Edge*, Dodge painted two versions of *Summer Serenade* (pl. 41).[249] The first was completed in 1960 in Glens Falls; the second and larger version was begun in Glens Falls and finished in Florida in 1963. In both works, four figures—two women and two men—are set at the water's edge and framed against a backdrop of a pier. The major difference between the two works is the color scheme of the paintings, about which Dodge commented in both his 1969 and 1990 lectures.[250] The women listen as the men play a trombone and a guitar. *Summer Serenade* recalls, of course, the rooftop pictures such as *Trio* and *The Key is Lost*; the serenade, however, has moved to the water's edge.

On the slides of details from *Summer Serenade* Dodge wrote the notation «passive half» to characterize the women and «active half» to characterize the men.[251] This recalls the artist's explanation of *The Nest* painted in 1951, where Dodge claimed that women are often the nest makers and the nurturers, while men are often the dreamers and the planners.[252] In *Summer Serenade* the women are indeed beautiful but passive objects, recipients of the men's playing; obviously implying several levels of meaning, which is what Dodge intended and has been noted in his explanation of the rooftop pictures.

It is abundantly evident in the works considered so far that Dodge preferred painting beautiful young women. He admitted:

> I must confess that, as a subject, the male of the species takes a distant second place to the female, as far as I'm concerned. However, he hasn't been entirely neglected. In 1964 I did this ink and watercolor sketch for a picture later named *The Sentinel*, showing a young man sitting on some rocks and holding a long pole of an unspecified nature in his hands.[253]

In the completed oil version of *The Sentinel* (1964), the viewer witnesses another canvas in which the study of stones plays a prominent role. The pole «of an unspecified nature,» held between the young man's face and the viewer, strikes a chord of mystery. Behind the central figure are two other fellows in the distance, one standing with an arm extended, the other climbing over the mass of enormous boulders. Dodge commented that unlike the preliminary watercolor sketch he made of the subject, he included:

> … more sky to give an impression of vastness. Here there are only two bands (or zones)—the sky, very plain, and the earth, very complicated. By this time, as you've probably noticed, rocks were coming to be as much a favorite subject for me as drapery and the body.[254]

Treasure Hunt, painted in the same year as *The Sentinel*, was inspired by the aftermath of Hurricane Dora that struck Jacksonville in 1964.[255] Dodge remembered:

> … after Hurricane Dora the beaches were a shambles. All sorts of stuff was dumped there to prevent further damage and erosion, and their rather eccentric shapes suggested this painting. After a storm people actually do find coins and jewelry and so forth on the beaches but that's only part of the subject here. I dearly love to compose in more or less horizontal bands or zones with perhaps different textures or shapes in each—like a band of smooth sand with the subtle arabesques of wave lines, opposed to a band of jagged, angular rip-rap, next to smoother but weathered concrete wall, and so forth. I also like solids and voids, the three dimensional ins and outs created by forms like these where children can come and go, sit and climb, hide and seek—and maybe find the treasures they're seeking.[256]

Treasure Hunt is related compositionally to *On the Edge*. In both paintings, figures are spaced at intervals among and against stones. Architecture crowns the top in each work, although Dodge's increasing tendency to include more of an expanse of sky is seen in *Treasure Hunt*. *On the Edge* and *Treasure Hunt*, along with *Summer Serenade* show Dodge's same affection for a geometrical framework achieved by the careful placement of forms and figures. Even the shadows become important compositional devices.

Lush Life (*The Good Life*) is more artificial, more self consciously classical. The sea is glimpsed at the left, but the stage on which the figures assume a variety of positions is a massive expanse of stone with its veins and sundry colorations painted with precise exactitude. A young woman in a bikini dries her back with a pink towel. Another young woman stands on a higher level of the rocks; her blonde hair is answered by her bright yellow dress. Her elbows flare outward as does her skirt. Her palms are held up next to her face. Is this a gesture of surprise? Of despair? In the middle distance a young boy crouches. A woman in a red shirt is careful to balance herself as she steps along the uneven surface of the boulders. A male figure, his head covered by a white hat, sits and leans on one of the boulders, returning the viewer's gaze. His features are those of the artist. Another woman in short shorts and a long-sleeved shirt cups her

hands to her mouth to call out, but to whom? Another male figure reclines, again recalling a Greek pediment figure. Cubic volumes of beach houses affirm an orderly perspective. Against the white wall of one of them sits a male in profile staring out to the sea.

A clear antecedent, both in compositional format and in general mood, is *By the Old Mill Stream* except that half the canvas is given to the sky. Dodge borrowed the title for *Lush Life (The Good Life)* from a ballad marked by «sophisticated lyrics of jaded loneliness,» written by Billy Strayhorn, Duke Ellington's life-long collaborator.[257] Dodge places himself almost centrally among the young attractive players in an idyllic respite characterized by the artist's typical lack of interaction.

Perhaps not coincidentally, Dodge lightened his palette and gave a greater prominence to the sky in his works after moving to Florida in 1962, although it is really during the seventies that these changes became pronounced. The artist's studio in Glens Falls had been in the basement of the Hyde House lit by artificial light. In Florida Dodge used natural light more consistently. He had always painted pictures inspired by his environment, as can be seen in *Glens Falls Rooftops* (1959, pl. 34) and the series derived from the quarry. After the move south, seascapes or coastal themes with single figures or with mutifigural compositions become much more prevalent.

In the mid-sixties Dodge's predilection for rocky coasts became entrenched, reaching a climax in the seventies and throughout the eighties. In a 1966 review of a one-man show at The Group Gallery in Jacksonville, Florida, the writer noted:

> Dodge … has chosen a wide spectrum of subject matter to represent him…. But perhaps most obvious is Dodge's splendid childlike fascination for golden beaches. About one-third of the dozen-plus new paintings have a beach setting: Warm orange-gold sand, cloudless skies yawning high above, people separated by a measured distance. One such work features a crumbling rock structure on the sand's edge, two boys and a girl—Dodge always peoples his pictures with young life—balancing out a triangular composition. The skies in Dodge's paintings are often huge, swallowing up most of the canvas in a wide blue gulp. The horizon line dips low. «That too comes from living in Florida,» he explains. «The land is so flat; when you're driving on the highway, what you see in your field of vision is ninety percent sky.» So he paints sky, plenty of sky.[258]

Although the move to Florida changed his work and encouraged him to explore the theme of the beach, Dodge's coastal scenes were not always drawn from the South. Dodge was quick to point out that he preferred the shorelines of New England, especially those of Rockport and Cape Ann, Massachusetts. The California coast near Carmel, Midway Point, and Point Lobos also enchanted him. There was, however, one particular stretch of Florida beaches that Dodge found intriguing and that was the area south of St. Augustine in Washington Oaks Park. The artist found:

> ... the rocks aren't very impressive in size but the formations are fascinating, and I've used them as material for several pictures. At any rate, the rocks are wonderful—and as something both to visit and to paint, have been all joy for me.[259]

Washington Oaks Park with its expanses of coquina inspired Dodge to paint *High Noon*, *Lady of the Rocks*, and *Rocky Beach with Two Figures* (all 1967). In the first two, a lone female figure, the red-haired Jeanne Klempf explores the beach. In *High Noon* the stone formations receive the major focus, while in *Lady of the Rocks*, the woman is centrally placed and climbs over the rocks holding her sheer blue dress, blown by the sea breeze behind her. This moment of animation as the woman steps, balances, and holds her dress while exposing a shapely thigh, results in a subtle choreography that brings the scene to life.[260]

The coquina formations are also found in *Rock Concert* (1975), a humorous title for a nude female and a clothed male, whose back is to the viewer as he strums his guitar. The instrument is pointed tellingly at his companion, much like a Cupid's bow. Once again, the man plays, the woman listens. The drawing *Coquina #1* (1973, pl. 60) is another example of Dodge's fascination with this site, as are the paintings *Interlude on the Rocks #4* and *There is a Tide* (1976, pl. 73).[261] Both paintings feature Jeanne. In *Interlude* she smiles out at the viewer, while in *There is a Tide* she appears to be lost in thought, the lower portion of her body obscured as she leans on the weathered forms that surround her. The paintings and drawings inspired by Washington Oaks are based on a series of photographs Dodge made, a major working method of his career. As he explained:

> Sketching takes too much time. Painting as slowly as I do, I can't really work outdoors or from a model. It makes me self-conscious to have someone sitting around while I am struggling with something. You can take 100 pictures at one particular place in the time I would take to do one sketch.

> A large percentage of my work is made up of components I have found in different places. I usually combine several photographs. It might be a background or a landscape that I took ten years ago. I might think it needs a certain figure or group of figures. So I look around for something I can use. Occasionally, I will see something in a magazine or newspaper—a figure or a pose or maybe a background; or I might just make up something. It varies to a great extent.[262]

Particularly in relation to *Interlude on the Rocks #4* Dodge explained, «I wanted to make the painting specific enough so that it looks convincing, but I'm not a Photo-Realist. It's always an imaginary idea, a fantasy world that I try to make look real.»[263]

In reviewing the list of Dodge's known works from the seventies, the number of paintings dedicated to the theme of the rocky coastline or the seashore is considerable. Selected examples include *Near Rockport* and *Interlude by the Sea* (both 1970); *Tidal Pool, Morning* (pl. 59); *East of the Sun* (pl. 57); and *Finding* (all 1971). *Tidal Pool, Morning* and *Finding* were based on photographs Dodge took along the New Hampshire coast, which figured among the literally thousands of photos, magazine clippings, and other images he had culled over a lifetime.[264]

Comparing the photographic model for *Tidal Pool* to the finished painting is instructive.[265] Dodge borrowed the positions of the two figures at the right from the photograph, but he undressed them and changed their genders. Much is similar in the foreground treatment of the rocks, including the carefully observed reflection of the figure, but the subtle changes and deletions illustrate how Dodge used an image as an imaginative springboard. The houses at the top of the picture have been simplified and streamlined. Clarity and harmony reign and the mood is one of bucolic repose transferred to the sea shore.[266]

Similar shifts were at work in *Finding*. Again the artist stayed true to many elements of the photograph while altering others. Dodge painted both of the children as little boys. Accents of color enliven the work in the pink of the house facade, the reddish bucket, absent in the photograph, and in yellow and orange shirts.

Interlude by the Sea and *East of the Sun* share the same male perched on a rock in an identical pose. Nude females appear in both paintings, but are separated in proximity from the male. The provocative pose of the nude female in *East of the Sun* is based on a photograph taken of Jeanne in a bathing suit. The title may refer to the setting of the sun with the golden band above a brilliant expanse of blue sky, but it may also be the artist's wish to equate the painting with the mood of the song of the same title.[267]

To this category of rocky coasts and seashores can be added *Low Tide, Morning*; *Goodharbor Beach*, based on a photograph taken at Cape Ann; *Maine Cove*; *Rocks at Cape Ann*, completed on the spot; and *Sunday Afternoon Promenade (Atlantic Beach*, pl. 62) inspired by a Jacksonville Beach scene; all dating to 1973.[268] In 1974 Dodge painted *Rockport from Doyle Cove* at Cape Ann, and in 1975, the year of *Rock Concert*, Dodge added *An August Afternoon* (pl. 65), *A Morning in May* (pl. 66) and *Rocks Near Rockport* (pl. 69). Selections from the last half of the decade include *Incoming Tide, Evening* and *Tranquil Shore, Cape Ann*, both painted in 1976, and the imposing *Rockscape Near Rockport* (1978, pl. 75). Of this last work, Jacksonville art critic Edelson wrote:

> Though Joseph Dodge may use camera records for reference, he does not attempt to imitate the camera as much as he competes with it. In *Rockscape Near Rockport* the expanse of eroded rock is handled with superb finesse to detail, which is executed with the artist's usual clean purity, we do not feel the effect is ever labored.[269]

In the eighties Dodge painted *Fishing Off the Jetties, Mayport* (1981), where a lone male, his back to the viewer, is silhouetted against the sky, waiting for a bite. *Inlet, Cape Ann* (1984), is devoid of human presence in its study of the undulating mass of the rocks. *Stranger on the Shore* (1985-86), evocative of the song by the same name, contains a woman dressed only in a shirt which is open to reveal her nude body beneath it.[270] *Seeking* (1986, pl. 85), based on photographs taken south of Los Angeles, has a beachcomber and a seated figure poised above the complexity of stones and against the simpler expanse of the sky like the figure in *The Sentinel*. In *August Morning, Cape Ann* (1987), four figures each follow his or her own casual pursuits at the edge of a wide expanse of beach at low tide.

In *Waiting* (1987, pl. 87), the contemplative calm is ever so slightly interrupted by the tension of the suspended beach ball. In this work, inspired by photographs taken at Daytona Beach, there is a rare absence of rock formations. The sky and sea seem to merge and the sky and its canopy of clouds vie for attention. Dodge was such a master of naturalism that the viewer may rarely notice his treatment of the skies. Upon careful scrutiny, however, a wide array of cloud formations and weather conditions become apparent in Dodge's painting. Some works are cloudless but in the complex skies in *Waiting*; *Inlet, Cape Ann*; and *Fishing off the Jetties, Mayport*; for instance, it is clear Dodge reveled in the variety of expressive possibilities above the stony coastlines.[271]

In *Rushing the Season* (1988), an eager child, unable to contain his excitement, tugs at his mother. The rock formations are similar to those in several of the other Cape Ann pictures such as *Stranger on the Shore*. In *Morning, Gulf Coast* (1988, pl. 88), the figure intently searching for shells or shark's teeth is joined by others in a setting inspired by a beach in Sarasota, Florida.

During the last two decades of the artist's life, the theme of the rocky coast continued, but it was no longer the dominant one. After his retirement from the position of director of the Cummer, Dodge traveled widely, and subjects from these journeys began to appear with greater frequency in his paintings and drawings. He continued his explorations of the female nude and the still life. One of his most interesting and inventive experiments is seen in his treatment of crumpled paper. Yet the «infinite pictorial variety» afforded by the sea, the coast, and rocky outcroppings presented irresistible attractions that Dodge relished and embraced until he was forced by illness to stop painting. The paintings of his last series, and the unfinished canvas on the artist's easel at the time of his death, were variations of figures on a rocky beach.

Sights and Sites

 Dodge immensely enjoyed traveling. With his breadth of knowledge of art and history, he delighted in experiencing a variety of monuments both man-made and natural. The paintings inspired by numerous trips and excursions reflect his ongoing attraction to stone edifices.

One of the first sites to capture Dodge's imagination was Fort Clinch. Dodge began painting Fort Clinch not long after he arrived in Jacksonville. Located on the north end of Amelia Island in northeast Florida, the fort is bordered by the Amelia River on the west, the Cumberland Sound on the north, and the Atlantic Ocean on the east. The fort, begun in 1847 and named after General Duncan Lamont Clinch, was built originally to «guard the mouth of the St. Mary's River, protect coastal and interior shipping, and defend the deep water port of Fernandina, Florida.»[272] It was occupied by Confederate troops in 1861 at the outbreak of the Civil War and retaken by Federal forces in 1862. It was opened to the public as a park in 1938.[273] Of the fort and his paintings of it, Dodge remembered:

> I suppose every painter in the realist tradition has succumbed at one time or another to the nostalgia and picturesqueness of the ruin, and I'm no exception.
>
> When I first saw Ft. Clinch near Fernandina, I fell in love with it immediately. Along with the rocks below St. Augustine, it's my favorite spot in Florida—a bit less so now, however, now that it's being restored. It was better, I think, a couple of years ago when it was more of a ruin, when it seemed like one was discovering it for oneself for the first time. I've painted a number of Ft. Clinch pictures.... There are really some wonderful compositions and shapes to be found there.
>
> I think the stark geometry of the fortifications, softened and given variety of texture by its state of neglect, makes a perfect background for figures, especially children. My own children enjoyed it with as much enthusiasm and rushed around pretty much as I've indicated here, with their imaginations completely unleashed—as was mine.[274]

Afternoon at Fort Clinch (1966), to which Dodge referred in the lecture as the «largest ... and probably the best» painting was purchased for a corporate collection and elicited special comment from reviewer Wayne Hamm:

> Mystery is another quality that attracts and holds attention, and companies may try to counter their matter-of-factness by displaying art that suggests secrets deeper than the annual statement. Koger Properties, for instance, owns a fine oil by Joseph Jeffers Dodge. *Afternoon at Fort Clinch* is rich and haunting. Painted in a robust style that I think of as characteristically American, it projects a strong sense of a particular moment in time. Arrested motion is frozen in a strange tableau. A modern looking young blonde in a sleeveless pink top and blue skirt stands squarely in front of the viewer—as if posing for a snapshot. A group of boys begins to climb the meticulously rendered bricks. In the distance another boy raises his arm. Is it a signal? Victory at reaching the top? Below the human complexities, the old fort slowly and somberly decays. Itself created by and for human conflict, the mouldering mass of masonry seems to contain and guard an enigma. Odd to find the lesson of Ozymandias in the corporate environment![275]

No wonder the artist reveled in this site. With its makeup of masonry, its placement at the edge of the sea, and the expanse of vast horizontal sky, the features of Fort Clinch clearly appealed to the artist's inherent preferences.[276] Future paintings of ruins and monuments would be based on sites much farther away.

Dodge did not make his first trip abroad until 1947, when he joined his parents in Europe. The elder Dodge was on official government business in Vienna as the United States minister to the quadripartite treaty convention. In his autobiographical musings Dodge devoted rich descriptive passages to his tour. The passages range from memories of a spectacular banquet in Vienna at the Belvedere Palace to a fling with his Parisian guide.[277]

It was not until Dodge's move to Florida and after his retirement from the Cummer in 1972 that his travels at home and abroad really increased. They included regular visits to Europe and throughout the United States. The West, especially California, and New England were his favorite destinations. Trips to Greece and the Yucatán Peninsula in the sixties provided inspiration for approximately fifteen works. About a dozen paintings and drawings resulted from Dodge's tours to Spain, Egypt, Sicily, and central Italy. Paintings derived from a September, 1981, trip to France, with a special emphasis on the exploration of Brittany, form a substantial part of the artist's output in the late eighties into the nineties. The Brittany works are marked by the identifiable characteristics of the artist: a precision of execution, a tendency to idealize, with the pronounced penchant for depicting coastal scenes, rocks, ruins, and monuments.

Paintings from Dodge's 1966 tour to Greece and his 1969 tour to the Yucatán were first exhibited at The Group Gallery in Jacksonville. A page of finely written descriptive text by Jacque Holmes accompanied the exhibit:

> Recent visits to Greece and the Yucatán have provided the inspiration for the majority of paintings in this exhibit. The sites of two ancient civilizations are subjects well suited to Mr. Dodge's style of painting which might be called classical realism. Simplification and idealization of natural forms—careful organization of these forms into beautifully correct compositions—all combine to create a unique interpretation of subject matter. Concern with intricate detail, such as the hundreds of rocks on an Aegean beach, indicates the artist's fantastic powers of observation. And yet within this detail, one must still be aware of the artist's own selectivity and distortion toward his ultimate re-creation of nature.
>
> Light is perhaps the single most important element in these paintings. The play of light and shadow over three dimensional forms—buildings, the ancient ruins, figures, the landscape—emphasizes the artist's great technical knowledge of his medium. Again his use of this knowledge is in the classical vein, tending to isolate each form within its own designated space. This space is very much limited to the picture plane created by the artist and the eye is aware of a two rather than a three dimensional surface. The use of sunlight on his subjects—its effect on colors and forms—is important in creating the mood of each scene. Throughout the exhibit, this mood is one of serenity and of eternity.[278]

In a long and perceptive article about this exhibit written by Elihu Edelson, the former arts writer for the now defunct *Jacksonville Journal*, seven of the eight paintings inspired by Greece and the Aegean Islands were mentioned or discussed.[279] One of the works was *On the Acropolis* (1967), in which Edelson observed «a good example of Dodge's classicism as applied to composition ... [it] has a strong underlying structure of verticals and horizontals.»[280] Without the title the viewer may be hard pressed to identify the location because *On the Acropolis* shows no recognizable monuments at all. Instead, a figure who is Dodge himself sits and sketches a modern day Aphrodite, a representation of life, and perhaps love, amidst the ruins. *From the Acropolis: The Propylea* (1968, pl. 50) shows the northern section of the grand gateway to the Acropolis cropped at the viewer's left much like a photographic view would be.[281] This painting; *The Agora, Athens* (1969); and *Aegean Island Town* (1970) are categorized by Edelson as «more simply picturesque.»[282]

Also included in The Group Gallery show were *Waiting, The Aegean* (1970, pl. 56); *Blues for Delos* (1968); and *Duo at Delos* (1970, pl. 55). Edelson described *Waiting, The Aegean* as:

> ... a strong departure from the prevailing landscapes. It portrays three older women sitting on a stony beach and waiting for their men to return from the sea. Their heads are covered with white, cowl-like shawls. Their gestures, and the expressions of one whose face is turned toward us, reflect resignation, patience, and anxiety at the same time. One clutches her rosary beads. In this painting there is also remarkable detail in the stones, which cover the entire beach.[283]

This painting of the three women, whose tight-knit placement forms a solid compositional pyramid, offers in its depiction of shared solitude a strong counterpart to the more romantic vistas Dodge painted of Greece and the islands. Lives played out near the sea and dependent on it know not only the enchanting beauty of its blue expanses, they know of its harshness and peril as well.[284]

Although he did not indicate specific titles, Dodge was probably referring to *Duo in Delos* and *Blues for Delos* in his 1969 lecture when he briefly discussed the Greek works. He explained:

> I've also painted four pictures based on a trip to Greece, of which this is the most recent. The scene depicted here is partly from photos taken on the sacred island of Delos, and partly made up—as are the figures. I must say that there's something about this great silent island, with its surrealist ruins, that seems to cry for someone to sing and play the blues. And, to me, those weathered and displaced stones are objects of immense fascination, provoking all sorts of reactions. They're no longer classical Greek but have somehow become bits of modern, abstract sculpture—assemblages, creating their own peculiar environment.[285]

In his review, Edelson found *Duo at Delos* to be «the most interesting painting here,» going on to describe it at length:

> ... it incorporates a touch of eroticism and symbolism. Here two young people make love amid classical ruins. Nearby, almost like witnesses, are four statues: but these could not even be stony observers as they are decapitated. The statues are in two pairs—a male and a female in each couple. One couple, only torsos, is depicted in the prime of life. The male, in classical tradition, is completely nude while the female is partly draped. The other pair represents an older couple, full length, wearing robes.[286]

The black hair and eyebrows of the man are similar to those of the guitar player in *Blues for Delos*. The woman with her red hair spread out lies on yellow drapery and appears to be the standard ideal Dodge beauty. As for symbolism, practically everything in the painting has a mate or is coupled in a pair: the sculptures mentioned by Edelson, the columns placed in the center and at both sides of the work, the column drums at the right, even the amphorae at the left. With the overriding emphasis on duality from the duo of the title to the configuration of figures and objects, could Dodge be cleverly alluding to the twins Apollo and Artemis? According to legend, Delos was the mythical birthplace of these Greek gods.

Duo at Delos is yet another pictorial essay on Dodge's absolute infatuation with stone. Indeed in all of the paintings derived from the Greek tour, Dodge anchors the compositions with solid forms whether they are ruins or modern architectural structures. This approach is also seen in the travel paintings drawn from the Yucatán Peninsula, Spain, and Italy.

In the 1970 Group Gallery exhibition there were also five Yucatán subjects, the result of a 1969 tour. From Edelson's review one learns:

> The *Orange Tree at Labna* is the largest painting in the show. Here we can observe many of the typical characteristics of Dodge's work. Clear, bright light brings out detail in sharp relief. There is generally a high key, though not so much as in other paintings where there is even much detail in the shadows. Here Dodge's love of detail is seen in the treatment of the leaves and oranges. An interesting architectural feature is the corbeled vault.[287]

Edelson's praise is punctuated with slight criticism as he continues:

> ... [a] similar vault is seen in *Steps to the Nunnery, Uxmal*. Here Dodge runs the risk which is seen in several of the recent paintings. He comes precariously close to the picturesque landscape photographs on calendars distributed by airlines. In *The Old and the New, Dzibilchaltun*, we see an interesting contrast between the ancient Indian ruins and those of a more recent church with its Romanesque vault.[288]

Interestingly, *Steps to the Nunnery* was the target of criticism again when it was included in The 9th Annual Major Florida Artists Show, staged by the Harmon Gallery in Naples, Florida, in 1972. Griffin Smith wrote:

> There were several surprises at the Harmon show ... and then the revelation (to me) of the week—Joe Dodge paints. I have had Joe Dodge mentally pigeon-holed as the Director of the Cummer Gallery, Jacksonville. Period. It develops that not only does the director direct, but that he has also had a recent one-man there. At the Harmon, Dodge is exhibiting a small oil, *Stairway to the Nunnery at Uxmal, Yucatan*.

It's a nice thing, pleasantly redolent of classical landscape painting, if a bit too tight and marred by two badly drawn figures.[289]

Photographs and slides of the Yucatán tour found in the artist's estate illustrate the claim made by Dodge that «rarely in the last sixty years or so have I just drawn or painted things as they were.»[290] As was demonstrated in the paintings of coastal scenes, the camera captured the views and then Dodge drew from those, combining and refining to produce this particular group of works as well.[291] The figures in the images of the Yucatán ruins can be compared to those in the slightly earlier paintings of Fort Clinch; individuals explore, stand, look, think, and rest much as they do on Dodge's beaches.

In 1975, three years after his retirement from the Cummer Gallery of Art, Dodge was given his second one-man exhibition there. *A Ten Year View* featured works from 1964 through 1974. Travel paintings from the Yucatán, Greece, Spain, and Guatemala were well represented. *Guatemala Valley* (1974, pl. 63) derived from a photograph made near San Cristóbal Acasaguastián, was illustrated in the exhibition catalogue.[292] About this work one reviewer claimed:

> *Guatemala Valley* shows the remarkable finesse which may be achieved with oil on paper. It is one of the most romantic of Dodge's compositions, depicting a distant mission church beyond a foreground of lush vegetation. There is a quality reminiscent of 19th Century American landscapists, like Martin Johnson Heade.[293]

Representative works from Dodge's trip to Spain include *Spanish Village* (1974), which is reminiscent of a Corot or Cézanne in its presentation of a walled city with its cubic volumes evincing solidity and endurance. In *Fisherman, Costa del Sol* (1975, pl. 68) and *Siesta, Costa del Sol* (1976), Dodge renders two coastal scenes. The latter is a composite derived from photographs Dodge had taken. The perspective is rendered with painstaking accuracy, as are other details. An almost hyper-realism dominates the absolute stillness of the scene showing fisherman slumbering alongside their colored boats.

Dodge was particularly taken by the ruins and the spectacular natural beauty he saw in southern Italy and Sicily. Two paintings, *Doric Column, Paestum* (1978, pl. 76) and *Old Olive Tree, Agrigento* (1981, pl. 79), showcase not the major monuments but subjects at the periphery.[294] In *Old Olive Tree*, a Greek temple is barely visible to the far right while the magnificent tree occupies the viewer's attention as if to say not all the glories are man-made. Yet Dodge evokes and captures the grandeur of the classical past in these paintings.

Many of the travel-inspired works pronounce the artist's enchantment with stone, fashioned and dressed as it was by the ancients. Stones stand as silent sentinels, eroded but often triumphant reminders of former glories. The continuum of time is inevitably implied. In *Roman Scene* (1987, pl. 86), a fragmented view of the Italian capital was based on photographs taken of the piazza dell'Esedra in front of the church of Santa Maria degli Angeli, which was built into the ruins of the second-century baths of Diocletian.[295] The painting contains references to an ancient monument, the pervasive presence of Catholicism, a fountain populated by celebratory references to mythological naiads. In the shadow of it all, one sees gesticulating Italians, their history a backdrop on a great stage.[296]

Not surprisingly, a tour in Egypt inspired Dodge to paint *Pyramids* (1986, pl. 84).[297] In a crook of the great pyramid, a young couple, dwarfed by the immensity of the structure, is nestled. They are lost in each other, seemingly oblivious to the grandeur and pageantry supporting and surrounding them. Other pyramids are barely perceptible in the distant horizon. In most of these paintings, the intervention of the contemporary is subtly rendered, if it is included at all. Typical of the approach of a classical artist, Dodge preferred to transmit the timeless qualities of his subject.

One of the most ambitious series of paintings inspired by travel was that of about a dozen works of Brittany created between 1988 and 1992. Many of these were first exhibited publicly at Dodge's third show at the Cummer, a retrospective celebrating his seventy-fifth birthday.[298] Dodge's affinity for stone found inspiration in the Neolithic megaliths of Carnac. *Prehistoric Monoliths, Brittany* (also known as *Past, Present and Nature, Brittany*, pl. 89) and *Some Prehistoric Menhirs near Carnac, Brittany* were painted in 1988. *Brittany*, also featuring the menhirs, or monolithic stones, dates from 1989. Upon close inspection of *Past, Present and Nature*, the viewer realizes that Dodge has used the nine ancient stones to establish a sense of continuity with the nine trees from nature and the nine houses from the present in the back-ground, which leads one back to the title.

In a 1992 Cummer Gallery of Art brochure in which Dodge's exhibition was discussed, the Brittany works were singled out by then assistant to the director, Mary Campbell Gristina:

> These paintings and drawings are indeed a feast for the eyes, and for the soul. For example, *Brittany Manor Springtime*, painted in 1990, portrays an architecturally enriched landscape, a landscape that is equally unified by the light, the clouds, and the shadows cast by the clouds. The building is brick, chimnied, towered, it combines simple forms into a comfortable geometric

Fig. 20 —**Joseph Jeffers Dodge home at Silversmith Creek**, 1983

whole. Soft baby-blue sky is covered by soft almost-white clouds that serve as a filter for sunlight in the mid-ground and shade in the foreground.

A field filled with rows that wind under the clouds carries the eye into the distance. Peace and quiet fill the air. The balance of warm to cool, sun to shade, sky to earth, recession, progression, and projection, is infinitely and finely tuned. The atmosphere is imbued by the artist with a unified presence and a noticeable spirituality. The harsh, mathematical principles of perspective do not intrude, though the geometric foundation of the painting lies like a ghost, felt but not seen.

The exhibition demonstrates that the artist is progressively adroit in terms of composition, in terms of lighting, in terms of distilling the essence of art. The artist excels in defining a creative vision that elevates and sets art apart from craft.

Joseph Jeffers Dodge is an outstanding craftsman. His paintings are marked by impeccable technical execution. In a lesser talent, the desire to conquer the craft might have extinguished the necessary light of creativity. Instead these paintings show a progression toward both craft and creative spirit; a growth that celebrates the seventy-five years living as an artist, art collector, and art museum director.[299]

Dodge's love of traveling and painting monuments prompted one critic to compare him to Poussin and Corot, who also painted temples, castles, cathedrals, and architectural settings.[300] In addition to the choice of subject matter, their methods and approaches to composition are two more essential elements that the three artists had in common. Dodge's favorite way of composing a picture was in horizontal bands, a way of ordering the picture that can be traced from painters such as Poussin, David, Ingres and Cézanne,

all the way back to Byzantine mosaics and Greco-Roman friezes. Discussing his own work, Dodge observed, «there's often an intellectual content and always a very strong tendency towards logic, clarity, balance, and order—which are basically characteristics of classicism.»[301]

Dodge realized these characteristics of classicism in the paintings of Brittany from the late eighties and early nineties. The ordering of horizontal bands is seen especially in *Breton Village* (1991, pl. 91) and in *Sea Wall, Echmuhl, Brittany* (1992, pl. 98). The viewer is afforded an open foreground allowing an unimpeded view of benign nature in which man's presence is confirmed and ordered by the presence of buildings and structures.

Green, varying in value and intensity, dominates many of the Brittany paintings. This is noteworthy because Dodge was partially color blind and had difficulty over the years recognizing some tints of red and green. When asked about the abundance of greens in the Breton works, the artist laughed and said, «Well, I can read the names of colors on the tubes. Maybe I'm going through a green period!» Of this color blindness, Dodge observed, «Handicaps, like limitations, can be an advantage and a challenge in a way. They do limit what I can do, but, at the same time, they make me concentrate and make the most of what I can do.»[302] Dodge also often relied on the advice of Jeanne Klempf, whom he not so jokingly called his color adviser when it came to mixing greens.[303]

In contrast to the verdant canvases of Brittany, Dodge made a body of paintings and drawings from several long tours of the American Southwest. In *Arizona High Country* (1978, pl. 74), subtle references to the passage of time are seen in the weathering, erosion, peeling, and flaking of the stone. The undulating crevices curling back upon themselves deny the sense of immutable stasis and obdurate permanence associated with stone.[304] In *High Noon, Monument Valley* (1987), the viewer is afforded a broad panoramic vista of the desert landscape, its imposing grandeur marked by utter stillness and the absence of any living forms.

Paintings inspired by Florida scenery include *Fallen Tree: Intracoastal Waterway* (1984, pl. 82).[305] In *Fallen Tree*, the viewer immediately recognizes Dodge's preference for broad horizontal bands of composition in the water of the Intracoastal, the marsh grasses, the trees, and the expansive sky interrupted by wisps of clouds, the sail, the wayward trunks, and the mass of twisted roots. The painting is serene with its allusion to gentle breezes and pleasurable pursuits.

Dodge's home also inspired him. The upstairs studio overlooked Silversmith Creek, a tributary of the Arlington River that in turn flows into the St. Johns River. Of *Silversmith Creek #2* (1982), Margaret Koscielny, Dodge's old friend, fellow artist, former assistant at the Cummer, and co-founder of Art Celebration!, wrote:

> Joseph Jeffers Dodge is an artist who retains a genuine sense of the distinctly American concern for atmosphere, and more specifically, the Luminists of the 19th Century.... Dodge's work also shows his respect for the technical rationality of 17th-century French landscapes, as well as other European models. However, *Silversmith Creek #2* is a work which is wholly American in its deep appreciation and awe of the wildness which still exists, even in pockets of Urbania, such as Arlington, Florida.[306]

The sites featured in this painting and in *The Osprey Nest, Silversmith Creek* (1984) are easily accessible in north Florida. Dodge enjoyed boating for many years and he knew this locale well. Visitors to his home on Silver Lake Terrace were beguiled by the constant activity of birds, alligators, and other creatures. In contrast to these two paintings with their panoramic view and expanses of sky is an earlier *Silversmith Creek* (1981, pl. 80), which presents the density of the swamp with barely any sky visible at all.

Dodge painted sights and sites throughout his lifetime. From the quarry near Glens Falls to the far reaches of Egypt, Greece, France, and Italy; from the inspiration of Mayan ruins to the grandeur of the American Southwest; from rocky beaches on both coasts of the United States to more immediate marvels such as Fort Clinch and Silversmith Creek, Dodge's paintings of such diverse places remain his «expressions of appreciation, acts of love, [and] personal savourings of the garden of earthly delights.»[307]

The Still Life Revisited

 The still life is conspicuously absent from Dodge's works in the seventies. After producing numerous still lifes from the forties through the sixties, the artist turned to paintings of Greece, the Yucatán, Spain, Guatemala, numerous coastal scenes, and nudes. In the eighties, he returned to the still-life genre.

In 1980 Dodge painted one of his most memorable still-life compositions, *Panetto Bolognese* (pl. 77) which means «Bread from Bologna» in Italian. Although this work presents neither a monument nor a picturesque vista, Dodge serendipitously discovered the subject on a 1978 tour to Italy.[308] Dodge recalled how he came across these fanciful shapes:

> When I was in Bologna, one day at lunch there was a basket of queer-looking Italian bread on the table. So I took it up to my room. The light was coming in the window, so I put these breads in different combinations with a piece of drapery and took 35 or 36 photographs of them.[309]

The dark negative space contrasts dramatically with the wrinkled, starkly white tablecloth. Curving, sinuous lines and the meticulous modeling of their surfaces seem to animate the two pieces of bread. Dodge's apparent animation of inanimate objects recalls a similar approach to his still lifes of the sixties, particularly *Pavane* where two apples appeared to be dancing.[310]

The motif of the cutting or stabbing knife also returns in the eighties in *Still Life: Bread in a Basket* (1984) and *Untitled (Still-Life: Bread, White Jug and Lemon*, 1985).[311] Dodge commented on a certain «ominous finality» recalling the similar use of the knife in *No Turning Back*.[312] The first painting shows the bread in a napkin-lined basket on a shiny table surface in which the reflections are carefully recorded. In the untitled work the bread rests on a white plate that is placed on a white tablecloth, the folds of which are like those in *Panetto Bolognese*. A bright source of light creates a network of angular shadows. In these paintings and in *Bolognese Bun and Napkin* (1983), diagonal lines on the walls indicate a strong light falling from the right. In *Bread and Napkin* (1987), the bread vies for attention with the napkin that surrounds it.[313] The focus on the napkins in these works recalls a similar preoccupation in earlier paintings such as *Apples and Knife* (1967), where incidentally, a knife is also shown cutting into the fruit.[314] In all of these works the placement of the knife adds a slightly disturbing element.

One of the most interesting and creative series Dodge created in the eighties was a group of paintings and drawings of single sheets of crumpled or wadded paper that he called paperscapes. Recalling his inspiration for this group he commented, «I was unwrapping a package and tore the paper. When the light happened to strike it a certain way I decided to take some photographs.»[315] In the works that resulted from this creative idea, Dodge transformed the banal object and its weightless character into miniature mountain ranges with the «same sparkling crevices, pits, and scars which characterize the rock paintings.»[316]

In *Paperscape #1*, an oil, this connection to Dodge's paintings of rocks in the Southwest, such as *Arizona High Country*, is striking. The paper is placed on a white marble table, the veins of color painted as carefully as the creases and folds in the brown packaging above it. The light blue wall suggests a sky. The very precise rendering invites the viewer to consider this common object anew in its monumentalized state. Dodge takes the similar approach of treating paper as a topographic study in *Green Paperscape* (1982) and *Golden Paperscape* (1983), both executed in colored pencil. In *Green Paperscape*, the definition of a horizontal surface is not signaled by a table but by the terrain of the paper itself. An oil, *Blue Paperscape* (1982), offers a different vantage point that is reminiscent of an aerial view, in which one looks down at the expanse.

Related to the paperscapes and in exploration of further approaches to the still-life genre, Dodge painted *White Jar with Violet Paper* (1983, pl. 81) and *It's Only a Paper Moon* (1986, pl. 83). In the first work, the variegated marble table is recognizable as the same surface as in *Paperscape #1*. Instead of filling the white jar with flowers as he had done in *Still Life with Hydrangea* (1966), the artist offers a bouquet of «violets» painted with lapidary strokes in the form of a ball of crushed paper. Dodge also made a conscious effort to experiment with complementary colors on the color wheel.

In *It's Only a Paper Moon*, a carefully formed globe of paper is suspended against a rich lapis blue background. Dodge seems to have sculpted the sphere's faceted surfaces. The subtle nuances of contrast in value used to define the hanging orb are another testament to the painter's craft. Even the sturdy string that is wrapped around the ball and used to hang it is rendered with meticulous definition, recalling not only the tradition of American still-life painting, but also that of the seventeenth-century Dutch. The whimsical title reflects not only Dodge's love of music but also his sense of humor.

Although Dodge's return to the still life in the eighties was limited to only about a dozen works, he brought a decidedly creative approach to the genre. The three paintings of round loaves on tabletops are among the more traditional of his still-life works, but even they show the artist's sustained interest in the varied

compositional possibilities of cloth. The use of the cutting knife to create a sense of tension, and disturb an otherwise placid subject is typical of his eighties still lifes. The true surprises are in the employment of the commonplace in new and unexpected ways. Dodge reinvigorated the still-life category in his inventive images of Bolognese bread and crumpled paper. He would continue to experiment with the genre in the nineties.

The Nineties

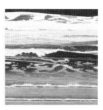 The nineties brought continued recognition of Dodge and his works, but were also punctuated by his major heart surgery in 1992; the tragic death of his eldest daughter, Tia, in 1993; and the diagnosis of his colon cancer in 1994. In assessing Dodge's artistic output of the nineties, one recognizes a consistent return to favorite subjects. There are numerous coastal scenes ranging from the site of Washington Oaks Park in Florida, to the western shores of California. He completed at least six paintings derived from the tour of Brittany. Other subjects included paintings of the Southwest, a group of trees from the Sonoma and the Big Sur areas of California, and images of Silversmith Creek near his studio. There are a variety of still lifes, several of which reflect new artistic directions. Lastly, it was during this late period that Dodge turned to self-portraits and a series examining the theme of the artist in his studio.

Dodge remained remarkably productive until about mid-1996 when, because of cancer, it became increasingly difficult for him to sit upright for any sustained length of time. The paintings he completed during his last years show no compromise in quality. That his powers of observation were just as acute as ever and his execution just as luminous and exacting can be seen in works painted during the last six years of his life.

Horizons (1990, pl. 90), was included in an exhibition titled *Jacksonville Creates* at the Jacksonville Art Museum in the same year.[317] One writer found Dodge's *Horizons* « ... lastingly impressive for its combination of solemn majesty and youthful longing, seen in a carefully rendered study of a youth gazing out at the ocean's edge.»[318] Dodge himself was particularly satisfied with the way the water turned out in this painting, remarking that he doubted he could ever paint it so successfully again.[319]

Additional coastal scenes include *Northern California Coast* (1990, pl. 91) and *Low Tide, Northern California* (1991). A number of earlier works also depict details of the West coast, where Dodge included isolated rock formations and sometimes tree fragments or gnarled root masses. Dodge had painted similar compositions two decades earlier in *Oregon Coast, Early Morning* (1974) and *Between Two Tides* (1975, pl. 67).[320] The four works are related not only in the obviously similar subject matter, but also in the careful rendering of atmospheric conditions. A relatively narrow range of hues, mostly neutrals, links them, although blue figures in several of them as well.

New to Dodge's repertoire of subjects was a group of paintings of trees derived from photographs he had taken in California. Four outstanding examples that demonstrate the skills Dodge honed over a lifetime are: *Along the Sonoma Coast* (1991); *Evening, Big Sur* (1991); *California Cypress* (1991, pl. 93); and *Carmel Cove (Monterey Cypress*, 1993, pl. 100). Typical of Dodge's ability to transform the mundane into images of sweeping beauty, these majestic stands of trees record another aspect of the California coast.

The Southwest was also represented in this late period in several works. In paintings such as *Late in the Day, Nevada* (1993), a visual first cousin to the paperscapes; the ambitious and highly detailed *Desert Trail* (1995, pl. 103), the title of which is a sly reference to the contrail left by an unseen plane; and one of Dodge's last completed works, *Canyon, New Mexico* (1996), the viewer recognizes Dodge's well established preference for rocky precipices and infinite panoramic vistas.

Closer to home are the paintings based on views of Dodge's back yard in which he reconsiders the osprey nest. In earlier paintings the nest appeared as a distinctive feature in the Florida landscape. In the late paintings the nest may have a more symbolic presence. The earlier of two nineties treatments of the osprey nest is *Osprey Nest, Silversmith Creek* (1992, pl. 97). Three bare cypresses are arranged in a row across the foreground, strikingly similar to countless depictions of the three crosses at Christ's crucifixion. The osprey nest is in the central and tallest tree. One is reminded of earlier paintings that featured the nest such as *The Renaissance* and *What Struggle to Escape*. In those the nest was very clearly a symbol of the promise of life and fecundity. In the 1992 painting, however, the contrast between the nest and leafless trees arranged in a trinity of sorts points at the cycle of birth and death, hinting at questions of the beyond. All of this would be understandable in light of Dodge's own health problems and the deteriorating condition of his daughter Tia's health as she battled the ravages of cancer.

The second painting, *Osprey Nest, Silversmith Creek* (1994-95), shows a much broader view from a vantage point that directs one skyward toward two references to flight: another contrail, and in the far distance, a yellow hot air balloon. Dodge had used the kite in earlier paintings such as *Gods of Our Fathers: The Christian Tradition* to signal the flight of the soul or heavenly allusions. The ascending balloon in the later painting conveys a similar message. This, coupled with the prominence of the tree holding the nest, results in a subtle but moving consideration of the cyclical rhythms of life.

In the nineties Dodge explored the still-life genre using powerful and poignant imagery. As a memorial tribute to his daughter, he painted *Tia's Rose* in 1993 shortly after her death and gave it to Tia's sister Julie. In his welcoming comments to those who had gathered to attend Tia's memorial service at Grace Cathedral in San Francisco on October 6, 1993, Dodge remembered his daughter as «a loving and lovable person,» who «struggled for three and a half years with infinite courage and determination ... much of it in pain; and knew full well the probable conclusion. To me, and perhaps to many others, she is a model and a hero.»[321] The painting was based on photographs Dodge had taken at Julie's upstairs apartment of the rose in a vase, which had been placed on an exterior banister. Tia was living with her sister at the end of her life and could look out the window to see the rose. *Tia's Rose* is shown in full bloom, its leaves reaching out like open arms. The uppermost leaf on the viewer's left is marred by holes left by an insect. Certainly this detail can be read as a straightforward dash of realism but it is also highly reminiscent of the established *vanitas* tradition in still-life painting in which the artist refers to the brevity and transience of material existence.[322]

In 1992 Dodge painted one of his late masterpieces, which is comprised of a pendant pair, *Dancing Pears I and II: Fandango*. In each painting, two pears wrapped in tissue are set on Dodge's marble tabletop against a bright blue wall. The two *Dancing Pears* sometimes remind viewers of the wrapped oranges by American artist William John McCloskey. Dodge's inspiration was borrowed not from McCloskey, «Master of the Wrapped Citrus,» but from the actual pears ordered from the *Harry and David* catalogues that arrive in many American homes with great regularity during the holidays.[323] The artist had refrigerated several of these mail-order pears, and when he removed them from the refrigerator, the condensation made the paper cling to the fruit. He was immediately struck by the artistic and expressive possibilities he saw, much as he had been when he recognized potential subjects in torn packaging and oddly shaped bread from Bologna.

Dodge took these simple wrapped pears and monumentalized them. His rendering of the paper wrapping recalls the wet drapery on Greek statues of female goddesses in the fifth century B.C. that reveal and conceal the voluptuous forms beneath. The subtitle *Fandango* refers to a lively Spanish dance, also suggested by the paper, which seems to twirl. This apparent movement pervades the composition with a dynamic élan. A similar approach can be seen in Dodge's earlier painting *Pavane* from 1960, in which two apples appear to twirl in a «stately old dance,» which is the meaning of pavane. In contrast, *Dancing Pears* convey a higher charge of energy. The paired canvases were among his most popular in the last exhibitions and Dodge himself admitted that he found them to be among his most successful late works.[324]

One of Dodge's last series, although he didn't set out intending to create a series, depicts the passage from the innocence of childhood to adolescence, and the awakening interest in the opposite sex. Even the titles suggest this passage from childhood to adolescence and beyond: *Safe Harbor* (1993, pl. 101), *Rising Tide* (1995, pl. 104), and *Setting Sail* (1995, pl. 105). In *Safe Harbor* a boy sits in the seawater surrounded by smooth expanses of coastal stone formations. He is gingerly dipping his small sailboat into the water. Intently absorbed by his toy he is snugly secure in and unaware of the calm beauty of his surroundings.[325]

In *Rising Tide* an older boy has been playing with his toy sailboat in a similar tidal pool. He perches on a large stone, his dangling foot barely creates a ripple. Reflections are studiously rendered. He turns and watches in the distance as three beauties toss a ball, their arms outstretched.[326] The blonde, brunette, and redhead recall the depiction of three bathing beauties in an earlier work, *Three Graces* (1954). In *Rising Tide* the boy's growing interest in girls is evident as he turns from his toy.

Setting Sail features a young red headed girl with a ponytail in a blue bathing suit. She has joined a boy whose attention has returned, for the moment anyway, to the small sailboat. The pretty girl reclines in the water supporting herself on an elbow. Is the boy about to launch the toy boat as the title implies? Will he let go of his childhood interests and launch into new ones? *Setting Sail* can also signal the youths' testing of the waters as they venture into the new, and here at least for the time being, still innocent world of adolescence. The trio of works reflects Dodge's preference for tranquil, serene, and timeless settings. Set in and on the water in compositions that are hallmarks of Dodge's mature style, *Safe Harbor*, *Setting Sail*, and *Rising Tide*, reflect the artist's consistent view of a benign and welcoming nature in which peace prevails and children can delight in the haven it provides.

Related to the three previous paintings was the painting in progress on Dodge's easel at his death. The painting served as a conversation piece at Dodge's memorial celebration held in his home on May 24, 1997.[327] Although the painting would have been the fourth in the series in order of completion, it would have been the first in the sequence by virtue

of the subject. In its preliminary state the painting shows a couple, presumably parents, perched on a boulder, while a boy, perhaps their son, sets out with his sailboat to find a suitable pool. At the end of his life, was Dodge recalling his own idyllic youth as an only child?[328] Dodge often declared his refusal to psychoanalyze his own works and he probably would have been the first to insist that there was no deliberate attempt to suggest such a meaning. The four paintings together, however, the untitled unfinished piece, *Safe Harbor*, *Setting Sail*, and *Rising Tide*, do present a compelling and poignant look at the inevitable path of the child toward independence and adulthood.

Also in the nineties, Dodge painted a number of self-portraits, incorporating the artist and model in variations on the subject. The genesis and evolution of this latter theme can be seen in four paintings where Dodge painted himself at the easel. In each of these the viewer finds the artist's real life muse, friend, and inspiration, Jeanne Klempf. In *Artist and Model, First Session* (1991), Dodge, who is dressed in a blue shirt and khaki shorts, stands at the easel painting with one hand and holds a large palette with another. Model and artist stand on a wooden floor in front of a white wall. Jeanne stands before him holding her drapery to reveal her nude body. Next to Dodge is a small table on which rests a jar holding paintbrushes.

In *Artist and Model, First Session, II* (1991), the hues have become primarily blue and the entire scheme is a visual essay in blues and browns. Here Dodge sits and holds his brush as if to measure something. Jeanne stands in much the same posture as before but her drapery obscures her body; only the artist can see her nude form. Dodge made this composition more complicated. There are paintings on the wall and on the floor, as there often were in Dodge's own studio, to the viewer's left. A geometrical pattern is formed in the shadows cast on the wall and echoes the lines of the easel.

The intricate shadows remain in *The Artist and his Muse* (1992, pl. 94). Dodge's head is placed at the center of a cross formed by the shadows. The painting is very clearly set in Dodge's studio. Here, though, Jeanne is behind the artist. She stands, breasts bared, her robe cascading but held in place by her hands. She looks toward Dodge and the easel with an almost beatific smile as if she were an allegorical personification of inspiration or some type of guardian angel. The treatment of her drapery and her pose is almost columnar, and Dodge may have intended to cast Jeanne in the guise of a classical muse.

Artist and Model (1992) illustrates Dodge's reductive sensibilities. Everything superfluous has been removed. The figures of model and artist have been moved close to the viewer and each is represented in his or her own panel resulting in a diptych. Dodge sits and paints.

The edge of the easel seems to jut out of the picture. Jeanne stands holding her robe, the light bathing her breasts and shoulders.

This series demonstrates Dodge's preference for reworking an idea and continuing to refine it. His celebration of beauty and the centrality of the human form to his work, especially the female nude and more especially the nude Jeanne, are seen. The paintings acknowledge the primacy of inspiration derived from the visual and the tangible, while they testify to the artist's role as arbiter and transformer of nature's objects. The later depictions and variations of the artist in his studio are heir to a long line of past and modern representations of the theme where artists confront, acknowledge, and consider the fundamental nature of the profession.

The self-portraits painted by Dodge at this time were executed as pictorial legacies. A few were executed as presents to family members and friends. *Self-Portrait* (1993) was given to his third daughter, Lisa. Derived from a photograph, the bust-length painting shows the smiling artist in his trademark blue shirt, here open-collared. He appears healthy, robust, and cheerful, characteristics that usually applied to Dodge. He has recorded himself as he had many of his still-life compositions—with a strong light source from the right and with the subject silhouetted against a negative space, in this case a light blue. [329] Other self-portraits present more distressing images that reflect the artist's losses and illness. *Self-Portrait* (1992, pl. 99) in particular shows Dodge's face drawn and lined; the head is set against a dramatic foil of bright red. Its expressionistic intensity presents a startling contrast to its earlier counterpart as it records the painter's failing health.

In 1995 the artist completed two paintings, which in their stark clarity, strong light effects, and dark backgrounds, recall his still lifes of the sixties. *The String* (*The Rope,* 1995) and *The Bundle* (1995, pl. 102) both hang from a point denied to the viewer's vision. *The String* is painted with such realism that it approaches *trompe l'oeil* in the manner of Dutch painters from the seventeenth century and American masters of the still-life genre. The completely convincing illusion is stayed only by the visible brushstrokes of the surface behind the rope. *The Bundle* is composed of a napkin in which there is what? A ball? Fruit? Dodge has left this to the viewer's imagination. The cloth has been gathered at the top, its corners arcing to the left, and tied with the twine from which it dangles.

The String and *The Bundle* formed the basis for a third painting, *Still Life: Bundle and Rope* (pl. 108), completed in 1996.[330] Elements of the two earlier works are combined in the third with slight modifications. Dodge has altered the background from black to deep mottled blue. The configuration of the rope is slightly different in the degree to which the ends are frayed.

The position of the bundle is turned so that the gathered corners cascade toward the viewer. Dodge has united the two objects by connecting them to a strand from the rope. Pieces of white string are then tied resulting in a geometric arrangement, suggesting square and trapezoid, while the bundle and rope hang, inviting the viewer's scrutiny and interpretation.[331]

One is reminded of the Three Fates who spin, weave, and then cut the thread of individual existences. Dodge intended a similar meaning.[332] The bundle represents the course of life with its promises, its potential, but also the unknown; it even brings to mind a baby, often called a bundle of joy. Dodge admitted the object within the bundle could be an egg with its many symbolic connotations, or it could suggest an embryo and birth, but he wished to leave that to the viewer's interpretation. The rope shown in all its contrast does represent the many turns and particularly the tangles of one's life, and ultimately life's end. The image is a stark one, yet it is indicative of Dodge's ability to approach well-established historical subjects, basically a *vanitas* still life in this case, in new, modern, and creative ways. The *Bundle and Rope* coincides thematically with the subtle intentions discussed above in Dodge's paintings of the osprey nest. Dodge also considered the titles *A Stilled Life* and *At Rope's End* for this painting. He clearly confronts his mortality in this work and other later works.

Dodge continued to be actively involved in exhibitions of his work in the nineties. In the autumn of 1992, approximately sixty of his paintings were shown at the Cummer Gallery of Art, reflecting his production since the time of his last exhibition at the museum in 1975.[333] At the same time, works in a variety of media from Dodge's own collection were displayed, illustrating another dimension of the painter and museum administrator. The next year Dodge exhibited «dazzling, meticulously detailed paintings» and shared the billing with David Engdahl, an architect, sculptor, friend, and fellow member of the Art Celebration! group in a two-man show at the Florida School of the Arts in Palatka, Florida.[334] *Paintings and Drawings from the 1940s to the Present* was the title of the retrospective at the University Gallery at the University of North Florida in Jacksonville, Florida, for which Dodge agreed to be interviewed by the gallery director, Paul Karabinis, and this author.[335] Also commemorating the retrospective at UNF was a videotape produced by Dodge's friend Taylor Hardwick.[336] The video records not only the images in the show but also brief comments from many of the artist's friends, collectors, museum and gallery professionals, architects, and fellow artists. Excerpts from Dodge's lecture in the University Gallery on November 8, 1995, are included on the videotape as well.

Works were selected for another university audience in 1996 when old friend and artist, Steve Lotz, professor of art and gallery director at the University of Central Florida in Orlando, invited Dodge to exhibit with long-time friend, fellow artist, and professor emeritus from the University of Florida, Hiram Williams.[337] Dodge had first come across the painting of Steve Lotz at a graduate exhibition at the University of Florida where the young artist was featured. Both Dodge and Cinder Hardwick served as mentors and patrons to Lotz, whom Hardwick convinced to stay in Florida. The coordination of the Dodge-Williams exhibition was a great tribute from Lotz to these old lions of the north Florida art landscape. In Lotz's comments about the exhibition titled *Two North Florida Master Painters: Jerry Dodge and Hiram Williams*, Lotz analyzed the two painters' dramatically different styles of painting comparing them to:

> ... Apollo and Dionysus. Dodge is the Apollonian part-ner, Williams is the Dionysian. Dodge is the Classicist, Williams the Romanticist. Dodge's classical and visionary materialism is very Apollonian. It is revealed by his confi-dent draftsmanship; his love for solid, sharp-edged sculp-tural forms; his clear Florida-Mediterranean light; his rig-orous compositions which are informed by underlying grids; the serene equilibrium of his figures' faces and postures; and the unity and purity of his forms. The total-ity of these stylistic tools imbues Dodge's civilized world with aristocratic simplicity, serenity and balance.

> Consistent with his Apollonian nature, Dodge works slowly and deliberately. He knows what he's doing and where he wants to go when he begins. Like that other great Apollonian American painter, Edward Hopper, Dodge understands that his creative task is to remain true to his original imagistic urge which first brought him to the canvas.... Apollo's attribute, the Lyre, is echoed in Dodge's passion for jazz (and especially, the jazz of Duke Ellington) which figures prominently in many of his works.[338]

Dodge attended the opening in a wheel chair accom-panied by dear friends; his second daughter, Julie; his younger son, Jeffers; and a grandson, Taz Brighton Dodge. Paintings from 1943 (the *Double Self-Portrait*) to his most recent works from 1995 and 1996 were shown. This exhibition was the last retrospective held while Dodge was living. Three months after its clos-ing, Dodge would be dead.

Conclusion

Found in the artist's files after his death was a message in the artist's handwriting on a small piece of note paper dated «October 17th (?) 96 Sunday night, Monday AM.» The underlining is Dodge's:

I'm having trouble breathing! Seems to be no fluid, mucus or other impediment, just that my lungs are not filling up with air. Even when I try to take a deep breath, and, if I stop consciously trying to breathe, that I'll just cease breathing. No other abnormal symptoms. Only this feeling that my lungs are not taking in the usual amount of air. Scary! Especially when I lie down—which I've been doing most of the day. This just started suddenly about 1/2 hour ago. Sitting up is better.

It's not the feeling of the air being blocked, but that the lungs are not pulling it in—only a little bit, about half as much as normal, leaving a slight feeling of nothing hap-pening in my lungs, that its normal pulling power is con-siderably diminished. I have a feeling that I might not wake up—and my will, etc. are not completed. I've made changes in the first part, which is being retyped, so please take it as accurate—my final wishes, etc. But the more detailed part about the disposition of my art and my collection hasn't been finalized in detail.

However, I've talked it over with my attorney Jeff Dunn and my good friend Laura Jeanne Klempf, and they know pretty much what I want done. If the worst happens, please let them make the decisions—To the Cummer: (remainder scratched out by artist)[339]

As Dodge's health deteriorated dramatically, he was clearly concerned about settling his affairs. With the assistance of Jeff Dunn, Dodge arranged for donations of his works and selections from his collection to be distributed to various institutions, family members, and friends. A reception honoring Dodge and his gifts to the Cummer Museum was held in November of 1996. Dodge was recognized by former director Kahren Jones Arbitman who expressed appreciation not only for the works of art, but also for the donation of Dodge's considerable library of art books, and for the establishment of a fund for the purchase of fine drawings for the museum collection.

Dodge received a number of letters and notes of con-gratulations for his generosity to the museum and the Jacksonville community. Artist and friend Steve Lotz was unable to attend, but writing on November 25, 1996, he paid tribute to his old mentor:

> You have spent your creative life so effectively! It is diffi-cult for me to imagine how you managed to paint as mindfully and, apparently, as steadily as you did during all the years of directing the Hyde and the Cummer. It is a remarkable achievement to have maintained that level of quality and intensity over such a long career.[340]

From fellow artist and Art Celebration! member, Allison Watson, came a note dated November 26, 1996, in which she stated, «You have been a lifelong inspiration to me and have influenced my life pro-foundly.»[341] Another note from painter professor emer-itus, Hiram Williams, read:

> Dear Jerry: Your works are wonderfully expressive of a life I've dreamed of: an examined life. My life always seems to be rather shabby and shoddy, full of elbows and

hurry and scurry. I believe you have known «the examined Life» from early on. I never took time to examine mine. We must bow to Roy Craven for introducing us. You have enriched my life far more than you know. It's important that you understand this. Love, Hiram.[342]

In Dodge's comments at Tia's 1993 memorial service, he made the following observations about life and death:

> At some time, after we were born, we are all confronted with the idea of our own mortality. We become aware of beginnings and endings, of cycles and rhythms, of unities and varieties, of the certainties and ambiguities, and seemingly cruel and inexplicable aberrations of life and nature.... But most of us are more immediately concerned and apprehensive about the climax of life's drama called death. Is it the end? Fini? Or is it part of a cycle, or continuum? Most of us don't know when or how it will happen and hope, understandably, that it will be quick and painless.[343]

Joseph Jeffers Dodge died at home on March 6, 1997, at the age of seventy-nine. Three of his children, Julie, Lisa, and Jeffers, were with him at his death. His last days were spent in and out of consciousness as his old friends came to say good-bye and pay their last respects. Dodge was able to speak with some of them and seemed to be aware of others' presence. When Jeff Dunn took his last leave, he said to Dodge, «I'll be seeing you.» Jerry replied by singing the next phrase from the old song, «in all those old familiar places.»[344]

A card designed by Dodge to announce his death was mailed in mid-March. It was decorated with *The String*. Inside the card, with the notice of Dodge's demise, were the words, «All that remains is good works and love.» A memorial dinner celebrating the life of Jerry Dodge was held in the artist's home on May 24, 1997. The day before, family members and close friends gathered to distribute Dodge's ashes on Silversmith Creek behind the artist's home. Yellow roses were thrown into the water as tributes. Dodge's remains rejoined the setting he had lived in, drawn inspiration from, and painted.

At the end of a lecture given by the author of this book on Dodge's works at the University of North Florida in 1995, an audience member asked an important question. Where does the work of Jerry Dodge fit and how will it be viewed by successive generations? The latter question obviously cannot be answered with complete assurance but the first can be answered fairly securely.

In reviewing Dodge's career, it has been demonstrated that his earliest works reflected a period of experimentation in which he dabbled in a variety of styles influenced by Bonnard, Picasso, and Dalí, in addition to Renaissance and Baroque masters. Responding to the popularity of Cubism and

Surrealism in the United States and abroad in the forties, Dodge adapted elements of both of these movements, relying on the visual idiom of Surrealism in his jazz pictures and the structural basis of Cubism in his Quarry series. Dodge's admiration for the *fête champêtre* tradition found in Venetian and French painting can be seen in his modernization of the theme in his rooftop pictures and in depictions of figures engaging in leisurely activities on beaches.

Dodge remained steadfast in his devotion to a thoroughly modern but basically classical mode of representation, both in his selection of subjects and in the treatment of those subjects. The artist remained resolutely tied to the construction of harmonious compositions using recognizable imagery. A consistent adherence to a contemporary classical realist approach forms the underpinnings of Dodge's works, which developed from the highly symbolic narratives of his early career to the acute clarity of vision that marked his late paintings. Many reviews of his exhibitions and writings about his work, particularly those by Edelson and Holmes, have noted these tendencies. Other writers, Hamm and Koscielny, for example, have compared his approach to that of a particularly American tradition that favors realism in the arts. Though Dodge would not have agreed, some have found a similarity in Dodge's paintings of introspective, lonely, and unsmiling individuals seemingly isolated even from immediate company, to selected works by Edward Hopper. Others have seen similarities to works by Balthus from the thirties, especially in Dodge's explorations of themes of incipient sexuality of female adolescents. Ultimately Dodge was his own master. His knowledge of art history was enviable and catholic but for him the beauty of an object, a figure, or a setting was the main and determining factor in what to paint or draw. Explaining his preference for working in a representational mode, Dodge observed:

> To me it is more satisfying to design a tightly-knit arrangement, using more or less real forms. I feel that geometry is enriched and nature made more visually interesting. To me, abstract painting is kind of like what they say about Chinese food; it's tasty but I'm usually hungry soon afterwards. And that, I think, is because most abstract art is primarily about taste. Esthetics rather than content. To me it simply isn't as rich or interesting as the geometry of Poussin or Rubens or Tiepolo or Cézanne. [345]

Although Dodge resisted labels for his work, he admitted that he was a classical romanticist or a romantic classicist. Throughout his long career he worked in a way akin to the classical approach of taking directly from nature but always refining its realistic elements into a harmonious synthesis. It is this insistence on idealizing nature that separates him from the photo-realists. As detailed as Dodge's works are, his goal was never to render exactly what he saw. The observed view was always a springboard and a point of departure.

Dodge took his inspiration from the visual world and transformed it in his imagination to present an image or images that were often charged with a heightened reality. He concurred with the following observation about realism, «Realism is a changing imaginative construct which, if it is still to be of some real use to us, ought to acknowledge that the imagination is an active agent of our perceptions.»[346]

For much of the twentieth century, those artists who rendered figural, landscape, and allegorical subjects in a naturalistic or classical fashion were often ignored by mainstream art criticism. Coverage of contemporary realist painters by major art journals had been very slow in coming, although recently there have been several articles considering renewed interest in the representational.[347] Whatever the name —figurative, content-bearing, or representational— realism in its various guises may have been dramatically overshadowed by abstraction, but it has never been entirely eclipsed by it. For decades artists like Dodge have been creating, detractors would say laboring, in this idiom, which was dismissed as outdated and irrelevant to the twentieth century.

Former Cummer staff member and art historian Mary Campbell Gristina wrote about Dodge and his work in a 1992 museum brochure:

> The artist's romance with representation, with realism, with naturalism, dates back decades. Even during the 1960s, when Dodge painted subjects with overt symbolism, the representation in his paintings was strong. He stayed out of step with the accepted movements of the time, preferring more conservative values.
>
> From the 1940s into the 1960s, representational realism, figural, landscape, and allegorical subjects were excluded from recognition by mainstream art criticism. Dodge pursued what was then viewed as a lost and archaic direction, a hollow receptacle of the past rather than (what was viewed at the time) as a creative vision of the future. But as so often happens, the future changed direction. The image was reintroduced. Representation, even photo-realism, received critical acclaim. Painting so that the subject is recognizable is no longer anathema.
>
> Dodge's sharpness of vision became more acute as his painting career continued. Devoted to painting full-time after his retirement, the artist's meticulous treatment of light, texture, surface, and composition fused more deeply. A unity of subject, surface and creative vision marks his later paintings with a casual, unselfconscious grandeur.[348]

Like those paintings inspired by the tour of Brittany, many of Dodge's works are small and jewel-like with exquisitely crafted and miniature details that invite close perusal and studied contemplation. There is often an introspective serenity implied in his images, which are concerned with the timeless, the universal, and the beautiful.[349] Dodge believed:

> Painting is a silent art, created in silence—and best experienced in silence. Perhaps—and this is just kind of a guess—some of us are artists, because we find words inadequate. We find that the visual, uncontaminated by words and unlimited by words is, in fact, our real world, our reality, our delight, perhaps our compensation, or refuge. And so we try to create, or recreate these things, try to make them real, make them exist through art, and in this way, express what we want to share with others and, at the same time, what we want to keep for ourselves. [350]

At seventy-nine, Dodge was intrigued but not at all surprised that there was such a resurgence of interest in representational and figurative art. He was heartened by the revival, and as a former museum professional, an artist for more than fifty years, and a veteran collector, he recognized the inevitability of the cyclical nature of styles.

In June of 1990, Dodge concluded his lecture at the Jacksonville Art Museum about his life and work with these observations:

> Sometimes, as I look at these things, I think how wonderful some of them are, and how did I ever invent, and do them, and that I've gone downhill ever since. Other times, I'm equally sure that the picture I've just finished is my best work, or, more often that the best will be the one I've just started, or have in mind to do soon—someday. But usually I feel lucky too that I have been able to paint what I like, and that often enough, I like what I paint. And if some other people do, too, at least, some of it, so much the better! I'm just that much luckier—which at this time in life is a pretty good way to feel![351]

Also in 1990, Dodge submitted a brief biography and commentary to the Fiftieth Anniversary Report for the Harvard Class of 1940:

> Although by no means spectacular in fame or fortune, my life since 1940 has been fulfilled and happy—replete with good paintings and good children created, jobs well done, and the enjoyment of wonderful friends and lovers, music and art, people, places and things. As for the world and our times, I'm truly sorry they haven't shared my good fortune.[352]

Jerry Dodge's succinct statement reflects a life well lived. For those who admire and enjoy the works of Joseph Jeffers Dodge, whether in private collections or in museums, for those who enjoy the art of The Hyde Collection and the Cummer Museum, for those who remember the artist's friendship, generosity, and laughter, Dodge's legacy continues and his good fortune becomes ours.

Fig. 21 —Joseph Jeffers Dodge studio at his Silversmith Creek home

Notes

1 Dodge, (untitled paper presented in conjunction with an exhibition of his works at the University of Florida, Gainesville, Florida, April 2, 1969). See the Joseph Jeffers Dodge Archives to be established at the Cummer Museum of Art & Gardens, Jacksonville, Florida. This l969 lecture will hereafter be cited as UF. UF, 63.

2 UF, 47.

Introduction

3 Sharon Weightman, «Chosen to Become an Artist's Muse,» *The Florida Times-Union* (Jacksonville) Sunday, August 14, 1994, E-4.

4 Dodge recorded the autobiographical tapes in February, 1995. They were transcribed by this author and various student assistants and corrected by Dodge between September 1995 and April 1996. As might be expected of an oral history, the notes, although mostly chronological in order, skip back and forth among various periods in the artist's life. At the writing of this text, the document is 201 pages. The length and pagination are subject to change with future editing. See Dodge Autobiographical Transcriptions, the Joseph Jeffers Dodge Archives to be established at the Cummer Museum of Art & Gardens, Jacksonville, Florida. These autobiographical transcriptions will be cited hereafter as Dodge.

5 The lecture consists of sixty-three typed pages. See the Joseph Jeffers Dodge Archives to be established at the Cummer Museum of Art & Gardens, Jacksonville, Florida.

6 Untitled paper presented at the Jacksonville Art Museum, Jacksonville, Florida, June 28, 1990. The Jacksonville Art Museum is now the Jacksonville Museum of Modern Art. The lecture consists of sixty-four typed pages. See the Joseph Jeffers Dodge Archives to be established at the Cummer Museum of Art & Gardens, Jacksonville, Florida. This 1990 lecture will hereafter be cited as JAM.

Joseph Jeffers Dodge—The Life of the Artist

From Detroit to Glens Falls: 1917-1941

7 Alan L. Otten and Charles B. Seib, «There Goes the Man who Cut the Budget,» *Nation's Business,* May, 1954, 43.

8 «Presidential Adviser Joseph Dodge, Man with a Puzzle,» *TIME*, January 24, 1955, 12-15. See also *Banking, Journal of the American Banker's Association*, October, 1947, where Mr. Dodge was featured on the cover and Duncan Norton-Taylor, «The Banker in the Budget Bureau,» *Fortune*, March, 1953, 134-136, 138, 144. Dodge's contributions to the restitution of the Japanese economy were cited in a January 9, 1990, *Wall Street Journal* article written by Peter Drucker, see «Japan's Not-So-Secret Weapon,» n.p.

9 Dodge, 71-72.

10 Ibid., 42 and 72.

11 JAM, 18.

12 Dodge, 8-9.

13 Ibid., 16. Dodge also noted that, according to family tradition, «Other ancestors include the founder, Nathaniel Foote, of the Burlington Free Press, in northern Vermont, still publishing after 150 years or so,—a couple of furniture makers in Vermont and Michigan,—a portrait painter who did one of Daniel Webster,—A dancing teacher whose studio in New York became the first home of the Metropolitan Museum of Art (and none of whose genes I inherited, obviously),—Robinson Jeffers, the famous poet of Carmel, California,—an architect who designed the St. Francis Hotel, among other buildings, in San Francisco,—Harriet Beecher Stowe, who lived for a time near here in Mandarin, [Florida].»

14 Dodge Photo Albums, Joseph Jeffers Dodge Archives to be established at the Cummer Museum of Art & Gardens, Jacksonville, Florida. Hereafter the photo albums will be cited as Dodge Photo Albums.

15 Diana Korzenik, *Drawn to Art, A Nineteenth-Century American Dream*, Hanover and London, 1983. My thanks to Jeanette Toohey who directed me to *Drawn to Art, A Nineteenth-Century American Dream*. Noting of the American character that the «unquenchable quest for improvement, whetted back in the nineteenth century, motivates us still» (260), Korzenik studies the increase in the popularity of art instruction in the United states. She observes «with the turn of the century and the burgeoning interest in psychology, art instruction was transformed from a skill or trade to a way of organizing thoughts and feelings» (258).

16 UF, 13.

17 See Donald R.Morris, «Thomason U.S.M.C.,» *American Heritage,* November, 1993, 52-66.

18 Alexander Dumas, *The Three Musketeers* (translated by William Robson, with 250 illustrations by LeLoir), New York and London, 1930. Dodge treasured this volume and kept it throughout his life. He left it to Jeff Dunn at his death. My thanks to Dunn for the citation.

19 Dodge, 15.

20 Ibid., 18-19.

21 Handwritten page by the artist, date unknown. Dodge Documents, Joseph Jeffers Dodge Archives to be established at the Cummer Museum of Art & Gardens, Jacksonville, Florida. Hereafter the documents will be cited as Dodge Documents.

22 Dodge, 13.

23 Marcia Corbino, «Joseph Jeffers Dodge,» *American Artist*, 47, June, 1983, 97. «When my eyes went bad, I thought that I could never go through architectural school with all the fine work involved. But as it happens, I now do very detailed work.»

24 JAM, 21.

25 Dodge, 23.

26 Dodge, 27-28.

27 JAM, 20. He did, in fact, design plans for a dream house on the California coast. Titled *Plan for Fantasy House on the Monterey-Carmel Coast*, pen and ink on paper, 10" x 14", it dates to 1941 and is in the artist's archives in the Cummer.

28 *The Helicon*, Detroit University School Yearbook, 1935, 72-73.

29 Portrait of Franklin Delano Roosevelt, pencil, 1936, autographed by the President, collection of Joseph M. Dodge II, Tallahassee, Florida.

30 JAM, 23.

31 Linda Bank Downs, *Diego Rivera: The Detroit Industry Murals*, New York and London, 1999.

32 *The Faculty* and *The Alumni* from the *Choate Yearbook*, 1936, both executed originally in pen and brush.

33 William Nye Swift (editor), *The Choate Literary Magazine*, November, 1935, volume 22, number 1, 41.

34 Guy B. Ewing (editor), *The Choate Literary Magazine Anthology Issue, 1915-1965*, 49.

35 Dodge, 52-53.

36 JAM, 34.

37 Letter from the elder Dodge to Leighton, August 24, 1936. Dodge Correspondence, Joseph Jeffers Dodge Archives to be established at the Cummer Museum of Art & Gardens, Jacksonville, Florida. Hereafter the files will be cited as Dodge Correspondence.

38 For works by Arthur Pope, see *The language of drawing and painting*, New York, c. 1949 (reprint 1969); *Art, artist, and layman; a study of the teaching of the visual arts*, Cambridge, Mass., 1937; and *Titian's Rape of Europa; a study of the composition and the mode of representation in this and related paintings*, Cambridge, (published for the Isabella Stewart Gardner Museum) 1960.

39 See Denman Waldo Ross, *On Drawing and Painting*, New York, 1912 and *The painter's palette: a theory of tone relations, an instrument of expression*, Boston and New York, 1919.

40 Eugene R.Gaddis, *Magician of the Modern: Chick Austin and the Transformation of the Arts in America*, New York, 2000, 42.

41 Dodge Notebooks, 1938. Joseph Jeffers Dodge Archives to be established at the Cummer Museum of Art & Gardens, Jacksonville, Florida. Hereafter the notebooks will be cited as Dodge Notebooks.

42 JAM, 26.

43 Ibid., 27.

44 Ibid.

45 Ibid., 25.

46 Gaddis, 42 and 436.

47 Dodge, 51-52.

47 JAM, 28.

Glens Falls and The Hyde Collection

49 James K. Kettlewell, *The Hyde Collection* Catalogue, Glens Falls, New York, 1981, ix.

50 Elizabeth B. Wilson, «Who Needs The Big City?,» *Art & Antiques*, November, 1998, 86.

51 Noel Suter, «The Surprising Hyde Collection,» *Museum Magazine*, September/October, 1982, 24.

52 Kettlewell, 46-48.

53 Ibid., 108-111.

54 See Steven Vincent, «The Crimson,» *Art & Auction*, January, 1996, 80.

[55] Dodge, 111-112.

[56] Ibid., 112. For the Fragonard, see Kettlewell, 142-143; for the Picasso works, see 180-183; for the Hassam, see 216-217; for Peto, see 202-203.

[57] Quoted in Suter, 25.

[58] Ibid.

[59] For the Raphael, see Kettlewell, 66-68; El Greco, 90-91; Tintoretto, 82-83; Rubens, 92-93; van Dyck, 102-103.

[60] For Eakins, see Kettlewell, 192-195; for Vedder, 196-201; for Homer, 204-207.

[61] Quoted by Frederick J. Fisher in Kettlewell, xi.

The Glens Falls Years: 1941-1962

[62] See «Art Week: Local Treasure,» *The Post-Star*, Glens Falls New York, November 5, 1959, «The term collection is used advisedly, Joseph J. Dodge, curator observes. The Hyde Collection is not a museum, but a home in which the owner lives, and the paintings and art objects to be seen there are arranged for enjoyment in the various rooms.»

[63] See Kettlewell, xi. The Glens Falls newspaper observed, «Critics rate the Hyde Collection as the third best collection of old masters in the state, ranking next to the Met Museum and the Frick Collection.» See *The Post-Star* (Glens Falls, NY), November 5, 1959.

[64] Suter, 26.

[65] For fond reminiscences of Bill Palmer, «a living gnome of a person ... perpetually smiling and happy,» see Dodge, 159-161.

[66] Refer to the listing of major exhibitions by Dodge in the appendices for a more comprehensive view of how active the artist was during these years.

[67] See Edward F. Fry, *David Smith, Painter, Sculptor, Draftsman*, 1982, and Rosalind E. Krauss, *Terminal Iron Works: The Sculpture of David Smith*, 1971. Dehner and Smith were married in December, 1927; they divorced in 1952.

[68] Dodge, 139.

[69] Ibid., 139-140. Dodge Photo Albums. See Dodge's family albums housed in the Cummer for photographs of the posed vignettes for Crockwell.

[70] Joan M. Marter, *Dorothy Dehner: Sixty Years of Art*, Katonah, New York, 1993, 7-8. «More than eighteen small egg tempera paintings depicting scenes from her daily routine at Bolton Landing, New York, ranged from allegorical to those conceived in the naive style of a folk artist.» For a brief biography on Dehner with mention of her *Life on the Farm* series based on medieval manuscripts, see «Dorothy Dehner's Legacy to the League,» by Joan Marter in *LINEA, The Newsletter of the Art Students League of New York*, Winter, 1998, 1, 7 and 14. See also Dodge, 147.

[71] Dodge, 147.

[72] Ibid., 146.

[73] See Dodge Files, the Joseph Jeffers Dodge Archives to be established at the Cummer Museum of Art & Gardens, Jacksonville, Florida. These files will be cited hereafter as Dodge Files. There is no indication of the source of this short blurb, torn from a newspaper, which reads, «Alan Lerner is flying to New York this weekend to attend the show of Painter Joseph Jeffers Dodge. And thereby hangs the tale. Lerner who wrote *An American in Paris*, got the inspiration from Dodge's own career and used much of the material from the young artist's life for the film. He even called the star of the picture Jerry Dodge, which is the actual name the painter's friends gave him.» In pencil at the bottom of the column is written the name of Hedda Hopper. In actuality, the central character is named Jerry Mulligan not Jerry Dodge, and the artist was given the nickname not by friends, but by family when he was an infant. A more recent citation can be found in Judy Wells's «The Wells Watch, Artistic likeness,» *The Florida Times-Union* (Jacksonville), Sunday, November 2, 1997, D-2. Lerner won the best picture Oscar for *An American in Paris* in 1952; see Edward Jablonski, *Alan Jay Lerner, A Biography*, New York, 1966, 63-69.

[74] Dodge, 165.

[75] UF, 43.

[76] UF, 15; JAM, 31.

Jacksonville and the Cummer Gallery of Art

[77] Corbino, 98.

[78] For information on the original Cummer mansion, see Wayne Wood, *Jacksonville's Architectural Heritage*, 150; additional information on Cummer Lumber Mill built in 1896 can be found on p. 370 along with an illustration of the Cummer Mausoleum in Evergreen Cemetery, «the purest example of the Egyptian Revival Style in Jacksonville.» Brief biographies of the Cummers are found in the museum handbook, Tanja Jones et al., *Cummer Museum of Art & Gardens*, 2000, 6-7.

[79] *Along the Strand* has hung for many years in the Cummer Museum's Tudor Room.

[80] Jean Hall Dodd, *Ninah May Holden Cummer* (pamphlet published by the Cummer Museum, September, 1997).

[81] See Jones et al., 7. It was a highly appropriate and important decision to change the name of the Cummer Gallery of Art to the Cummer Museum of Art & Gardens in 1994, thereby reflecting the history, beauty and significance of these gardens.

[82] Ibid.

[83] Dodge Files. Selected catalogues include (all exhibitions were held at the Cummer unless otherwise noted): *Five Hundred Years of Flowers and Gardens in Western Art* (October 17-November 25, 1962); The introductory text notes «The Cummer... is pleased to present this esthetic bouquet as part of the celebration of our First Anniversary.» Within Dodge's copy were eleven typed pages of a lecture on the exhibition given by Dodge; *Courtenay Hunt,* September 24th- October 13th, 1963; *Sculpture through the Ages*, January 1963; *Paintings by Lee Adams*, 1963; *Young American Realists*, January 7-February 2, 1964; *Artists of the Paris Salon*, January 7-February 2, 1964; *French Art of the Sixteenth Century, Commemorating The Fort Caroline Quadricentennial*, June 27-September 30, 1964, (with forward by Charles Bennett and essay «The Art of Sixteenth Century France,» by William R. Crelly, Yale); *Harold Hilton Memorial Exhibit*, October 6-November 1, 1964, (brochure); *Mun Quan*, November 11-29, 1964 (brochure); *William E. Parker, Works:1960-1964; Diminutive Studies, 1965*, May 4 to May 30th, 1965; *Sheldon Bryan*, September 15-October 17, 1965; *Artists of Victoria's England*, February 2-March 14, 1965; *Six American Sculptors*, January, 1966; *Exhibitions, Lectures, Concerts*, 1965-1966; *Mid-nineteenth Century American painting from the Collections of Henry M. Fuller and William H. Gerdts*, July-August, 1966; *Four Photographers: Gefter, Kwilecki, Parker, Uelsmann*, May 30-July 2, 1967; *Landscapes of the Norwich School*, (title page: Landscapes of the Norwich School, An American Debut, 1967, Essay, Chronology, and Catalogue by Norman L. Goldberg, M.D.); *From Palace Walls, An Exhibition of Tapestries and Antique Furnishings*, lent by French & Company, Inc., February 14-March 31, 1968; *American Paintings of Ports and Harbors, 1774-1968*, (frontispiece: Organized by Joseph Jeffers Dodge, Director, Cummer Gallery of Art, Foreword by Henry Bryan Caldwell, Director, Norfolk Museum of Arts and Sciences, February 4-March 16, 1969; Norfolk Museum of Arts and Sciences, Norfolk, Virginia, April 5-May 11, 1969); *The Age of Louis XIII* (frontispiece: The Age of Louis XIII, October 29-December 7, 1969 & The Museum of Fine Arts, St. Petersburg, Florida, January 5-February 8, 1970); catalogue written and compiled by Dodge and staff; *Remnants of Things Past* (inside cover: Remnants of Things Past, The Museum of Fine Arts, Saint-Petersburg, Florida, January 8-February 7, 1971, the Cummer Gallery of Art, Jacksonville, Florida, February 16-March 14, 1971; foreword by Joseph Jeffers Dodge); *William Palmer, Two Decades of Painting*, Munson-Williams-Proctor Institute, Utica, New York, January 3-February 7, 1971; Cummer Gallery of Art, Jacksonville, Florida, March 20-April 25, 1971; *Edmund W. Greacen, N.A., American Impressionist, 1876-1949* (title page: Edmund W. Greacen, N.A., American Impressionist, An Original Exhibition organized by the Cummer Gallery of Art, Jacksonville, Florida, April 11, 1972-May 20, 1972, foreword by Joseph Jeffers Dodge; «A Biography,» Elizabeth Greacen Knudsen); *1822 Sesquicentennial Exhibition, Part I, Cummer Gallery of Art* (title page: 1822 Sesquicentennial Exhibition, January 11, 1972-February 2, 1972; foreword by Joseph Jeffers Dodge).

[84] Jones et al., 54-55.

[85] Ibid., 102-103.

[86] The painting is illustrated in Jones, et al., 64-65. A valuable source of information is found in a videotaped interview with Dodge conducted in the museum galleries by former Cummer director Henry Adams in 1996. It currently exists in an unedited state. Dodge discusses the acquisition of works by Vibert, Barrias (believed to contain a portrait of the young Degas), Heade, Cropsey, and Rombouts. He noted that he bought the Gobelins-style tapestry in New York on his way down from Glens Falls not only because of its quality but because it would cover a considerable amount of wall space, an important consideration in the early days of the museum when there was more building than collection.

[87] See Mary Campbell Gristina, *The Wark Collection: Early Meissen Porcelain*, Jacksonville, Florida, 1984 and Jones et al., 202-205.

The Jacksonville Years: 1962-1997

[88] Robert W. Schlageter, introduction made at the Cummer Museum of Art & Gardens, Jacksonville, Florida, December, 5, 1976. Copies in Dodge Files.

[89] Dodge served as a juror for numerous exhibitions throughout Florida including shows in Mandarin, Saint Augustine, Cedar Key, and Melbourne among others. Following a pattern established in Glens Falls, he continued to give lectures at museums, universities, and other organizations, for example at the University of Florida in 1969 and at the Waweatonong Club in Detroit in 1979, where Jerry's old friend Dave Mills introduced him. In 1983 Dodge was invited to participate in a symposium at The Hyde Collection titled *American Art Collectors: From Avocation to Institution*; other speakers included Hilton Kramer and Everett Fahy. In 1987 Dodge gave a lecture series at the Jacksonville Art Museum titled «Drawing: The International Language.» He gave an updated version of his 1969 lecture about his life and his work at the museum in June of 1990. Dodge was a regular contributor to the Channel 7 auction to benefit the WJCT public television station in Jacksonville. His diverse activities ranged from contributing an image of his painting *Finding* (1971) to be included in a calendar for the Children's Miracle Network at University Hospital in Jacksonville, to serving on an advisory committee for the Barnett Bank.

[90] See Bob Phelps, «Classical music has rich history in Jacksonville, Frederick Delius tops century of ties,» *The Florida Times-Union* (Jacksonville, Florida), June 20, 1999, D-1 and D-3.

[91] Dodge Files. Copies of both programs, the first dating January 31, 1963, the second dating January 29-February 7, 1969 are in the artist's files.

[92] See Catherine Enns, «Artist inspired by Delius,» *The Florida Times-Union* (Jacksonville), February 24, 1984, D-1 and D-4.

[93] Enns, D-1, «'I liked Delius' music and am very much interested in the Delius Association and so it was something I liked to begin with,' he said. 'But I'm really not a poster artist. I knew it wasn't my field.'» The painting, which is in the collection of Mrs. John Donahoo, Jacksonville, was reproduced on the poster for the 1984 Delius Festival, March 7-10. It features the exceptional breadth of the St. Johns River at that point—almost four miles—and the steamy tropicality of the location. In including four African Americans (the women are based on old photographs of Billie Holiday and Ethel Waters), Dodge acknowledged the profound inspiration Delius found in the spirituals sung by the African American workers on his father's grove, an influence that was to influence his compositions long after his return to England. Dodge's friend, attorney Dave Mills noted in reviewing this manuscript, «in one of his trips to France he spent the better part of two days tracking down or looking for sites where Delius had lived or composed.»

[94] Judy Wells Martin, «Art Celebration! will begin on Saturday,» *The Florida Times-Union and Journal* (Jacksonville), 1981. Other members in the Art Celebration! group included Charlie Brown, Charles Charles, Mark Howard, Steve Lotz, Allison Miraglia (Watson), Marilyn Taylor, Ben'H Usry, Ger Williamson, Ray Wiley, and Memphis Wood. Over the years special invitations would be issued to new member artists; these included Enzo Torcoletti, Mary Ann Bryan, David Engdahl, Robin Shepherd, and Peter Rumpel. Guests artists included Hiram Williams, Steve Lotz, Henry «Pete» Petersen, Vance Shrum, and Louise Freshman Brown.

[95] In addition to Dodge and Koscielny, artists listed in the 1979 Art Celebration! exhibition at the Le Moyne Foundation were Charlie Brown, David Engdahl, Mark Howard, Allison Miraglia (Watson), Marilyn Taylor, Ben'H Usry, Ray Wiley, and Memphis Wood. A non-exhibiting member of the group was Jeffrey D. Dunn, an attorney. As is noted in the introduction, Dunn, with Jeanne Klempf and architect Taylor «Cinder» Hardwick, was one of Dodge's closest friends and confidants during the Jacksonville years. Dunn also became the personal representative of Dodge's estate and negotiated the artist's bequests to various museums including the Cummer, The Museum of Arts and Sciences in Daytona Beach, The Hyde Collection, and the Fogg Museum at Harvard. Dunn has distinguished himself as a leader in the arts. He has been Chairman of the Board of Trustees of the Jacksonville Art Museum (now the Jacksonville Museum of Modern Art); he was Chairman of the Florida Arts Council; he is active in the Southern Arts Federation and currently serves as its Chairman.

[96] Corbino, 50-54, 95-99.

[97] Carole Katchen, «Exploring Technique, Joseph Jeffers Dodge: Evolving into Simplicity,» *Painting Faces and Figures*, New York, 1986, 54-61.

[98] Jacque Holmes, also a co-founder of the Arts Assembly, later renamed the Cultural Council, went on to found Art Sources, which was located in the former Gulf Life Tower. She moved her business to her Orange Park home in 1981. She continues to be a prominent figure in the community, has served as Chair of the Board of the Ringling Museum in Sarasota, Florida, and still does corporate art consulting. Cinder Hardwick was one of Jerry Dodge's closest friends in Jacksonville. A distinguished architect, Hardwick designed Jacksonville's downtown Main Library, Friendship Park and Fountain on the south bank of the St. Johns River, five area high schools, and Little Hall at the University of Florida campus in Gainesville, among many other structures. When Dodge purchased his home on Silversmith Creek, it was Hardwick who designed the additions to provide the artist's studio and other improvements. Hardwick and Dodge lunched together once a week for many years. Hardwick's tribute to his old friend can be seen in a video he produced and directed of Dodge's exhibition at the University of North Florida in 1995. Interviews of many of Dodge's oldest friends are included, as is film footage of the works in the exhibition.

[99] *Joseph Jeffers Dodge, A Ten Year View, The Cummer Gallery of Art, 1975*, (exhibition catalogue with essays by Russell B. Hicken and William E. Parker), Jacksonville, 1975.

[100] See Pamela Paige, «Dodge of Cummer: The director's first one-man local exhibit goes on display,» *The Florida Times-Union Sunday Magazine* (Jacksonville, February 16, 1964, 12; and Yvonne Parker, «Man Still Remains Focal Point For Artists,» *Jacksonville Journal*, Thursday, March 5, 1964, 27.

[101] Sharon Weightman, «Arts supporters honored», *The Florida Times-Union* (Jacksonville), April 26, 1996, B-3. Writing in support of the nomination were former United States Representative, The Honorable Charles E. Bennett; architect and author Robert C. Broward; artist and museum director John S. Bunker; Mrs. John W. Donahoo, widow of Mrs. Cummer's attorney and chair of Cummer board; Jeffrey Dunn; Taylor Hardwick; Jeanne Klempf; attorney and collector Carle Felton and his wife, Nancy; former museum directors Russell B. Hicken and Robert Schlageter; artists Margaret Koscielny, Steve Lotz, and Allison Watson; Edward W. Lane Sr., the only surviving member of the original board of trustees of the Cummer and his wife Helen; Sally Ann Freeman, gallery director; and the author.

[102] Dodge Correspondence. Selected excerpts include: «The Cummer Gallery coming to Jacksonville was the most significant advance in the city's cultural history. Jerry Dodge, who became director of the Cummer in 1962, made this advance real and solidly anchored for the future. He inspired a resurgence of artistic appreciation unequaled in our past. Moreover his own paintings have become a part of the area's heritage because of their excellence» (from The Honorable Charles E. Bennett, former United States Representative). «Mr. Dodge has dedicated his life to the celebration and promotion of the fine arts. He has opened new horizons for everyone who has known him, by setting an example with his lifetime of masterful drawings and paintings. He is a man and artist who celebrates excellence in all the varied facets of life. His work has continuously expressed this personal belief» (from Robert C. Broward, architect and author). «Jerry Dodge has been a major force in the art world in Jacksonville and the State of Florida since he moved to Jacksonville in 1962 to become director of the Cummer Gallery of Art. Jerry was the Cummer's director during the first ten years of existence, and he built the foundation of the Cummer Collection. Jerry is an outstanding artist, being written about and having works of his regularly reproduced in books and magazines. He was a founder of Art Celebration! in 1972 which was a major breakthrough in the display and sale of Jacksonville artists to a wider public. His works are in collections through the United States and Europe. He is a major collector of art from Old Masters to contemporary. He regularly lends to major museums shows ... and currently has a work in an exhibition at the Museum of Fine Arts, St. Petersburg. He is the only individual collector included in this major show with such museums as the Louvre and the Metropolitan Museum of Art» (from Jeffrey D. Dunn, attorney, arts advocate and collector). «Jerry Dodge has been my friend and colleague since we met in 1962. His friendship and collegiality in those early years was a huge contribution to the establishment of tranquility in a sometimes turbulent and unseemly art climate. During my terms as Director of the Jacksonville Art Museum I experienced an immense spirit of cooperation and support from Jerry and I give him a lot of credit for the impressive strides experienced in the arts for that period» (from Russell B. Hicken, arts administrator and art dealer). «I first met Jerry in 1963. At that time I was finishing my graduate degree work at the University of Florida, and Jerry happened to visit Gainesville and see a three-person exhibition of work in which I participated. He was enthusiastic about what I was attempting and he very generously included my work in an exhibition (*Young American Realists*) which he was putting together for the Cummer. He also encouraged me and my bride, Gretchen, to move to Jacksonville—which we did. That encounter, and the move to Jacksonville, began a thirty-plus year friendship/mentorship which has continued to enrich my life and and my art. Jerry's superb taste, as an artist, collector, and museum director, is founded on a cultural awareness which is of a breadth and depth which I have not encountered in any other person. The stamp of his sure taste clearly defines the astute acquisitions which he has

made to the Cummer Collection during his tenure as director. The same visual intelligence informs every work which issues from his studio» (from Steve Lotz, artist, professor of art and gallery director). All excerpts date between February and March of 1996 and are taken from correspondence directed to the author or to the Cultural Council of Jacksonville in support of Dodge's award nomination. The application and original letters are in the artist's archives.

Dodge the Collector

[103] Nancy Belote Felton, «A Man's Domain,» *Antiques Show Magazine*, December, 1988, Jacksonville, Florida, 74-75. For a color plate of *Greek Amphitheater at Taormina, Sicily* by Emil Holm, see the Cummer handbook, Jones, et al., 98-99.

[104] Cummer brochure: *The Collections of Joseph Jeffers Dodge, Sept. 11-Oct. 25, 1992, Cummer Gallery of Art*, with foreword by Robert Schlageter, director, «The Collection,» by Debra Murphy-Livingston, and «Collector's Statement,» by Dodge.

[105] Dodge referred to the sculpture by Smith as *Snaggle Toothed Woman #2*. For a color illustration see the Cummer handbook, Jones, et al., 188-189.

[106] Joshua C. Taylor et al., *Perceptions and Evocations: the Art of Elihu Vedder*, Washington, 1979, 48 and figure 35. Dodge was originally given the Vedder by one of Mrs. Hyde's sisters. Thanks to Jeff Dunn for this information.

[107] Kettlewell, 196-201.

[108] The text is from an invitation announcing the exhibition at the Hyde Collection. Dodge's painting, *Hudson River Town*, 1959, also given to the museum by the artist, is featured in color on the cover.

[109] Jennifer Hardin, *The Lure of Egypt: Land of the Pharaohs Revisited*, Museum of Fine Arts, St. Petersburg, Florida (exhibition catalogue), January 10-June 9, 1996, 8-9 and 23. Dodge gave the *Colossi of Memnon* to the Cummer. It is illustrated in Jones et al., 96-97. The fanciful name of Memnon, son of Aurora or the dawn, came from the curious bell-like sound the figures—especially the northern one—were purported to make at sunrise. The site served the Romantic poet, Percy Bysshe Shelley (1792-1822) as inspiration for his poem *Ozymandias*.

The Artist's Work

Early Paintings and Photographs from Glens Falls

[110] Dodge, 104-107. «Museums Without Walls» is contained in *The Voices of Silence* by André Malraux, (translated by Stuart Gilbert), New York, 1953. Part of his experimenting can be seen in *Breakfast by a Window*, where the artist's homage to Bonnard is especially obvious in the coloring and composition. The whereabouts of this painting are unknown.

[111] *And Then There Were Two* is in The Museum of Arts and Sciences in Daytona Beach, Florida. *La Vie* by Pablo Picasso is in the Cleveland Museum of Art. See John Richardson, *A Life of Picasso*, volume I, 1881-1906, New York, 1991, 268-277.

[112] UF, 14; JAM, 30

[113] UF, 15; JAM, 30. *The Hour of Parting* is in the Cummer Museum.

[114] Mr. Mills wrote these observations in the margin of the manuscript as he was reviewing it; the author is grateful for these insights and many others.

[115] The location of *Art Student* is unknown. It may have been one of the works stolen. The only trace of the work in the artist's files is a color transparency. Dodge Transparencies, Joseph Jeffers Dodge Archives to be established at the Cummer Museum of Art & Gardens, Jacksonville, Florida from here on will be cited as Dodge Transparencies.

[116] For a color plate of the Giorgione portrait, see *The Golden Century of Venetian Painting* by Terisio Pignatti, pages 48-49.

[117] UF, 17. Dodge also cites the influence of Eugene Berman, Pavel Tchelitchew, Giorgio de Chirico and Salvador Dalí. Dodge was responsible for the acquisition of a painting by Berman for the Cummer. *Wreckage and Debris on the Beach*, 1935, is illustrated in the museum handbook, Jones et al., 178-179.

[118] *Maternity* is in the Cummer Museum collection.

[119] Dodge examined the subject matter of *The Classical Tradition* in two small paintings completed at the end of the 1940s and are titled *Gods of Our Fathers: The Classical Tradition* and *The Christian Tradition*.

[120] Dodge Files. Found in the artist's files the newspaper clipping, no date, was titled «Hammonds win first honors in camera contest,» Dodge received honorable mention for the Classical Tradition. A paragraph was devoted to «Crucifixation [sic] one of three photograms made by Mr. Dodge was also given honorable mention in the miscellaneous class.» The Cummer Museum also houses several of Dodge's photograms.

The «Jazz» Paintings

[121] Dodge, 62.

[122] See Sidney Janis, *Abstract & Surrealist Art in America*, 1944, 87.

[123] Dorothy C. Miller and Alfred H. Barr (editors), *American Realists and Magic Realists*, New York, 1943 (reprint 1969), 5.

[124] Ibid.

[125] UF, 18.

[126] JAM, 34.

[127] Margaret Breuning, «The Cerebral Approach to Portraiture,» *Art Digest*, April 15, 1945, 13.

[128] *Moon Mist* was purchased by Mr. and Mrs. A.C. Flood in Birmingham, Michigan; its current whereabouts are unknown. *Black and Tan Fantasy* was a gift from Dodge to Choate Rosemary Hall (the Choate School) in Wallingford, Connecticut.

[129] *Surrealism* by Patrick Waldberg, London, 1978, contains a sound introduction to the principal figures and history of the movement.

[130] Clippings in Dodge's files regarding *Moon Mist* and its sale to the Floods contain no dates. Dodge Files.

[131] *Christian Science Monitor*, December 28, 1946 issue of the paper, no page included.

[132] *Catalogue of the One Hundred and Fortieth Annual Exhibition of Painting and Sculpture*, January 19 through February 25, 1945, the Pennsylvania Academy of the Fine Arts, Philadelphia.

[133] *Black and Tan Fantasy* was composed by Ellington and James «Blubber» Miley in October, 1927; see John Edward Hasse, *Beyond Category: the Life and Genius of Duke Ellington*, New York, 1993, 97. Ellington explains the meaning of *Black and Tan Fantasy* in Mark Tucker (ed.), *The Duke Ellington Reader*, Oxford and New York, 1993, 89. The title referred to «night clubs patronized by both white and coloured amusement seekers ... these are colloquially known as 'black and tans'.»

[134] The annual exhibition was held at the DIA between November 28 and December 24, 1944. The clipping in Dodge's files has no source or date. Written at the top is «Joseph Jeffers Dodge exhibits *Black and Tan Fantasy*,» Wed. News; «Art and Artists in Detroit.» Dodge Files.

[135] UF, 19.

[136] Ibid. See also Robert Hughes, «Seeing Life in Jazz Tempo,» *Time*, January 20, 1992, 60-61.

[137] Dodge, 62.

[138] Geoffrey C. Ward and Ken Burns, *Jazz: The Story of America's Music*, New York, 2000, 269. Although Holiday sometimes claimed to have written the song herself, the poem was composed by Abel Meerpol, a «young, leftist high-school teacher» in 1939.

[139] Ward and Burns, 269-270.

[140] Ibid.

[141] For Thomas Wright «Fats» Waller, see Joel Vance, *Fats Waller, His Life and Times*, New York, 1977.

[142] Vance, 70.

[143] UF, 20.

[144] Robert G. Wheeler, «Art in Albany,» *Sunday Times-Union* (Albany, NY), October 9, 1949, D-5.

[145] Two albums recorded by Reed include *Susan Reed Sings Old Airs*, released by the Elektra label in 1954 and *Susan Reed*, also released by Elektra, n.d. Information provided in the former album noted her acting career in *Brigadoon, Finian's Rainbow* and *Our Town*.

[146] Dodge Photo Albums. In one of Dodge's photo albums housed at the Cummer there are several pages devoted to Reed. One clipping is from *Life*, 1945, n.p.; the caption reads, «New Folk singer—Susan Reed is nightclub hit with her singing of old ballads.» The article notes, «[This] fall the pet of Manhattan nightclubbers is a chubby, freckled-face redhead of 18 named Susie Reed,» and, «she wears no makeup when performing.» Another clipping titled «Who Sings to One Clear Harp in Divers Tones» refers to her as «a voice as pure as spring waters,» *Esquire*, December, 1945, n.p.

[147] Dodge, 151-153.

[148] Ibid. It is interesting to study the preliminary drawings associated with the *Elegy* painting. A number show Reed standing admiring herself in a full-length mirror while a male (Dodge?) sleeps alone or watches from a bed. Dodge Drawings, Joseph Jeffers Dodge Archives to be established at the Cummer Museum of Art & Gardens, Jacksonville, Florida. Hereafter the drawings will be cited as Dodge Drawings.

[149] Dodge, 151-153.

[150] The painting was exhibited widely and was included in the artist's exhibitions at the Wildenstein Gallery in New York in 1952; the Albany Museum in 1956; and the Cummer in the artist's retrospective exhibition in 1964, where it was reproduced as number 5 in the accompanying catalogue. More recently it was seen at exhibitions at the University of North Florida, the University of Central Florida, and at the Cummer in a small posthumous show. It is in the Cummer Museum.

[151] John Edward Hasse, *Beyond Category: The Life and Genius of Duke Ellington*, New York, 1993, 157.

[152] UF, 21; JAM, 41.

[153] At the time of his death Dodge had amassed an extensive collection of books and articles on Marilyn Monroe.

[154] Dodge, 66.

[155] Dodge occasionally used the same title for different works. In addition to *Black and Tan Fantasy*, he also used *Fugue* and *Interlude* several times.

[156] The painting was originally purchased by Dr. and Mrs. Irving (Pete and Kathleen) Juster. It had been exhibited at the Crandall Library in Glens Falls. The painting is now in a private collection.

[157] Taken from notes on an index card in the artist's records. Dodge Files.

[158] The painting was given to Mr. and Mrs. Sherwin B. French as a wedding present about 1948 or 1949. After their divorce the painting remained with Dodge's longtime friend «Bill» French, an accomplished drummer and musician in his own right. Dodge Photo Albums.

[159] Dodge, 30.

[160] Dodge, 31.

[161] Dodge Photo Albums. In one of his photo albums Dodge saved the article about this concert; see «Duke's Bagful of Music Rocks Palace,» *The News, Mexico City*, December 9, 1971, 16.

[162] Dodge, 31-32.

The «Rooftop» Paintings

[163] This writer is indebted to Taylor Hardwick's notes about this.

[164] See Betty B. Jean, *The Jacksonville Symphony Orchestra: Fifty Years of Great Music*, Jacksonville, 1999, 80-81.

[165] Taylor Hardwick's recounting of this was most helpful.

[166] For information about the funeral see also Janna Tull Steed, *Duke Ellington, A Spiritual Biography*, 1999, 3-13. In attendance there were «enough musicians to have staged a marathon performance of stellar quality,» including Pearl Bailey (who represented President Nixon), Count Basie, and Ella Fitzgerald who, accompanied by Billy Taylor at the piano, sang» Just a Closer Walk with Thee.»

[167] *Trio* and *A Place in the Sun* are in The Hyde Collection, *The Key is Lost* is in the Cummer Museum.

[168] UF, 25.

[169] Dodge, 152.

[170] JAM, 43; to elaborate on the UF lecture, *The Pastoral Symphony*, c. 1510, Musée du Louvre, Paris, has also been more recently attributed to Titian with some scholars asserting that both Giorgione and Titian painted portions of the canvas. See Patricia Fortini Brown, *Art and Life in Renaissance Venice*, New York, 1997, 138-139.

[171] UF, 27.

[172] Edward Jablonski, *Alan Jay Lerner, A Biography*, New York, 1996, 316-317.

[173] *An Exhibition of Paintings by Joseph Jeffers Dodge*, April 1-May 14, 1953, Wildenstein, 19 East 64th Street, New York City.

[174] From a clipping in the artist's files. It had no source, date, or page. The initials E.G. indicate the author. Handwritten at the bottom was «Tribune May 2.» See Dodge Files.

[175] The blurb is signed with the initials H.L.F. and a black and white illustration of *A Place in the Sun* is included with the descriptive fragment «allegories of adolescence.» Dodge Files.

[176] *I Have Immortal Longings in Me*, 1948 is in the collection of Amy Thompson Finneran of Washington, D.C., according to Dodge's records. The work shows a nude woman seated on the sand next to a large clump of roots. The beach is in the distance. A man plays a clarinet. The woman looks to the viewer's right at a figure flying a kite. *I Have Immortal Longings in Me* is related to *Interlude* (1947), David N. Mills collection, in which a similar root mass is placed in the center of the composition, also a beach. A nude woman is either hanging a dress on a branch or taking it down; the red garment partially obscures her body. A bright moonlight casts dramatic shadows. As in the other painting, a seated male plays an instrument, here a trombone, in the middle distance. The locations and dates of *How High the Moon* and *Fugue* are unknown. *Young Man with a Horn* (1945), also titled *Bix Beiderbeck in a Blue Landscape*, shows a solitary figure seated at the end of a curving row of posts that lead to a clump of trees. There is a building in the central distance. The horizon line is low and in the yawning space the figure seems quite small in lonely isolation. The painting was originally in the collection of Alan Jay Lerner; its location is unknown.

[177] «Joseph Jeffers Dodge,» *Art Digest*, May 1, 1952, 21.

[178] Dodge, 34.

What Struggle to Escape, No Turning Back, and Related Works

[179] *What Struggle to Escape* is in the Museum of Arts and Sciences in Daytona Beach, Florida. *No Turning Back* is in the Cummer.

[180] UF, 31.

[181] UF, 40-41; JAM, 52-53.

[182] JAM, 53.

[183] Dodge, 137. Dodge remembered, « ... Derinda, who modeled for me and for the class for about four or five years, maybe. She was relatively uninhibited and didn't seem to expect anything particularly. I mean she wasn't flirtatious or suggestive in any way. A couple of the other girls had been a little bit. She was pretty matter-of-fact about it all and she seemed to enjoy it. She was a little bit of an exhibitionist, I guess and she realized she had a great figure and a pretty face. She didn't mind being admired. She was kind of an uneducated girl. I don't know what happened to her. I remember hearing later on that she became an airline stewardess at one point. Maybe she's entered the glamorous world of whatever. I hope the best for her.» Coincidentally Dodge did discover what became of Duross. When he was invited to exhibition at the Ormond Memorial Art Museum in the fall of 1995, he found that the wife of Pierre LeRoy, the director, was Duross's cousin. Apparently Duross had died a short time before.

[184] Originally purchased by Alan Jay Lerner, *Day Before Spring* was titled after the Lerner and Lowe musical of 1945 and features a half-nude standing holding a potted geranium.

[185] The author thanks Catherine Blanton Freedberg who graciously provided the title, correct date, and dimensions of this painting.

[186] Dodge Files.

[187] This idea is credited to Jeff Dunn who suggested it to me in conversation on January 21, 2000. Dunn also suggested that the van Gogh work could refer to Freedberg's new marriage and the blossoming of romance.

[188] UF, 25-26.

[189] Ibid.

[190] UF, 28, JAM, 57. Related to this group is *Susanna and the Elders* (1952), which started out as a horizontal picture of a nude on a sheet but when the artist saw the canvas turned on end one day, the subject matter came to him. He realized later that in the biblical passage there are only two elders but he was still struck by the «contrast between youthful innocence and beauty and vulgar prurience and hypocrisy.» The four figures are compressed in a shallow space. Susanna clings to the white sheet, a symbol of her innocence, as she stands in what barely qualifies as a puddle of water (alluding to her bath). The lecherous expressions of the elders border on caricature. These three could be the grown up versions of the boys in *The Classical Tradition*. The story of Susanna and the Elders is from the Old Testament Apocrypha. See James Hall, *Dictionary of Subjects & Symbols in Art*, New York, 1979, 294. Dodge gave the painting to his daughter Lisa Dodge, who resides in Nashville. See UF, 30; JAM, 58.

[191] Kenneth Clark, *The Nude: A Study in Ideal Form*, New York, 1956, 25.

[192] Clark, 23. One of Dodge's earliest depictions of the nude female is seen in *Cat Nap*, 1945. The title is a witty one with the small black cat curled up to the viewer's right. Dodge's model closes her eyes as she reclines. Her hands are behind her head and the curves of her breasts and hips answer those of her elbows. A yellow cloth tacked in three places hangs on the wall; its folds at the right signal Dodge's interest in painting drapery in the coming years. The red bedspread matches the color of the flower and also the polish on the model's toenails (the red and yellow colors used here are the same in another early Dodge painting, *Poetry*, from 1944, also known only from a transparency). This area of cloth falls in such a way to accentuate the pose of the nude even more emphatically. The dark haired figure shows armpit hair usually associated with cultures other than American. In addition to evoking nudes from art history, the depiction may also conjure up photographs of «pin-up» girls popular during World War II and after. There are awkward passages in this early work. The edge of the bed is not clearly defined and the nude seems to float slightly. As one of the artist's earliest nudes, it is an ambitious anatomical study, and one in which the figure displays an earthy sensuality. There is a self-conscious air to it and one may wonder where precisely this figure fits in Clark's categories of nude and naked.

[193] UF, 42.

[194] Examples of partially clad nudes include *Girl in a Blue Robe* (1958) and *Girl in a White Robe* (1960), or in the act of disrobing as in *Girl Removing Robe* (1959-1960). See also *Girl in a Wing Chair* (1963), whereabouts unknown; *Girl in a Wing Chair II*, also 1963 but in pencil and watercolor, whereabouts unknown; *Girl Dozing* (1963), ink, and *Girl Resting in a Red Tapestry Chair* (1963-1966), whereabouts unknown (a note on a slide of this work indicates it was sold in the Ch. 7 radio auction in 1975 for $1,360).

[195] UF, 43. For Balthus see Jean Leymarie, *Balthus*, New York, 1979 and Richard Covington, «Balthus,» *Art & Antiques*, November, 1994, 70-77.

[196] Dodge, 137.

Portraits of the Artist's Children

[197] Dodge, 55.
[198] Ibid.
[199] Ibid., 55-56.
[200] The painting was also exhibited as *Four Young Dodges* in exhibitions at the Cummer Museum and in Orlando. Dodge gave the painting to the Cummer.
[201] When Dodge showed this work in Gainesville, Florida, in 1969 he described it simply, «All four of them are shown here (in rare harmony), in 1958, when the oldest, in the orange dress, was seven, and the youngest, holding the apple was about two»; see UF, 44. In JAM 55 he noted «Tia on the left, the happy one and Julie, the introverted one in the box on the right. The individual figures here and in the group of four were from photographs which I'd taken.»
[202] Ted Weeks, *Folio*, '96: in pre-edited comments sent in correspondence to the artist, August 8, 1996.
[203] UF, 45. The painting was in the collection of Dorothy M. Dodge; at her death it was given to Julie Dodge. *Tia and Julie* was reproduced in the catalogue of the artist's retrospective exhibition of 1964 at the Cummer, number 49. A photograph showing Dodge in front of this painting is found in «Preview of Art Show at Fort Edward,» *The Post-Star*, Glens Falls, New York, June 1, 1960.

The Still Life

[204] Dodge, 126-127.
[205] Ibid., 127.
[206] Ibid., 127-128.
[207] Dodge Files. From records listing his works, there are several still-life paintings from the forties for which the whereabouts are unknown, for example, *Philodendron*, c. 1946-48, given to C. Malcolm Alber as a wedding present. Comments about the artist's early attraction to the still life genre can be found in Dodge, 127-129.
[208] Mr. and Mrs. Lyman Beeman Sr., Glens Falls, New York, originally owned the painting; it was reproduced in the 1964 Cummer retrospective catalogue, number 11.
[209] JAM, 49; UF, 26-27.
[210] See Esther Davis, ed. *The Scout*, Finch, Pruyn and Company, Inc., Glens Falls, New York, volume 7, number 2, September, 1962.
[211] Ibid., 2.
[212] Stephen E. Ambrose, *Eisenhower, Soldier and President*, 1990, 373-385.
[213] See H.W. Brands, «Eisenhower and the Problem of Loose Ends,» in *Eisenhower*, Stephen E. Ambrose and Günter Bischof (eds.), 127.
[214] Brands, 129.
[215] Ambrose, 34.
[216] See Dodge, 192-193.
[217] UF, 37.
[218] *Still-Life with Coffee Grinder* is in the collection of Joseph Morrell Dodge II, Tallahassee, Florida.
[219] UF, 38. Although it is not known which still life by Derain influenced Dodge, a comparison can be seen in Derain's *Still Life with Fruit* (1938) in the Stanford University Museum of Art; see Jane Lee, *Derain*, 1990, page 78, figure 53.
[220] See UF, 38. The painting is in the Cummer Museum collection; it was purchased by the museum from the artist's estate.
[221] Ibid., 39.
[222] Ibid.
[223] The reliance on recognizable symbolism is apparent. The rose is often associated with Mary, who because of her Immaculate Conception, was known as the rose without thorns (meaning without the stain of original sin). Regarding *No Turning Back* Dodge noted, «the cut roses symbolize love, or the full bloom of life, and finally death,» which could also assume Christian symbolism with the placement of the flower here. The bread and wine are references to the mass symbolizing the body and blood of Christ. The three daffodils refer to the Trinity and the general distribution of the flowers evoke the cross of the Crucifixion, and possibly even Christ and the two thieves. The three eggs can also refer to the Trinity with the broken egg referring to Christ as man. JAM, 52.
[224] UF, 39.
[225] See *Portrait of Jeanne* in the text for additional information.

Paintings of Jeanne

[226] Sharon Weightman, August 14, 1994, E-1 and E-4.
[227] Ibid.
[228] UF, 60-63.
[229] Elihu Edelson, «Dodge's show at Group Gallery is 'Cool',» *Jacksonville Journal*, April 25, 1968, 14.

[230] W.C. Burton, «It's Realism as High Art in Winston-Salem Exhibit,» *Greensboro Daily News*, October 12, 1969, B12. In addition, Dodge showed selections of the *Portrait of Jeanne* at his exhibitions at the University of Florida in 1969; Rollins College in Winter Park, Florida, in 1971; *Artists of the Jacksonville Area, Sesquicentennial Exhibition, Part II*, Cummer Gallery of Art, 1972; The Hyde Collection in 1973; *A Ten Year View*, a one-man exhibition at the Cummer Gallery of Art, 1975; Jacksonville University, 1976; and the Hollywood Art and Culture Center in 1977, among others.
[231] Weightman, August 14, 1994, E-4.
[232] Conversation between Mrs. Klempf and the author, 1996.
[233] Weightman, August 14, 1994, E-4.
[234] Clark, 23.
[235] Elihu Edelson, «Works of Joseph Dodge on Exhibition,» *Jacksonville Journal*, Saturday, May 31, 1975.
[236] *Study for Laura in a Deck Chair* measures 8 x 8 inches; it is ink on paper. It was sold through the Harmon Gallery in Naples, Florida. Its present whereabouts are unknown. *Laura Jeanne in a Deck Chair*, is 9 x 9 inches; it is colored pencil and is in a private collection in Sanibel, Florida.
[237] Elizabeth Chase Morrow, «'Twentieth Century Painting on view at Cummer,» *The Florida Times-Union* (Jacksonville) Friday, December 15, 1989, «Coasting,» 10. Formerly in the collection of the late Dr. M. Anwar Kamal.
[238] JAM, 44.
[239] For example, *The Nude, a New Perspective* by Gill Saunders was in Dodge's library. Dodge often wrote commentary in the margins of his books. Many times Dodge seemed to be responding in a conversational and sometimes combative manner to an author's points. Among the many responses Dodge wrote in the Saunders book include, «Art is the objectification of voyeurism; all visual artists are, to a degree, voyeurs,» (page 94), and «Woman as a personification of nature, or as a muse, is a natural response of the male artist; so what's unnatural or wrong about that? And in history so far there have been many more male than female artists-so it is inevitable. What if the reverse had been true?» (also page 94). This article was also found in a file in the artist's papers: Cathleen McCarthy, «The Problems and Potentials in Painting Nudes,» *American Artist*, April, 1990, 34-39, 68-70. Many of Dodge's art books from his library are housed in the Cummer library.

Rock Transformed

[241] Corbino, 54.
[242] UF, 35.
[243] Dorothy Adlow, «Quarry with Swimmers: An Oil Painting by Joseph Jeffers Dodge,» *The Christian Science Monitor*, June 8, 1960; an illustration of *Quarry with Swimmers*, 1955, was featured on the front page of «The Home Forum» section with Adlow's comments.
[244] The painting is in the collection of Dugald MacArthur, brother of Dodge's second wife, Dorothy.
[245] JAM, 48. One of Dodge's favorite old master paintings in America, *Feast of the Gods* by Venetian painter Giovanni Bellini, is in the National Gallery of Art, Washington, D.C. There are snapshots of the picnic on Dollar Island in Lake George in a Dodge photo album, Dodge Photo Albums.
[246] Russell's comments were taken from «Centuries of Blue Skies O'er a 'Pastoral Landscape',» *The New York Times*, Sunday, November 13, 1988, H35-36. Russell cites David Rosand reference in a catalogue essay to «pastoral inaction.»
[247] JAM, 59.
[248] UF, 47; JAM, 59.
[249] *Bathers* from 1955, which was damaged and cut up by the artist in 1976, was also related to this group. A slide of the *Bathers* exists in the Dodge Archives, Dodge Transparencies.
[250] UF, 48-49; Dodge recounted, «There's one thing in particular that I want to mention because the casual viewer might not be aware of it and that's the composition, or the palette. Usually my color range is rather limited, and deliberately so. I use the earth yellows, the umbers, the siennas, Venetian red, cobalt blue, black and white. These are systematically arranged and I rarely deviate—except occasionally to add accents of other colors if needed. In this picture, however, I added approximately one part of cadmium yellow to four parts of each other color that I used-including black and white (about the proportions of a good martini). This, of course, meant a lot of premixing before each painting session but the results in color harmony were worth it, I think.» See also JAM, 62.
[251] Slide, *Summer Serenade*, 1960, Dodge Transparencies.
[252] For Dodge's comments see UF, 28.

253 UF, 51.

254 Ibid.

255 Hurricane Dora, a category one storm, came ashore shortly after midnight on September 9, 1964; see P. Douglas Filaroski, «It did happen here, Hurricane Dora destroyed myth of a storm-proof city,» *The Florida Times-Union* (Jacksonville) Sunday, May 30, 1999, D-1 and D-6.

256 UF, 49.

257 Hasse, 288. See also Ward and Burns, 286-287. Thanks to Jeff Dunn for pointing out the source of the title *Lush Life.*

258 Shirrel Rhoades, *The Florida Times-Union* (Jacksonville) Entertainment Showcase, April 17, 1966, 16. The review considered Dodge's one-man exhibition of paintings and drawings at The Group Gallery.

259 UF, 50.

260 Related to *Lady of the Rocks* is *The Rocks at Washington Oaks II*, 1968, purchased by Dr Bernard Kaye in 1971 from an auction to benefit public radio station Channel 7. In *The Rocks*, Jeanne is shown in the same blue dress standing at the water's edge. A young man is asleep on a rock in the middle of the picture. This painting is now in the collection of the St. Augustine Art Association.

261 *Interlude on the Rocks #4* remained in the collection of the artist until he gave it to the Cummer in 1996. The painting was featured as a color illustration in the Corbino article about the artist, 50-51.

262 Corbino, 54.

263 Ibid. This process can be seen clearly when the preliminary drawing (based on the photograph) is compared to *Interlude on the Rocks #3*, which is an ink study. Here the position of the model is the same, but she is dressed in a short blue skirt and her headband or scarf is blue, whereas in #4 the model is nude and adjusts a yellow towel around her head.

264 Dodge left thousands of images in his studio from a variety of sources, including magazine and newspaper clippings, plates torn out of books, and of course, the thousands of slides and photographs he had made. Dodge Files.

265 For *Tidal Pool*, Dodge had taped a piece of paper to the photograph with the notation, «J.J. Dodge, photo on which *Tidal Pool, Morning* was based.» The photograph is dated July 29, 1968 and it is labeled Hampton Beach, N.H. This photograph and others discussed here were filed in a box labeled «J.J.Dodge, Photos, etc. used for drawings and paintings.» Dodge Files.

266 Elihu Edelson, «'The Human Presence' at Museum,» *Jacksonville Journal*, Saturday, September 21, 1974, 15. Edelson observed: «The two small paintings *Tidal Pool* and *A Time Remembered* (1974) continue the artist's recurrent theme of contemporary waterfront landscapes with figures in a classical style. However, there appears to be a subtle change toward more saturated color, while the figures look even more cool, hard and polished-almost like store-window manikins without cracks at the joints. (This is not intended to be derogatory, but simply a way of creating a mental picture with words.)»

267 *East of the Sun (West of the Moon)* was written by B. Bowman.

268 *Sunday Afternoon Promenade* was featured in the 1983 Corbino article, 53.

269 Elihu Edelson, «There are several kinds of realism,» *The Florida Times-Union and Journal* (Jacksonville) Sunday, November 19, 1978, E-8.

270 *Stranger on the Shore* is loosely based on a photograph taken at Cape Ann. *Stranger on the Shore* was written by author/songwriter Acker Bilk.

271 Found in Dodge's files in his studio after his death was an entire file devoted to clippings, photographs, drawings, and articles devoted to rendering clouds and skies, including those by the English artist John Constable (1776-1837). Dodge Files.

Sights and Sites

272 «History of Fort Clinch, 1847-1945,» brochure prepared by the staff of Fort Clinch State Park.

273 «Fort Clinch State Park,» brochure provided by the Florida Department of Environmental Protection, Division of Recreation and Parks. Fort Clinch is considered one of the best preserved examples of what is referred to as Third System fortification built with masonry and stone; see «History of Fort Clinch» cited above.

274 UF 56-57. In 1964 Dodge painted two versions of Fort Clinch. *Fort Clinch* shows the complex of buildings from the vantage point of the parapet looking down into the common area with the sea and coastline visible at the horizon. The view in *Fort Clinch: The Steps* shows an arrested moment in which a girl stops on the steep steps of a rampart, her shadow creating an interesting counterpoint. A male explores below; a seated female sits above in isolation, her head projecting above the long line that demarcates sea and sky.

275 Wayne Hamm, «The Corporation collections,» *Jacksonville Journal*, January 3, 1985.

276 Included in this group is also *Ramparts, Fort Clinch*, 1968. The painting went from Winthrop Bancroft to Duncan L. Clinch; at the death of Duncan Clinch, the painting was sent to his cousin Nicholas Bayard Clinch in Dallas, Texas, by Jacksonville historian Dena Snodgrass. Dodge Correspondence.

277 Dodge, 165-175.

278 Jacqueline B. Mullikin (Holmes), *Joseph J. Dodge, Recent Paintings, April 4-22, 1970*, The Group Gallery, Inc., Jacksonville, Florida (exhibition notes).

279 Elihu Edelson, «'Classical Realism' By Cummer's Director,» *Jacksonville Journal*, Saturday, April 25, 1970, 28.

280 Ibid., 1970

281 When the author asked Dodge why he turned his back on the Parthenon, one of the most famous monuments in the world, he laughed and shrugged, saying that there had been plenty of painters who specialized in views, in a kind of tourist vista; he much more preferred to select something on the periphery.

282 Edelson, 1970, 28.

283 Ibid.

284 The figures of the women in *Waiting, The Aegean* can be compared to those in *Aegean Harbor*, 1970 (originally in the collection of Ralph Wark); the distribution and placement of the figures are different but it is obvious they are drawn from the same series of images.

285 UF lecture, 57.

286 Edelson, 1970, 28.

287 Ibid.

288 Ibid.

289 Griffin Smith, «A Solid Look at Major Florida Painters,» *The Miami Herald*, Sunday, January 23, 1972, 2-M. The exhibit at the Harmon was held from January 16-February 12, 1972. Smith noted at the beginning of his article, «the annual invitational, which is rather highly regarded as the best of its type ... is showcasing dominant figures on major Florida campuses-Hiram Williams ... with studio names like Karl Zerbe, Syd Solomon, and the late Jon Corbino.»

290 JAM, 22.

291 To this group should be added *Ruins of a Spanish Church and Mayan Buildings, Dzibilchaltun* (1969); a small oil , it is similar to the right half of *The Old and The New* (1969) in a private collection. In addition, see *Near Sisal, Yucatan* (1969), private collection, Jacksonville; this painting was reproduced in the 1970 Edelson article quoted above.

292 *Joseph Jeffers Dodge, A Ten Year View*, the Cummer Gallery of Art, 1975 (exhibition dates: May 13-June 29); *Guatemala Valley* is illustrated on page 21.

293 Edelson, 1975, 7.

294 *Old Olive Tree* was reproduced in color in the June 1983, *American Artist* article, 52.

295 Related works and preliminary studies for *Roman Scene* are located in The Museum of Arts and Sciences in Daytona Beach. Dodge was never satisfied with the title for this work and hoped to find another one. Mario Rutelli was the sculptor of the *Fountain of the Naiads*, 1901, in the Piazza della Repubblica or Piazza Esedra; the nudity of the sculptures originally provoked a controversy. See *Rome* (Knopf Guides), 1994, 333-334.

296 Other paintings of Rome include *Roman Forum* (1978), and *Ave Roma* (1988), with a couple of young lovers set against the backdrop of the view from the Janiculum.

297 *Pyramids* is large (36" x 36") for a Dodge painting.

298 Debra Murphy-Livingston, *Joseph Jeffers Dodge: An American Classicist* (exhibition catalogue, September 11-October 25, 1992). Cummer Gallery of Art, Jacksonville, Florida.

299 Mary Campbell Gristina, Cummer Gallery of Art brochure and calendar, September, 1992.

300 Corbino, 53.

301 UF, 37.

302 Corbino, 1983, 96.

303 In Dodge's papers was found filed the following article by Richard Schilling: «Coping with Color Blindness, Practical ways to compensate for—and create with—color impairment,» *The Artist's Magazine*, March, 1994, 36-38.

304 A color reproduction of this work was in the Corbino *American Artist* article, June, 1983, 52.

305 *Fallen Tree: Intracoastal Waterway* was featured in the article by Sharon Weightman, «Artist, lecturer, author and educator ... Joseph Jeffers 'Jerry' Dodge,» *The Florida Times-Union* (Jacksonville) Sunday, August 4, 1994, E1. Two additional works inspired by Florida scenery are *Near Cedar Key* (1986) and *Early Spring, Near Cedar Key* (1989). For *Early Spring, Near Cedar Key* see *Holland & Knight Art Collection, Jacksonville*, n.d., 16.

306 Margaret Koscielny, *The M. Anwar Kamal Collection of Art, Twentieth Century Painting* (exhibition catalogue), the Cummer Gallery of Art,

November 29-December 31, 1989, n.p. Arlington is an area in the eastern part of Jacksonville.

[307] Dodge, see *Joseph Jeffers Dodge, A Ten Year View* (exhibition catalogue), the Cummer Gallery of Art, 1975, 3. The quote is taken from the «Statement from the Artist.»

[308] The tour was coordinated and led by the author while she was an instructor in art history at Jacksonville University in Jacksonville, Florida.

[309] This was quoted in the 1983 Corbino article, page 97, although the author misquoted Dodge as saying he «took five or six photographs of them.» In actuality he took about three rolls of film. *Panetto Bolognese* was illustrated in color in this article, page 54.

[310] Related to this work are a pencil drawing from the same year, *Pane piccolina da Bologna* (1980) and another painting, *Bolognese Bun and Napkin* (1983).

[311] *Still Life: Bread in a Basket*, is in the Cummer collection. *Untitled (Still-life: Bread, White Jug and Lemon)* is in the collection of David N. Mills.

[312] UF, 40-41; JAM, 52-53.

[313] *Bread and Napkin* was featured in color on the invitation for *Joseph Jeffers Dodge, an Exhibition*, held at the Alexander Brest Museum at Jacksonville University, Jacksonville, Florida, from February 23 to April 1, 1988.

[314] It comes as no surprise that among Dodge's many files of clippings, articles, and photographs, a paperback book on napkin folding was found; see *A Guide to Napkin Folding* by James Ginders, Boston, 1979.

[315] Corbino, 96-97

[316] Ibid., 96.

The Nineties

[317] *Jacksonville Creates* was held at the Jacksonville Art Museum May 31 through August 12, 1990; there were seventy-eight pieces by forty-one artists.

[318] Anne Leighton, «Best and Brightest,» *Folio Weekly*, July 17, 1990. *Horizons* was illustrated in an accompanying advertising supplement to *Folio Weekly*, page 6.

[319] Conversation between Dodge and Jeff Dunn in 1990.

[320] *Between Two Tides* was also labeled *Tree Stump on Oregon Beach* on Dodge's slide of the work.

[321] Dodge Files. Dodge's comments at Tia's memorial service consist of two typed pages. Dodge painted two oil studies and one finished portrait of Tia. All show the sitter leaning against the back of a chair (the chair is seen in other Dodge works especially those based on photographs of Jeanne). In one study and in the finished work, the right hand hangs over the chair's back and the left hand is pressed to the face of the artist's thirty-three year old daughter. In all three the colors are somber and muted with dulled complements of blues and oranges. Characteristic of Dodge's approach to portraits and still lifes are the placement of Tia in front of a blank wall, which serves to define the clarity of the contours of the figure, and light pouring in from the viewer's right, its effects carefully observed and modeled. Tia is shown in a pensive and contemplative posture that echoes her father's depiction of her as a child in the 1958 group portrait. Although Dodge's paintings of his eldest daughter were realized eight years before her death, they serve as poignant testimonies to her brief life.

[322] During Dodge's tenure as the director of the Cummer, the *Vanitas* still life by Dutch painter Jacques Grief, called de Claeuw (active 1641-1676) was purchased. Dodge once referred to it in conversation as a «textbook example» of the genre. Its many *memento mori*, or reminders of death, include an hourglass and a candle that has just been snuffed out. See Jones et al., 74-5. Dodge would have also known well the *Vanitas Still Life* by another Dutch painter (active 1673-1702) Edwaert Colyer in The Hyde Collection. See Kettlewell, 119.

[323] See Eleanor H. Gustafson, «Museum accessions,» in *Antiques*, November, 1993, 612 for an illustration of McCloskey's *Oranges in Tissue Paper*; William Gerdts is responsible for McCloskey's nickname. The company Harry and David is based in Medford, Oregon.

[324] From conversation between the artist and this author.

[325] When the author asked Dodge in the autumn of 1995 if this painting could have been a wistful response to his recent bout of difficulties, his daughter's death, heart surgery, a diagnosis of cancer, he replied that the painting was not the result of a yearning for the peace of childhood, at least not consciously.

[326] Dodge borrowed this detail from a clipping of a color photograph from an unidentified magazine showing four young women tossing a beach ball in the air. From the hairstyles and the swimsuits, the photograph probably dates from the fifties. Only a portion of the caption below the picture can be read: « ... hills and a Canadian Lake set a perfect stage for holiday fun!» Dodge Files.

[327] Dodge left specific instructions in his will that all unfinished paintings be destroyed after his death. This painting was among that group.

[328] Attorney Carle Felton posited this suggestion. He and his wife, Nancy, own several of Dodge's works.

[329] A related work, *Self-Portrait, 1994* is in the Cummer collection; for an illustration see «Dodge collection at Cummer,» *The Florida Times-Union* (Jacksonville) November 24, 1996, F-3.

[330] *Still Life: Bundle and Rope* was among those given by the artist to the Cummer Museum in 1996. The title *A Stilled Life* appears in the artist's notes and lists in preparation for the exhibition in Orlando at the University of Central Florida, November 4-December 6, 1996. Dodge Files.

[331] In 1986 Dodge painted a hanging object in *It's Only a Paper Moon*, and his fascination with the wrapped object continued throughout his career as did his undisguised pleasure in painting drapery. From the fifties, *Still Life with Coffee Grinder* (1955) shows a coffee mill wrapped in material. As late as 1992, Dodge painted in ink and acrylic two napkins twisted and knotted around unidentifiable objects, titling them *The Strollers, Strolling* or *The Promenade* (private collection, Jacksonville). In *The Promenade*, hints of mystery and anticipation are suggested as the viewer wonders exactly what the cloths encase and hide. The composition in *The Bundle and Rope* is similar to that in *Panetto Bolognese* and the *Dancing Pears I and II*. In all of these works, two inanimate objects are placed against a dark wall.

[332] From conversation with the artist in December of 1996 with the author, Dodge Files.

[333] See Murphy-Livingston, and exhibition catalogue with essays by Russell B. Hicken and William E. Parker, *Joseph Jeffers Dodge, A Ten Year View, The Cummer Gallery of Art, 1975*, Jacksonville, Florida, 1975.

[334] The exhibition *David Engdahl/Sculpture-Joseph Jeffers Dodge/Paintings* was held from February 17 to March 26, 1993. The description of Dodge's work is from «Bob Phelp's people,» *The Florida Times-Union* (Jacksonville) Monday, February 22, 1993, B-1.

[335] See Karabinis and Murphy-Livingston, «An Interview with Joseph Jeffers Dodge,» (published in conjunction with the exhibition *Joseph Jeffers Dodge, Paintings and Drawings: 1940s to the Present*, October 17-November 9, 1995), University Gallery, University of North Florida, Jacksonville.

[336] Taylor Hardwick, *Joseph Jeffers Dodge* (videotape), 1995. Commentary on Dodge was provided by Judith Gefter, Jeffrey Dunn, Helene Baker, Paul Karabinis, Robert Shircliff, Laura Jeanne and Edward Klempf, Nancy and Carle Felton, John Bunker, Margaret Koscielny, Sally Ann Freeman, William Marshall, Ted Weeks, Robert Broward, Phil May, Hiram Williams, Steve Lotz, David Mills, and this author.

[337] See Robert A. Larson, *Hiram Williams, Images of Compassion*, 1998; *Two North Florida Master Painters: Joseph Jeffers Dodge and Hiram Williams, November 4-December 6, 1996*. Art Gallery of the Department of Art, University of Central Florida, Orlando (exhibition brochure with Introduction by Steve Lotz); «An Interview with Joseph Jeffers Dodge» by Karabinis and Murphy-Livingston, comments about Williams by Lotz and statements by Williams).

[338] Steve Lotz, Introduction to exhibition catalogue, *Two North Florida Master Painters: Jerry Dodge and Hiram Williams*, November 4-December 6, 1996. Art Gallery of the Department of Art, University of Central Florida, Orlando.

Conclusion

[339] Dodge Files.

[340] Dodge Correspondence.

[341] Ibid.

[342] Roy C. Craven Jr. was a professor of art at the University of Florida and director of the University Gallery.

[343] Dodge Files.

[344] Conversation between Jeff Dunn and the author, May, 1997.

[345] JAM, 62.

[346] John Yau, *Robert Birmelin: Opening the Door* (exhibition catalogue), Contemporary Realist Gallery, San Francisco, California, November 2-December 2, 1995, New York, 1995.

[347] See Ruth Bass, «When a Rose *Is* a Rose,» *ARTnews*, February, 1996, 93-94, and also Andrea Codrington, «Figuratively Speaking,» *Art & Auction*, June, 1996, 76-91.

[348] Gristina, 1992.

[349] In a eulogy read for collector and friend, Anwar Kamal, M.D., on January 4, 1991, Dodge noted, «Beauty, in the contemporary art scene, is not a fashionable word, or concept, and this says a lot, I think, about much of what passes for art these days.» Found on page 2 of document. Dodge Files.

[350] JAM, 8 and 10.

[351] Dodge, UF, 64; this quote is also cited in Murphy-Livingston, 1992.

[352] *Harvard Class of 1940, Fiftieth Anniversary Report*, Cambridge, MA, 1990, 146-147.

Fig. 22— *Portrait of Jeanne: Facial Expressions*, UF Exhibit, April, 1969

THE GALLERY

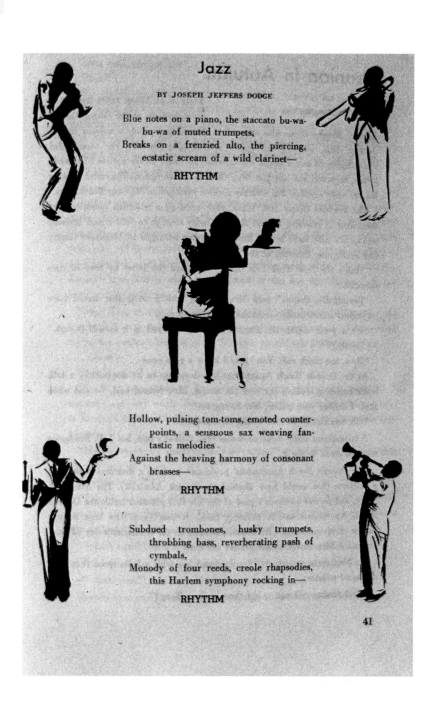

Jazz

BY JOSEPH JEFFERS DODGE

Blue notes on a piano, the staccato bu-wa-
  bu-wa of muted trumpets,
Breaks on a frenzied alto, the piercing,
  ecstatic scream of a wild clarinet—

RHYTHM

Hollow, pulsing tom-toms, emoted counter-
  points, a sensuous sax weaving fantastic melodies
Against the heaving harmony of consonant
  brasses—

RHYTHM

Subdued trombones, husky trumpets,
  throbbing bass, reverberating pash of
  cymbals,
Monody of four reeds, creole rhapsodies,
  this Harlem symphony rocking in—

RHYTHM

41

Plate 1 — *Jazz*, 1935
Poem and drawings published in *The Choate Literary Magazine*
Cummer Museum of Art & Gardens,
Joseph Jeffers Dodge Archives

Plate 2 — ***President Roosevelt***, 1936
Pencil on paper
Signed by Roosevelt
Collection of Joseph Morrell Dodge II

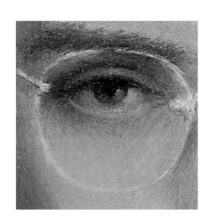

Plate 3 — **Self-Portrait**, June 1939
Oil on panel, 11 x 8 ½
AG2001.3.1
Cummer Museum of Art & Gardens

Plate 4 — **_And Then There were Two_**, 1942
Oil on masonite, 31 x 24 ¾
1996.10.2
The Hyde Collection
Glens Falls, New York

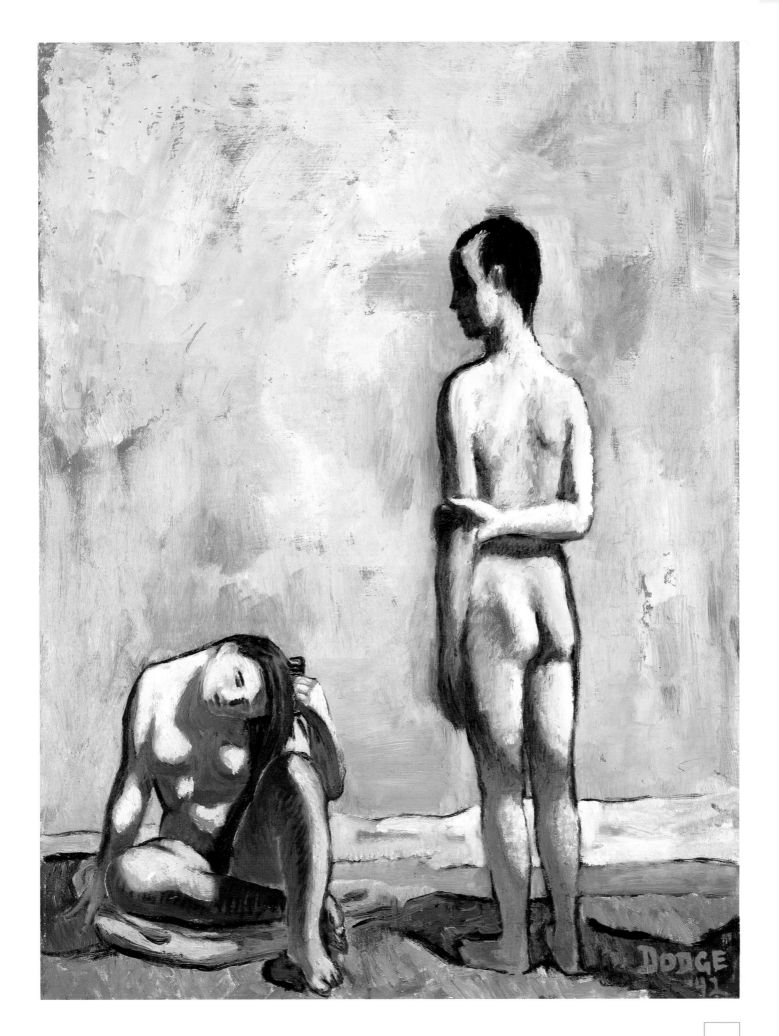

Plate 5 — ***The Hour of Parting***, 1942
Oil, pastel, pen and ink on board, 30 x 24
AG1996.2.25
Cummer Museum of Art & Gardens

Plate 6 — **Double Self-Portrait**, 1943
Oil on panel, 27 ½ x 20 ½
AG1996.2.26
Cummer Museum of Art & Gardens

Plate 7 — *Jazz Quintet (The Black and Tan Fantasy)*, 1943
Oil on canvas, 36 x 40
Private Collection

Plate 8 — **Black and Tan Fantasy**, 1944
Oil, 32 x 40
Collection of Choate Rosemary Hall

Plate 9 — ***Moon Mist (Moonlight Madness or Mad Moonlight)***, 1944
Oil, 20 x 32
Location Unknown

Plate 10 — *The Renaissance*, 1944
Oil on canvas, 12 x 8
Collection of Mr. and Mrs. Edward Klempf

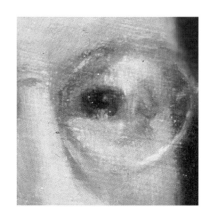

Plate 11 — **Self-Portrait**, 1944
Oil on paperboard, 18 x 15 ¾
1996.10.1
The Hyde Collection
Glens Falls, New York

Plate 12 — **Self-Portrait**, 1944
Oil
Destroyed by the artist

Plate 13 — **Art Student**, 1945
Location Unknown

Plate 14 — **Black and Blue**, 1946
Oil on canvas, 14 x 12
AG1996.2.29
Cummer Museum of Art & Gardens

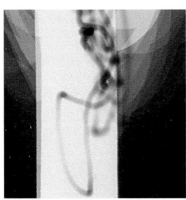

Plate 15 — **Crucifixion**, 1946
Photogram, 12 ¾ x 10 ½
AG1996.2.30
Cummer Museum of Art & Gardens

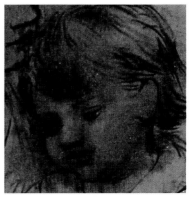

Plate 16 — **Maternity**, 1946
Photograph, 13 ¼ x 10 ⁵⁄₁₆
AG1996.2.32
Cummer Museum of Art & Gardens

Plate 17 — **Another Autumn**, 1947
Oil on canvas, 18 ¼ x 10 ⅛
Collection of Mrs. Sydney J. Freedberg

Plate 18 — **Elegy**, 1947
Oil on canvas, 20 x 26
Munson-Williams-Proctor Arts Institute, Museum of Art, Utica, New York, 50.3

Plate 19 — **_Frankie and Johnny (In Memory of «Tricky Sam» Nanton)_**, 1947-48
Oil on canvas, 28 ¼ x 36 ½
AG1996.2.34
Cummer Museum of Art & Gardens

Plate 20 — *Trio*, 1947
Oil on canvas, 15 ½ x 29
1996.10.3
The Hyde Collection
Glens Falls, New York

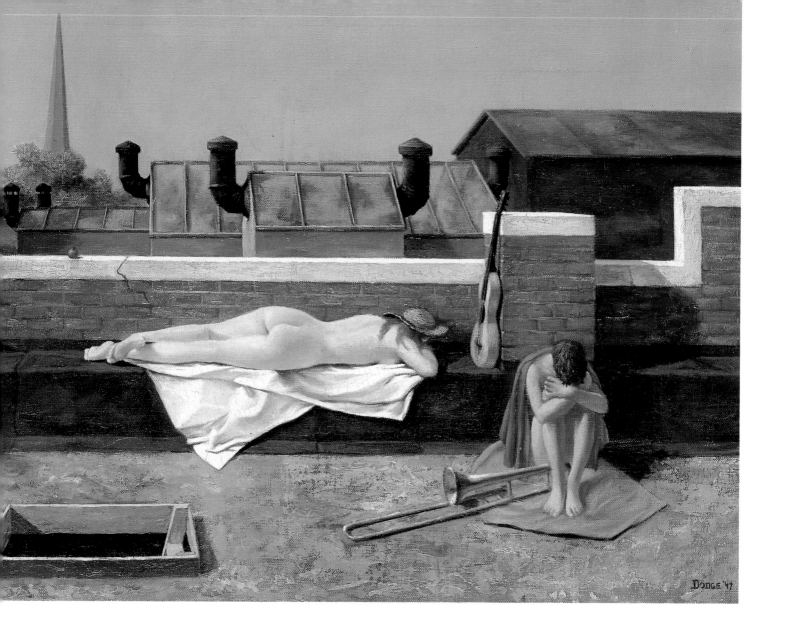

Plate 21 — ***Gods of Our Fathers: The Christian Tradition***, 1949-50
Oil on canvas, 12 x 16
Collection of Mr. and Mrs. Edward Klempf

Plate 22 — ***Gods of Our Fathers: The Classical Tradition***, 1949-50
Oil on canvas, 12 x 16
Collection of Mr. and Mrs. Edward Klempf

Plate 23 — **Lake George Picnic**, 1949
Oil, 20 x 24
Collection of Professor Dugald V. MacArthur

Plate 24 — **The Key is Lost**, 1950-51
Oil on canvas, 20 x 24
AG1996.2.35
Cummer Museum of Art & Gardens

Plate 25 — ***By the Old Mill Stream***, 1951
Oil on canvas, 22 x 28
1996.10.5
The Hyde Collection
Glens Falls, New York

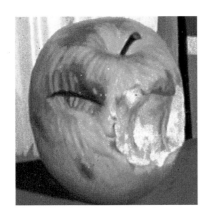

Plate 26 — *The Fruit of Knowledge*, 1951
Oil on board, 11 x 20
Location Unknown

Plate 27 — **The Nest**, 1951
Oil on panel, 8 x 10
AG1996.2.36
Cummer Museum of Art & Gardens

Plate 28 — ***What Struggle to Escape***, 1953-55
Oil on canvas, 34 ¼ x 46
From the Collection of The Museum of Arts and Sciences, Daytona Beach
Gift of Joseph Jeffers Dodge

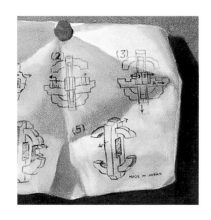

Plate 29 — ***The Chinese Puzzle (Still Life with Wooden Chinese Puzzles)***,
1954
16 x 20
Courtesy Dwight D. Eisenhower Library

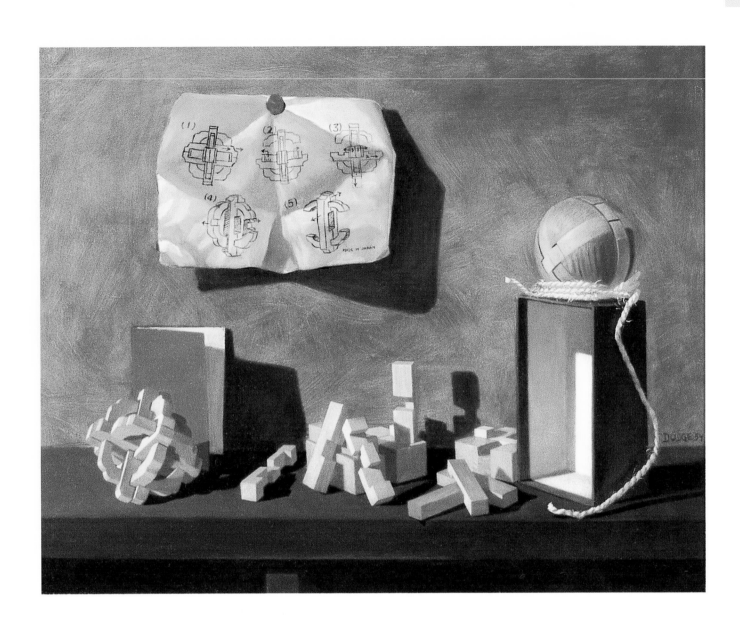

Plate 30 — **The Awakening**, 1955
Oil on canvas, 28 x 36
Location Unknown

Plate 31 — *Girl with a Blue Cloak*, 1955
Oil on canvas, 32 x 27
AP1997.1.1
Cummer Museum of Art & Gardens

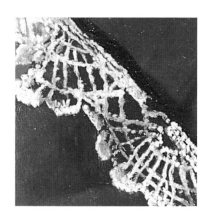

Plate 32 — **Sewing Basket (Work Basket)**, 1955
Oil on masonite, 16 x 11 ¾
Collection of Mr. and Mrs. B. Friedman

Plate 33 — **The Artist's Children: Tia, Jeff, Lisa and Julie**, 1958
Oil on canvas, 24 ¼ x 36 ½
AG1996.2.40
Cummer Museum of Art & Gardens

Plate 34 — ***Glens Falls Rooftops***, 1959
Oil on canvas, 16 ¼ x 18 ⅛
Collection of Lawrence Lovett, Venice, Italy

Plate 35 — **Hudson River Town**, 1959
Oil on canvas, 24 x 30
1996.10.15
The Hyde Collection
Glens Falls, New York

Plate 36 — **No Turning Back**, 1959
Oil on canvas, 32 x 42
AP1964.15.1
Cummer Museum of Art & Gardens

Plate 37 — **On the Edge**, 1959
Oil on canvas, 24 x 30
From the Collection of The Museum of Arts and Sciences, Daytona Beach
Gift of Joseph Jeffers Dodge

Plate 38 — ***Tia and Julie***, 1959
Oil on canvas, 46 ¾ x 61 ¼
Collection of Julie Dodge

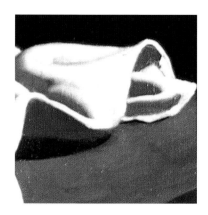

Plate 39 — **Bell Peppers**, 1960
Oil on canvas, 20 x 24
Location Unknown

Plate 40 — ***Still Life with Lemons and Yellow Tulips***, 1960
Oil on canvas, 28 x 30
Location Unknown

Plate 41 — **Summer Serenade**, 1961-63
Oil on canvas, 36 ¼ x 45
AG1996.2.42
Cummer Museum of Art & Gardens

Plate 42 — ***Sunday Afternoon at Fort Clinch***, 1964
Oil, 16 x 20
Collection of Gretchen and Steve Lotz

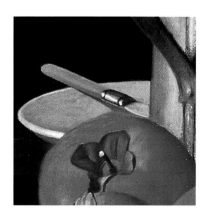

Plate 43 — **Still Life with Three Persimmons**, 1964
Oil on canvas, 20 x 24
Collection of Mr. and Mrs. Philip S. May, Jr.

Plate 44 — ***Easter Still Life***, 1965
Oil, 48 x 48
Location Unknown

Plate 45 — **_Lush Life (The Good Life)_**, 1966
Oil on canvas, 36 x 50
AG1996.2.43
Cummer Museum of Art & Gardens

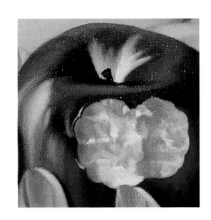

Plate 46 — ***Hand Holding Apple***, 1967
Oil on canvas, 12 x 20
Collection of Mr. and Mrs. Edward Klempf

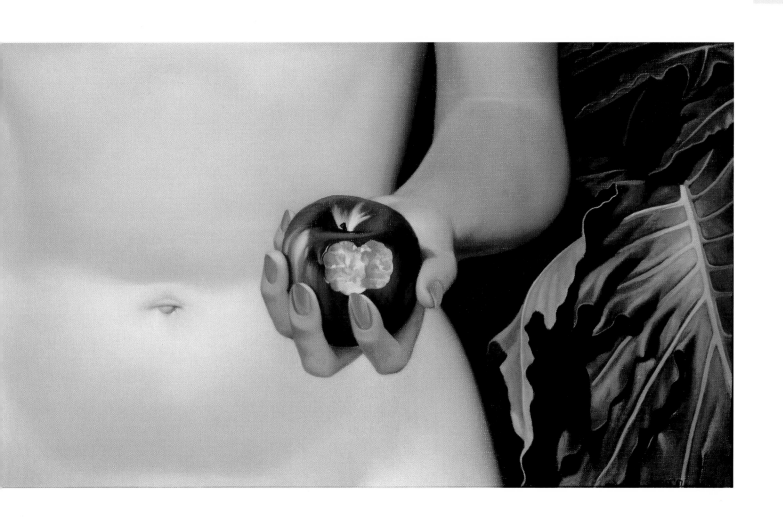

Plate 47 — **Portrait of Jeanne: Draped**, 1967
Oil on canvas, 32 x 24 ⅛
Collection of Mr. and Mrs. Edward Klempf

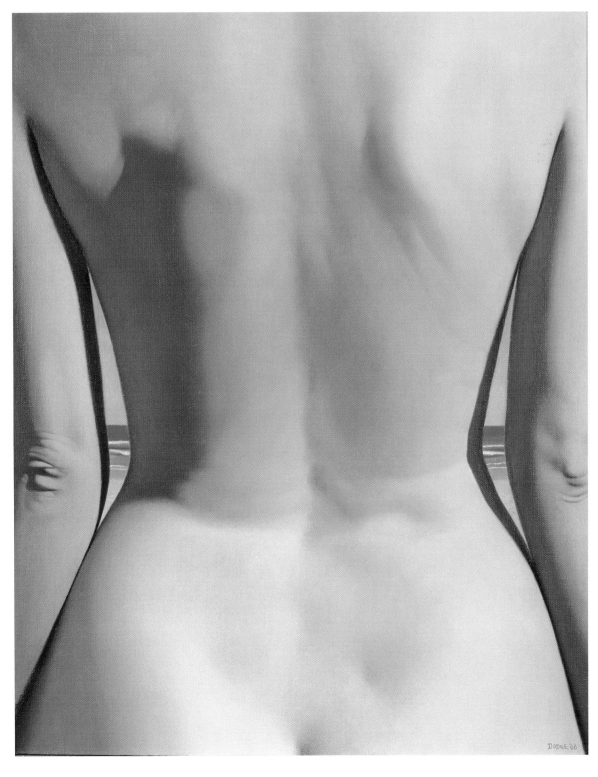

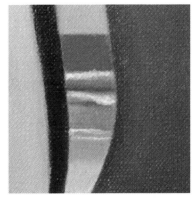

Plate 48 — ***Portrait of Jeanne: Back***, 1968
Oil on canvas, 20 x 16
Collections of Mr. and Mrs. Edward Klempf

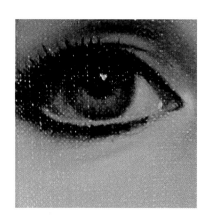

Plate 49 — ***Portrait of Jeanne: Bust***, 1968
Oil on canvas, 18 x 5
Collection of Mr. and Mrs. Edward Klempf

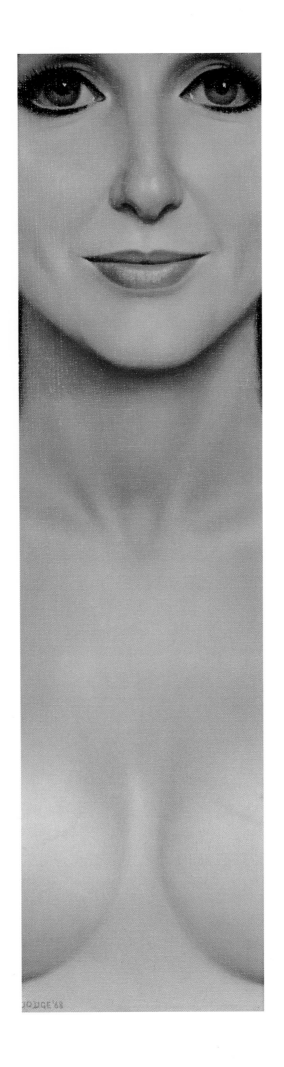

Plate 50 — *From the Acropolis: The Propylaea*, 1968
Oil
Collection of Lawrence Lovett, Venice, Italy

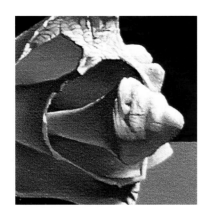

Plate 51 — *Crinum Lily and Shells*, 1969
Oil on canvas, 28 x 22
Location Unknown

Plate 52 — **Dixie Eggs: Portrait of Edward Klempf and his Father**, 1969
Oil on canvas, 9 x 12
Collection of Mr. and Mrs. Edward Klempf

Plate 53 — **Mushrooms**, 1969
Oil on canvas, 9 x 18
Collection of Mr. and Mrs. Anthony H. LaRoche

Plate 54 — ***Orange Tree at Labna, Yucatan***, 1969
Oil, 36 x 52
Location Unknown

Plate 55 — ***Duo at Delos***, 1970
Oil on canvas, 18 x 24
Collection of Felix R. and Debra Murphy Livingston

Plate 56 — ***Waiting, The Aegean***, 1970
Oil on canvas, 18 x 24
Collection of Mr. and Mrs. Edward Klempf

Plate 57 — **East of the Sun**, 1971
Oil, 16 x 16
Collection of Gretchen and Steve Lotz

Plate 58 — **Finding**, 1971
Oil on canvas, 16 x 16
Collection of Russell B. Newton, Jr.

Plate 59 — **_Tidal Pool, Morning_**, 1971
Oil on canvas, 16 x 16
Collection of Mr. and Mrs. Taylor Hardwick

Plate 60 — *Coquina #1*, 1973
Pencil on paper, 16 x 20
From the Collection of The Museum of Arts and Sciences, Daytona Beach
Gift of Joseph Jeffers Dodge

Plate 61 — **_Near Andrews Point, Cape Ann_**, 1973
Acrylic on paper, 16 x 20
Location Unknown

Plate 62 — ***Sunday Afternoon Promenade (Atlantic Beach)***, 1973
Oil, 16 x 16
Private Collection

Plate 63 — **Guatemala Valley**, 1974
Oil on paper, 19 ½ x 25 ¼
AG2000.3.1
Cummer Museum of Art & Gardens

Plate 64 — **Nude in Blue Victorian Chair**, 1974
Oil on paper, 21 ½ x 29 ½
Private Collection

Plate 65 — **An August Afternoon**, 1975
Oil, 16 x 16
Location Unknown

Plate 66 — *__A Morning in May__*, 1975
Oil on canvas, 24 x 26
Collection of Micheal and Julia Suddath-Ranne

Plate 67 — **Between Two Tides**, 1975
Oil on paper, 19 x 25
Collection of Jeffrey D. Dunn

Plate 68 — **_Fishermen, Costa del Sol_**, 1975
Oil on canvas, 24 x 30
AP1975.4.1
Cummer Museum of Art & Gardens

Plate 69 — **Rocks Near Rockport**, 1975
Oil on paper, 14 ¾ x 19 ½
Collection of Mr. and Mrs. Carle A. Felton, Jr.

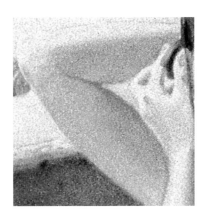

Plate 70 — ***Interlude on the Rocks #3***, 1976
Pencil on paper, 16 x 20
Location Unknown

Plate 71 — **Interlude on Rocks #4**, 1976
Acrylic on paper, 21 ½ x 29 ½
AG1996.2.47
Cummer Museum of Art & Gardens

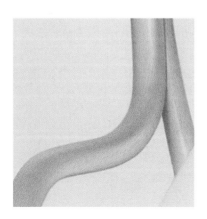

Plate 72 — ***Laura Jeanne in a Bentwood Chair***, 1976
Pencil on paper, 28 x 22 (sight)
Collection of Jeffrey D. Dunn

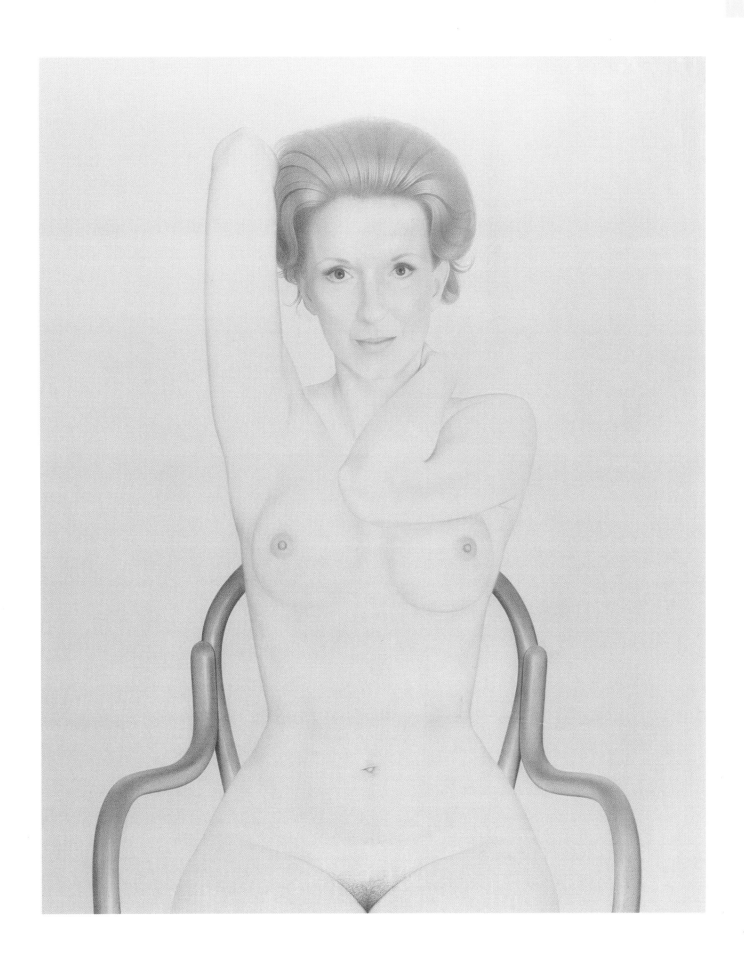

Plate 73 — *__There is a Tide__*, 1976
Oil on paper, 22 x 28
Private Collection

Plate 74 — *__Arizona High Country__*, 1978
Red pencil and acrylic on paper, 21 x 29
Collection of the Clarence Nussbaum Trust

196

Plate 75 — ***Rockscape Near Rockport***, 1978
Oil on paper, 21 x 29
Location Unknown

Plate 76 — **Doric Column, Paestum**, 1978
Oil on paper, 31 x 38 (frame)
Private Collection

Plate 77 — **Panetto Bolognese**, 1980
Oil on paper, 20 x 14
Collection of Mr. and Mrs. Carle A. Felton, Jr.

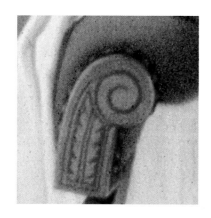

Plate 78 — ***After the Bath #2***, 1981
Oil on paper, 9 x 9
Collection of Mr. and Mrs. Edward Klempf

Plate 79 — **Old Olive Tree, Agrigento**, 1981
Oil on mounted paper, 21 x 29
Private Collection

Plate 80 — **Silversmith Creek**, 1981
Oil on paper, 16 ¼ x 17 ¾
Location Unknown

Plate 81 — **White Jar with Violet Paper**, 1983
Oil on paper, 18 ¼ x 14 ¼
Collection of Mr. and Mrs. J. Shepard Bryan, Jr.

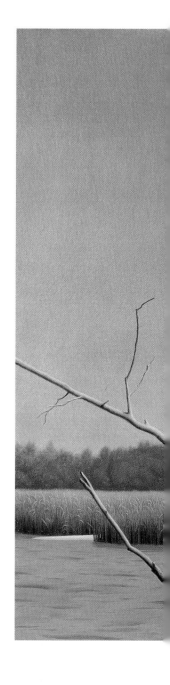

Plate 82 — **Fallen Tree: Intracoastal Waterway**, 1984
Oil on paper, 18 ⁷⁄₁₆ x 29 ¾
Collection of Mr. and Mrs. Robert T. Shircliff

Plate 83 — **It's Only a Paper Moon**, 1986
Watercolor and acrylic on paper, 29¼ x 21¼
Collection of Russell B. Newton, Jr.

Plate 84 — **Pyramids**, 1986
Oil, 36 x 36
Collection of David N. Mills

Plate 85 — **_Seeking_**, 1986
Acrylic and pastel on board, 20 x 30
Collection of St. Johns Country Day School, Orange Park, Florida

Plate 86 — **Roman Scene**, 1987
Oil on board, 16 x 19
Collection of Felix R. and Debra Murphy Livingston

© DODGE '87

Plate 87 — **Waiting**, 1987
Oil, 36 x 48
Location Unknown

Plate 88 — ***Morning, Gulf Coast***, 1988
Oil, 30 x 40
Location Unknown

Plate 89 — **_Prehistoric Monoliths,_**
Brittany (Past, Present and Nature, Brittany), 1988
Oil on canvas, 30 x 36
AG1996.2.56
Cummer Museum of Art & Gardens

Plate 90 — **Horizons**, 1990
Oil on paper, 21 ½ x 24
AG1996.2.57
Cummer Museum of Art & Gardens

Plate 91 — **Northern California Coast**, 1990
Oil on paper, 7 x 10
Location Unknown

Plate 92 — **Breton Village**, 1991
Oil on canvas, 16 x 20
Collection of Mr. and Mrs. Robert T. Shircliff

Plate 93 — ***California Cypress***, 1991
Oil on paper, 12 ¼ x 16 ¼
Collection of Jeffrey D. Dunn

Plate 94 — *The Artist and Muse*, 1992
Oil on canvas, 36 x 36
AG1996.2.60
Cummer Museum of Art & Gardens

Plate 95 — ***Dancing Pears I: Fandango***, 1992
Oil on panel, 16 x 20
AG1996.2.58
Cummer Museum of Art & Gardens

Plate 96 — ***Dancing Pears II: Fandango***, 1992
Oil on panel, 16 x 20
AG1996.2.59
Cummer Museum of Art & Gardens

Plate 97 — **Osprey Nest, Silversmith Creek**, 1992
Oil on paper, 17 x 19 ½
Private Collection

Plate 98 — **Sea Wall, Echmuhl, Brittany**, 1992
Oil on canvas, 20 x 24
Collection of Jeffrey D. Dunn

DODGE '92

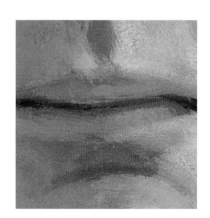

Plate 99 — **_Self-Portrait_**, 1992
Oil on paper, 10 x 10 (sight)
Collection of Marsha M. Coarsey

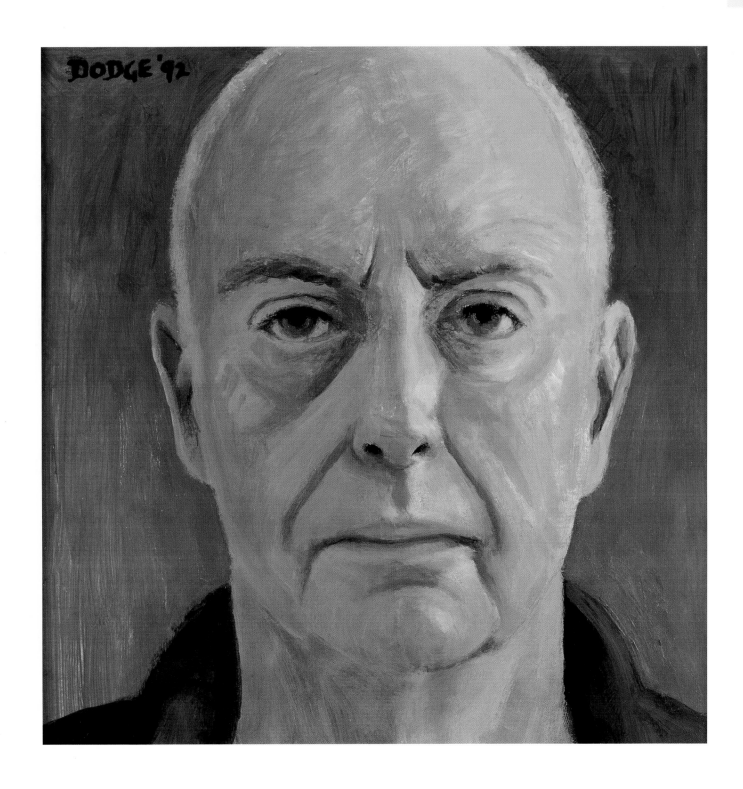

Plate 100 — ***Carmel Cove (Monterey Cypress)***, 1993
Oil on canvas board, 14 ⅛ x 18 ⅛
Collection of Evelyn H. Nehl

Plate 101 — **Safe Harbor**, 1993
Acrylic on paper, 19 x 26 (sight); 31 x 37 (frame)
Collection of Mr. and Mrs. Edward W. Lane, Jr.

Plate 102 — **The Bundle**, 1995
Oil on paperboard, 24 x 19 ⅞
Private Collection

Plate 103 — **Desert Trail**, 1995
Oil on paperboard, 18 ½ x 24 ½
AG1998.1.3
Cummer Museum of Art & Gardens

Plate 104 — **_Rising Tide_**, 1995
Oil on illustration board, 22 ¾ x 30 ½
AG1996.2.62
Cummer Museum of Art & Gardens

Plate 105 — **Setting Sail**, 1995
Oil on canvas, 24 x 30
Collection of Russell B. Newton, Jr.

Plate 106 — ***View of Silversmith Creek from my Studio***, 1995
Oil on gesso panel, 16 x 20
Collection of Mr. and Mrs. Taylor Hardwick

Plate 107 — ***Rockscape with Beach in Foreground***, 1996
Oil on canvas
Unfinished, destroyed as per instructions of artist

Plate 108 — **Still Life: Bundle and Rope**, 1996
Oil on canvas, 24 x 30
AG1996.2.63
Cummer Museum of Art & Gardens

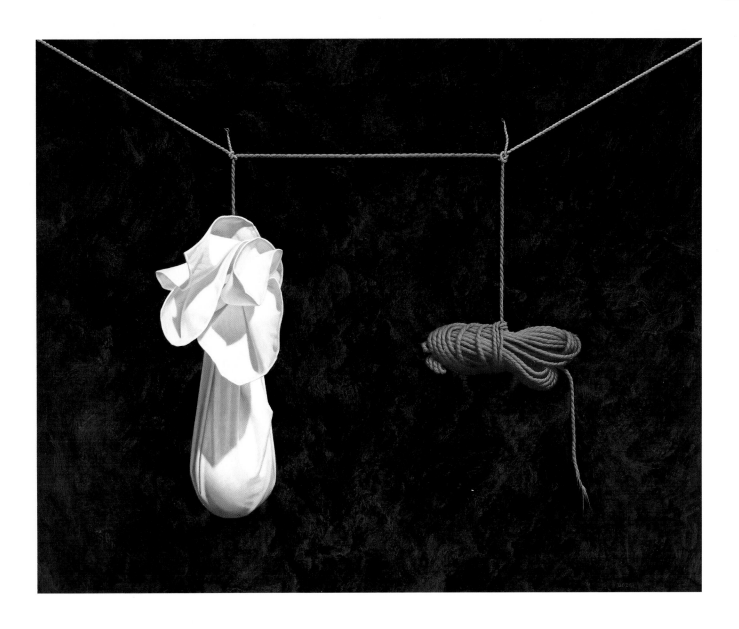

Works of Art

Plate 1 — *Jazz*, 1935
Poem and drawings published in *The Choate Literary Magazine*
Cummer Museum of Art & Gardens,
Joseph Jeffers Dodge Archives

Plate 2 — *President Roosevelt*, 1936
Pencil on paper
Signed by Roosevelt
Collection of Joseph Morrell Dodge II

Plate 3 — *Self-Portrait*, June 1939
Oil on panel, 11 x 8 ½
AG2001.3.1
Cummer Museum of Art & Gardens

Plate 4 — *And Then There were Two*, 1942
Oil on masonite, 31 x 24 ¾
1996.10.2
The Hyde Collection
Glens Falls, New York

Plate 5 — *The Hour of Parting*, 1942
Oil, pastel, pen and ink on board, 30 x 24
AG1996.2.25
Cummer Museum of Art & Gardens

Plate 6 — *Double Self-Portrait*, 1943
Oil on panel, 27 ½ x 20 ½
AG1996.2.26
Cummer Museum of Art & Gardens

Plate 7 — *Jazz Quintet (The Black and Tan Fantasy)*, 1943
Oil on canvas, 36 x 40
Private Collection

Plate 8 — *Black and Tan Fantasy*, 1944
Oil, 32 x 40
Collection of Choate Rosemary Hall

Plate 9 — *Moon Mist (Moonlight Madness or Mad Moonlight)*, 1944
Oil, 20 x 32
Location Unknown

Plate 10 — *The Renaissance*, 1944
Oil on canvas, 12 x 8
Collection of Mr. and Mrs. Edward Klempf

Plate 11 — *Self-Portrait*, 1944
Oil on paperboard, 18 x 15 ¾
1996.10.1
The Hyde Collection
Glens Falls, New York

Plate 12 — *Self-Portrait*, 1944
Oil
Destroyed by the artist

Plate 13 — *Art Student*, 1945
Location Unknown

Plate 14 — *Black and Blue*, 1946
Oil on canvas, 14 x 12
AG1996.2.29
Cummer Museum of Art & Gardens

Plate 15 — *Crucifixion*, 1946
Photogram, 12 ¾ x 10 ½
AG1996.2.30
Cummer Museum of Art & Gardens

Plate 16 — *Maternity*, 1946
Photograph, 13 ¼ x 10 ⁵/₁₆
AG1996.2.32
Cummer Museum of Art & Gardens

Plate 17 — *Another Autumn*, 1947
Oil on canvas, 18 ¼ x 10 ⅛
Collection of Mrs. Sydney J. Freedberg

Plate 18 — *Elegy*, 1947
Oil on canvas, 20 x 26
Munson-Williams-Proctor Arts Institute, Museum of Art, Utica, New York, 50.3

Plate 19 — *Frankie and Johnny (In Memory of «Tricky Sam» Nanton)*, 1947-48
Oil on canvas, 28 ¼ x 36 ½
AG1996.2.34
Cummer Museum of Art & Gardens

Plate 20 — *Trio*, 1947
Oil on canvas, 15 ½ x 29
1996.10.3
The Hyde Collection
Glens Falls, New York

Plate 21 — *Gods of Our Fathers: The Christian Tradition*, 1949-50
Oil on canvas, 12 x 16
Collection of Mr. and Mrs. Edward Klempf

Plate 22 — *Gods of Our Fathers: The Classical Tradition*, 1949-50
Oil on canvas, 12 x 16
Collection of Mr. and Mrs. Edward Klempf

Plate 23 — *Lake George Picnic*, 1949
Oil, 20 x 24
Collection of Professor Dugald V. MacArthur

Plate 24 — *The Key is Lost*, 1950-51
Oil on canvas, 20 x 24
AG1996.2.35
Cummer Museum of Art & Gardens

Plate 25 — *By the Old Mill Stream*, 1951
Oil on canvas, 22 x 28
1996.10.5
The Hyde Collection
Glens Falls, New York

Plate 26 — *The Fruit of Knowledge*, 1951
Oil on board, 11 x 20
Location Unknown

Plate 27 — *The Nest*, 1951
Oil on panel, 8 x 10
AG1996.2.36
Cummer Museum of Art & Gardens

Plate 28 — *What Struggle to Escape*, 1953-55
Oil on canvas, 34 ¼ x 46
From the Collection of The Museum of Arts and Sciences, Daytona Beach. Gift of Joseph Jeffers Dodge

Plate 29 — *The Chinese Puzzle (Still Life with Wooden Chinese Puzzles)*, 1954
16 x 20
Courtesy Dwight D. Eisenhower Library

Plate 30 — *The Awakening*, 1955
Oil on canvas, 28 x 36
Location Unknown

Plate 31 —***Girl with a Blue Cloak***, 1955
Oil on canvas, 32 x 27
AP1997.1.1
Cummer Museum of Art & Gardens

Plate 32 —***Sewing Basket (Work Basket)***, 1955
Oil on masonite, 16 x 11 ¾
Collection of Mr. and Mrs. B. Friedman

Plate 33 —***The Artist's Children: Tia, Jeff, Lisa and Julie***, 1958
Oil on canvas, 24 ¼ x 36 ½
AG1996.2.40
Cummer Museum of Art & Gardens

Plate 34 —***Glens Falls Rooftops***, 1959
Oil on canvas, 16 ¼ x 18 ⅛
Collection of Lawrence Lovett, Venice, Italy.

Plate 35 —***Hudson River Town***, 1959
Oil on canvas, 24 x 30
1996.10.15
The Hyde Collection
Glen Falls, New York

Plate 36 —***No Turning Back***, 1959
Oil on canvas, 32 x 42
AP1964.15.1
Cummer Museum of Art & Gardens

Plate 37 —***On the Edge***, 1959
Oil on canvas, 24 x 30
From the Collection of The Museum of Arts and Sciences, Daytona Beach. Gift of Joseph Jeffers Dodge

Plate 38 —***Tia and Julie***, 1959
Oil on canvas, 46 ¾ x 61 ¼
Collection of Julie Dodge

Plate 39 —***Bell Peppers***, 1960
Oil on canvas, 20 x 24
Location Unknown

Plate 40 —***Still Life with Lemons and Yellow Tulips***, 1960
Oil on canvas, 28 x 30
Location Unknown

Plate 41 —***Summer Serenade***, 1961-63
Oil on canvas, 36¼ x 45
AG1996.2.42
Cummer Museum of Art & Gardens

Plate 42 —***Sunday Afternoon at Fort Clinch***, 1964
Oil, 16 x 20
Collection of Gretchen and Steve Lotz

Plate 43 —***Still Life with Three Persimmons***, 1964
Oil on canvas, 20 x 24
Collection of Mr. and Mrs. Philip S. May, Jr.

Plate 44 —***Easter Still Life***, 1965
Oil, 48 x 48
Location Unknown

Plate 45 —***Lush Life (The Good Life)***, 1966
Oil on canvas, 36 x 50
AG1996.2.43
Cummer Museum of Art & Gardens

Plate 46 —***Hand Holding Apple***, 1967
Oil on canvas, 12 x 20
Collection of Mr. and Mrs. Edward Klempf

Plate 47 —***Portrait of Jeanne: Draped***, 1967
Oil on canvas, 32 x 24 ⅛
Collection of Mr. and Mrs. Edward Klempf

Plate 48 —***Portrait of Jeanne: Back***, 1968
Oil on canvas, 20 x 16
Collections of Mr. and Mrs. Edward Klempf

Plate 49 —***Portrait of Jeanne: Bust***, 1968
Oil on canvas, 18 x 5
Collection of Mr. and Mrs. Edward Klempf

Plate 50 —***From the Acropolis: The Propylaea***, 1968
Oil
Collection of Lawrence Lovett, Venice, Italy.

Plate 51 —***Crinum Lily and Shells***, 1969
Oil on canvas, 28 x 22
Location Unknown

Plate 52 —***Dixie Eggs: Portrait of Edward Klempf and his Father***, 1969
Oil on canvas, 9 x 12
Collection of Mr. and Mrs. Edward Klempf

Plate 53 —***Mushrooms***, 1969
Oil on canvas, 9 x 18
Collection of Mr. and Mrs. Anthony H. LaRoche

Plate 54 —***Orange Tree at Labna, Yucatan***, 1969
Oil, 36 x 52
Location Unknown

Plate 55 —***Duo at Delos***, 1970
Oil on canvas, 18 x 24
Collection of Felix R. and Debra Murphy Livingston

Plate 56 —***Waiting, The Aegean***, 1970
Oil on canvas, 18 x 24
Collection of Mr. and Mrs. Edward Klempf

Plate 57 —***East of the Sun***, 1971
Oil, 16 x 16
Collection of Gretchen and Steve Lotz

Plate 58 —***Finding***, 1971
Oil on canvas, 16 x 16
Collection of Russell B. Newton, Jr.

Plate 59 —***Tidal Pool, Morning***, 1971
Oil on canvas, 16 x 16
Collection of Mr. and Mrs. Taylor Hardwick

Plate 60 —***Coquina #1***, 1973
Pencil on paper, 16 x 20
From the Collection of The Museum of Arts and Sciences, Daytona Beach. Gift of Joseph Jeffers Dodge

Plate 61 —***Near Andrews Point, Cape Ann***, 1973
Acrylic on paper, 16 x 20
Location Unknown

Plate 62 —***Sunday Afternoon Promenade (Atlantic Beach)***, 1973
Oil, 16 x 16
Private Collection

Plate 63 —***Guatemala Valley***, 1974
Oil on paper, 19 ½ x 25 ¼
AG2000.3.1
Cummer Museum of Art & Gardens

Plate 64 —***Nude in Blue Victorian Chair***, 1974
Oil on paper, 21 ½ x 29 ½
Private Collection

Plate 65 —***An August Afternoon***, 1975
Oil, 16 x 16
Location Unknown

Plate 66 —***A Morning in May***, 1975
Oil on Canvas, 24 x 26
Collection of Micheal and Julia Suddath-Ranne

Plate 67 —***Between Two Tides***, 1975
Oil on paper, 19 x 25
Collection of Jeffrey D. Dunn

Plate 68 —***Fishermen, Costa del Sol***, 1975
Oil on canvas, 24 x 30
AP1975.4.1
Cummer Museum of Art & Gardens

Plate 69 —***Rocks Near Rockport***, 1975
Oil on paper, 14 ¾ x 19 ½
Collection of Mr. and Mrs. Carle A. Felton, Jr.

Plate 70 —*Interlude on the Rocks #3*, 1976
Pencil on paper, 16 x 20
Location Unknown

Plate 71 —*Interlude on Rocks #4*, 1976
Acrylic on paper, 21 ½ x 29 ½
AG1996.2.47
Cummer Museum of Art & Gardens

Plate 72 —*Laura Jeanne in a Bentwood Chair*, 1976
Pencil on paper, 28 x 22 (sight)
Collection of Jeffrey D. Dunn

Plate 73 —*There is a Tide*, 1976
Oil on paper, 22 x 28
Private Collection

Plate 74 —*Arizona High Country*, 1978
Red pencil and acrylic on paper, 21 x 29
Collection of the Clarence Nussbaum Trust

Plate 75 —*Rockscape Near Rockport*, 1978
Oil on paper, 21 x 29
Location Unknown

Plate 76 —*Doric Column, Paestum*, 1978
Oil on paper, 31 x 38 (frame)
Private Collection

Plate 77 —*Panetto Bolognese*, 1980
Oil on paper, 20 x 14
Collection of Mr. and Mrs. Carle A. Felton, Jr.

Plate 78 —*After the Bath #2*, 1981
Oil on paper, 9 x 9
Collection of Mr. and Mrs. Edward Klempf

Plate 79 —*Old Olive Tree, Agrigento*, 1981
Oil on mounted paper, 21 x 29
Private Collection

Plate 80 —*Silversmith Creek*, 1981
Oil on paper, 16 ¼ x 17 ¾
Location Unknown

Plate 81 —*White Jar with Violet Paper*, 1983
Oil on paper, 18 ¼ x 14 ¼
Collection of Mr. and Mrs. J. Shepard Bryan, Jr.

Plate 82 —*Fallen Tree: Intracoastal Waterway*, 1984
Oil on paper, 18 ⁷⁄₁₆ x 29 ¾
Collection of Mr. and Mrs. Robert T. Shircliff

Plate 83 —*It's Only a Paper Moon*, 1986
Watercolor and acrylic on paper, 29 ¼ x 21 ¼
Collection of Russell B. Newton, Jr.

Plate 84 —*Pyramids*, 1986
Oil, 36 x 36
Collection of David N. Mills

Plate 85 —*Seeking*, 1986
Acrylic and pastel on board, 20 x 30
Collection of St. Johns Country Day School, Orange Park, Florida

Plate 86 —*Roman Scene*, 1987
Oil on board, 16 x 19
Collection of Felix R. and Debra Murphy Livingston

Plate 87 —*Waiting*, 1987
Oil, 36 x 48
Location Unknown

Plate 88 —*Morning, Gulf Coast*, 1988
Oil, 30 x 40
Location Unknown

Plate 89 —*Prehistoric Monoliths, Brittany (Past, Present and Nature, Brittany)*, 1988
Oil on canvas, 30 x 36
AG1996.2.56
Cummer Museum of Art & Gardens

Plate 90 —*Horizons*, 1990
Oil on paper, 21 ½ x 24
AG1996.2.57
Cummer Museum of Art & Gardens

Plate 91 —*Northern California Coast*, 1990
Oil on paper, 7 x 10
Location Unknown

Plate 92 —*Breton Village*, 1991
Oil on canvas, 16 x 20
Collection of Mr. and Mrs. Robert T. Shircliff

Plate 93 —*California Cypress*, 1991
Oil on paper, 12 ¼ x 16 ¼
Collection of Jeffrey D. Dunn

Plate 94 —*The Artist and Muse*, 1992
Oil on canvas, 36 x 36
AG1996.2.60
Cummer Museum of Art & Gardens

Plate 95 —*Dancing Pears I: Fandango*, 1992
Oil on panel, 16 x 20
AG1996.2.58
Cummer Museum of Art & Gardens

Plate 96 —*Dancing Pears II: Fandango*, 1992
Oil on panel, 16 x 20
AG1996.2.59
Cummer Museum of Art & Gardens

Plate 97 —*Osprey Nest, Silversmith Creek*, 1992
Oil on paper, 17 x 19 ½
Private Collection

Plate 98 —*Sea Wall, Echmuhl, Brittany*, 1992
Oil on canvas, 20 x 24
Collection of Jeffrey D. Dunn

Plate 99 —*Self-Portrait*, 1992
Oil on paper, 10 x 10 (sight)
Collection of Marsha M. Coarsey

Plate 100 —*Carmel Cove (Monterey Cypress)*, 1993
Oil on canvas board, 14 ⅛ x 18 ⅛
Collection of Evelyn H. Nehl

Plate 101 —*Safe Harbor*, 1993
Acrylic on paper, 19 x 26 (sight); 31 x 37 (frame)
Collection of Mr. and Mrs. Edward W. Lane, Jr.

Plate 102 —*The Bundle*, 1995
Oil on paperboard, 24 x 19 ⅞
Private Collection

Plate 103 —*Desert Trail*, 1995
Oil on paperboard, 18 ½ x 24 ½
AG1998.1.3
Cummer Museum of Art & Gardens

Plate 104 —*Rising Tide*, 1995
Oil on illustration board, 22 ¾ x 30 ½
AG1996.2.62
Cummer Museum of Art & Gardens

Plate 105 —*Setting Sail*, 1995
Oil on canvas, 24 x 30
Collection of Russell B. Newton, Jr.

Plate 106 — *View of Silversmith Creek from my Studio*, 1995
Oil on gesso panel, 16 x 20
Collection of Mr. and Mrs. Taylor Hardwick

Plate 107 — *Rockscape with Beach in Foreground*, 1996
Oil on canvas
Unfinished, destroyed as per instructions of artist

Plate 108 — *Still Life: Bundle and Rope*, 1996
Oil on canvas, 24 x 30
AG1996.2.63
Cummer Museum of Art & Gardens

Photographs from the Joseph Jeffers Dodge Archives of the Cummer Museum

Photographs

The Artist's Work Icon

Detail Plate 7 —***Jazz Quintet (The Black and Tan Fantasy)***, 1943
Oil on canvas, 36 x 40
Private Collection

Icons Used in the Copy

Detail Plate 3 — ***Self-Portrait***, June 1939
Oil on panel, 11 x 8 ½
AG2001.3.1
Cummer Museum of Art & Gardens

Detail Plate 28 — ***What Struggle to Escape***, 1953-55
Oil on canvas, 34 ¼ x 46
From the Collection of The Museum of Arts and Sciences, Daytona Beach. Gift of Joseph Jeffers Dodge

Detail Plate 12 — ***Self-Portrait***, 1944
Oil
Destroyed by the artist

Detail Plate 33 — ***The Artist's Children: Tia, Jeff, Lisa and Julie***, 1958
Oil on canvas, 24 ¼ x 36 ½
AG1996.2.40
Cummer Museum of Art & Gardens

Detail Plate 11 — ***Self-Portrait***, 1944
Oil on paperboard, 18 x 15 ¾
1996.10.1
The Hyde Collection
Glens Falls, New York

Detail Plate 26 — ***The Fruit of Knowledge***, 1951
Oil on board, 11 x 20
Location Unknown

Detail Plate 6 — ***Double Self-Portrait***, 1943
Oil on panel, 27 ½ x 20 ½
AG1996.2.26
Cummer Museum of Art & Gardens

Detail Plate 49 —***Portrait of Jeanne: Bust***, 1968
Oil on canvas, 18 x 5
Collection of Mr. and Mrs. Edward Klempf

Detail Plate 99 — ***Self-Portrait***, 1992
Oil on paper, 10 x 10 (sight)
Collection of Marsha M. Coarsey

Detail Plate 45 — ***Lush Life (The Good Life)***, 1966
Oil on canvas, 36 x 50
AG1996.2.43
Cummer Museum of Art & Gardens

Detail Plate 94 — ***The Artist and Muse***, 1992
Oil on canvas, 36 x 36
AG1996.2.60
Cummer Museum of Art & Gardens

Detail Plate 50 — ***From the Acropolis: The Propylaea***, 1968
Oil
Collection of Lawrence Lovett, Venice, Italy.

Detail Plate 4 — ***And Then There were Two***, 1942
Oil on masonite, 31 x 24 ¾
1996.10.2
The Hyde Collection
Glens Falls, New York

Detail Plate 77 — ***Panetto Bolognese***, 1980
Oil on paper, 20 x 14
Collection of Mr. and Mrs. Carle A. Felton, Jr.

Detail Plate 6 — ***Double Self-Portrait***, 1943
Oil on panel, 27 ½ x 20 ½
AG1996.2.26
Cummer Museum of Art & Gardens

Detail Plate 90 — ***Horizons***, 1990
Oil on paper, 21 ½ x 24
AG1996.2.57
Cummer Museum of Art & Gardens

Detail Plate 24 — ***The Key is Lost***, 1950-51
Oil on canvas, 20 x 24
AG1996.2.35
Cummer Museum of Art & Gardens

Detail Plate 107 — ***Rockscape with Beach in Foreground***, 1996
Oil on canvas
Unfinished, destroyed as per instructions of artist

Exhibition History

An Exhibition of Works by Joseph Jeffers Dodge, Museum of Arts and Sciences, Daytona Beach, Florida, August-September 18, 1998.

Two North Florida Master Painters: Jerry Dodge and Hiram Williams, Art Gallery of the Department of Art, University of Central Florida, Orlando, November 4-December 6, 1996.

Joseph Jeffers Dodge: A Florida Legend, Cummer Museum of Art & Gardens, Jacksonville, Florida, 28 June-24 October, 1996.

Joseph Jeffers Dodge: A Retrospective (also referred to as *Joyful Serenity-Paintings by Joseph Jeffers Dodge*), Ormond Memorial Art Museum, Ormond Beach, Florida, March 22-May 5, 1996.

Joseph Jeffers Dodge: Painting and Drawings 1940s to the Present, University Gallery, University of North Florida, Jacksonville, Florida, October 17-November 9, 1995.

Jacksonville Airport Exhibition, Jacksonville, Florida, March, 1994.

Collectors' Showcase Exhibition at the Cummer, Jacksonville, Florida, September 30-November 20, 1993.

Sense & Sensuality, Gallery 88, Ponte Vedra Beach, Florida, June 13-July 23, 1993.

David Engdahl, Sculpture/Joseph Dodge, Paintings, Florida School of the Arts, Palatka, Florida, February 17-March 26, 1993.

Holiday Tables, Jacksonville Art Museum, Jacksonville, Florida, November 20, 1992-January 3, 1993.

Joseph Jeffers Dodge, An American Classicist, Cummer Gallery of Art, Jacksonville, Florida, September 10-October 25, 1992.

Recent Works on Paper, Gallery Contemporanea, Jacksonville, Florida, September 18-November 1, 1992.

Florida Crown Treasures: The Works of Senior Professionals, Gallery 88, Ponte Vedra Beach, Florida, January 12-February 5, 1992.

Art Celebration! Jacksonville, Florida. The group exhibited 9 times from 1973-1992 at various venues, mostly in Jacksonvile. Specific dates are: 1992, 1988, 1987, 1981, 1979, 1978, 1976, 1974, 1973.

Our Concerns, Gallery Contemporanea, Jacksonville, Florida, April 4-22, 1991.

Jacksonville Creates, Jacksonville Art Museum, Jacksonville, Florida, May 31-August 12, 1990.

Foster Harmon Galleries of American Art, Sarasota, Florida:
The 29th Annual Florida Artists Show, January 12-31, 1992
The 28th Annual Major Florida Artists Show, January 13-February 1, 1991
Four Exhibitions: The Sea, February, 1990.
The 27th Annual Major Florida Artists Show, January 7-February 2, 1990
The 24th Annual Major Florida Artists Show, January 11-30, 1987
The 23rd Annual Major Florida Artists Show, January 12-31, 1986
The 22nd Annual Major Florida Artists Show, January 13- February 1, 1985
The 21st Annual Major Florida Artists Show, January 8-27, 1984
Summer Exhibitions 1984 (Galleries I and III) July 23-August 10, 1984.
Three July Exhibitions, Works by 31 Florida Artists, 1982.

The Harmon Gallery, Naples, Florida:
7 Realists, 2 Shows, 2 Openings: The Harmon Gallery, February 15-21, 1983
The Nude in American Art, January 4-16,1982
Contemporary American Realists, February 24-March 1, 1980
The 16th Annual Major Florida Artists Show, January 14-February 3, 1979
The 15th Annual Major Florida Artists Show, January 15-28, 1978
20th Century American Realists, January 30-February 11, 1978
Florida Realists, 1977
The 9th Annual Major Florida Artists Show, January 16-February 12, 1972.

The M. Anwar Kamal Collection of Art, Twentieth-Century Painting, Cummer Gallery of Art, Jacksonville, Florida, November 29-December 31, 1989.

Selections from the M. Anwar Kamal Collection of Drawings and Sculpture, Cummer Gallery of Art, Jacksonville, Florida, June 22-July 30, 1989.

Joseph Jeffers Dodge: An Exhibition, Jacksonville University, Alexander Brest Museum, Jacksonville, Florida, March, 1988.

Arts Sampler, sponsored by the Arts Assembly, coordinated by the Jacksonville Coalition of the Visual Arts at the Jacksonville Landing, Jacksonville, Florida, September 8-12, 1987.

Razzle Dazzle Ramses, Gallery Contemporanea, Jacksonville, Florida, November 21-December 31, 1986.

A Month in the Country, an exhibition of landscape paintings at Lee & Williams Fine Arts, Jacksonville, Florida, October 14, 1985-February 25, 1986.

Drawings by Jacksonville Artists, Jacksonville Art Museum, Jacksonville, Florida, November 14-January 5, 1985.

Jacksonville Collects: A Salute to Corporate Collections, Jacksonville Art Museum, Jacksonville, Florida, December 13, 1984-January 27, 1985.

Solano Grove, Early Evening exhibited at the Cummer Gallery of Art during the Delius Festival, Jacksonville, Florida, March, 1984.

Manatee Junior College Presents 28 Florida Artists from the Foster Harmon Galleries of American Art, Manatee Junior College, Bradenton, Florida, September 7-October 28, 1983.

Art League of Manatee County: Florida Realists, Bradenton, Florida, October 23-November 16, 1983.

Jacksonville Artists, Drawing Exhibition, Cummer Gallery of Art, Jacksonville, Florida, 1981.

Eight Jacksonville Artists by the Art League of Daytona Beach at the Daytona Beach Art Center, Barre Barrett, Marcelle Bear, John Bunker, Joseph Jeffers Dodge, Gretchen Ebersol, William Proctor, Mun Quan, Dorothy Stewart, Daytona Beach, Florida, November 30-December18, 1980.

Contemporary Realists, Art Sources, Inc., Jacksonville, Florida, November 8-December 1, 1978.

Florida 10 plus 5, works by Florida Artists presented by The Friends of Art and Culture Center of Hollywood, Florida, September 11-October 11, 1977.

Joseph Jeffers Dodge, College of Fine Arts, Jacksonville University, Alexander Brest Museum, Jacksonville, Florida, June 3-18, 1976.

Joseph Jeffers Dodge, A Ten Year View, Cummer Gallery of Art, Jacksonville, Florida, May 14-June 29, 1975.

The Human Presence, Jacksonville Art Museum, Jacksonville, Florida, September 5-29, 1974.

Artrain, a presentation of the Michigan Council for the Arts, on tour for the Southern Growth Policies Board, 1974.

Joseph Jeffers Dodge, Recent Paintings, (1966-1973), The Hyde Collection, Glens Falls, New York, May 27-June 24, 1973.

Artists of the Jacksonville Area, Sesquicentennial Exhibition, Part II, Cummer Gallery of Art, Jacksonville, Florida, June 27-September 30, 1972.

Gibbes Art Gallery, Carolina Art Association, Charleston, South Carolina, February 1972.

Florida Creates 1971-1972, a touring exhibition throughout the south-eastern states cosponsored by Florida Gas Company and the Florida Art Museum Directors Association, 1971-1972.

Spring Festival of the Arts, The American Tradition, Rollins College, Winter Park, Florida, April 16-28, 1971.

Exhibition of Nine Paintings by Joseph Jeffers Dodge, Jacksonville Naval Air Station, Jacksonville, Florida, January, 1971.

St. Augustine Art Center, St. Augustine, Florida, October 11-November 3, 1970.

Joseph J. Dodge, Recent Paintings, The Group Gallery, Inc., Jacksonville, Florida, April 4-22, 1970.

Realist Invitational, The Gallery of Contemporary Art, Winston-Salem, North Carolina, October, 1969.

Dodge was featured guest artist, St. Augustine Art Association, St. Augustine, Florida, March 2-April 9, 1969.

University of Florida, Gainesville, Florida, April 1969.

Four guest artists, Joseph Jeffers Dodge, Mun Quan, John McIver, and Jean Troemel, St. Augustine Art Association, St. Augustine, Florida, November 1969.

Mint Museum of Art, Charlotte, North Carolina, September-October 20, 1968.

Joseph J. Dodge, Recent Paintings, The Group Gallery, Inc., Jacksonville, Florida, April 6-26, 1968.

Paintings by Joseph Jeffers Dodge, Gallery 31, Inc., Birmingham, Alabama, April 1967.
Traveling Exhibition, Florida Artist Group, Inc., 1966-1967.

Joseph J. Dodge, St. Augustine Art Association, St. Augustine, Florida, January, 1966.

Joseph J. Dodge, Recent Paintings and Drawings, The Group Gallery, Inc., Jacksonville, Florida, April 14-May 14, 1966.

Exhibition of works by Joseph Jeffers Dodge and J. J. Tharrats, Tampa Art Institute, Tampa, Florida, July 1965.

Joseph Jeffers Dodge, Retrospective, Paintings and Drawings
Presented by the following museums:
Columbus Museum of Arts and Crafts, Columbus, Georgia, February 7-23, 1965
George Thomas Hunter Gallery of Art, Chattanooga, Tennessee, March 7-24, 1965
Georgia Museum of Art, Athens, Georgia, April 4-25, 1965
Columbia Museum of Art, Columbia, South Carolina, May 9-31, 1965.
Mirrell Gallery, 3421 Main Highway-Coconut Grove, Miami, Florida, November, 1964.

Joseph Jeffers Dodge, Paintings and Drawings, Cummer Gallery of Art, Jacksonville, Florida, February 26-March 22, 1964.

25th Annual Exhibition of Contemporary Paintings, Society of the Four Arts, Palm Beach, Florida, December 7-29, 1963.

The Continuing Tradition of Realism in American Art, Hirschl & Adler Galleries, Inc., New York City, Part I March 6-24, 1962; Part II April 3-21, 1962.

The Pioneer Gallery, Cooperstown Art Association, Cooperstown, New York, 1961 season.

64th American Exhibition: Paintings, Sculpture; The Art Institute of Chicago, Chicago, Illinois, January 6-February 5, 1961.

Joseph Jeffers Dodge, Recent Paintings, Hirschl & Adler Galleries, New York City, January 11-28, 1961.

Ft. Edward Art Center, (preview exhibit for upcoming show at Hirschl & Adler scheduled for later in the year), June 1-3, 1960.

24th Regional Exhibition by Artists of the Upper Hudson, Albany Institute of History and Art, Albany, New York, April 22-May 24, 1959.

Southern Vermont Art Center, Manchester, Vermont, July 4-13, 1958.

New England and New York State Exhibition, Southern Vermont Art Center, Manchester, Vermont, June 29-July 14, 1957.

Albany Institute of History and Art, Albany, New York, January 19-February 13, 1956.

Joseph Jeffers Dodge: One-Man Show, Schenectady Museum, Schenectady, New York, November 8-24, 1955.

An Exhibition of Paintings by Joseph Jeffers Dodge, Wildenstein Gallery, New York City, April 16-May 14, 1952.

13th Annual Exhibition, Artists of Central New York Art Gallery, Munson-Williams-Proctor Institute, Utica, New York, February 4-26, 1950.

Joseph Jeffers Dodge, Albany Institute of History and Art, Albany, New York, September 20-October 2, 1949.

12th Annual Exhibition of Work by Artists of Central New York, Munson-Williams-Proctor Institute, Utica, New York, February 6-27, 1949.

11th Annual Exhibition of work by Artists of Central New York, Munson-Williams-Proctor Institute, Utica, New York, February 1-29, 1948

XII Upper Hudson Annual, Albany Institute of History and Art, Albany, New York, May 1-June 1, 1947.

Annual Exhibition for Michigan Artists, The Detroit Institute of Arts, Detroit, Michigan, November 11-December 14, 1947.

Annual Exhibition for Michigan Artists, The Detroit Institute of Arts, Detroit, Michigan, November 12-December 15, 1946.

XI Upper Hudson Annual, Albany Institute of History and Art, Albany, New York, May 1-June 2, 1946.

The One Hundred and Fortieth Annual Exhibition of Painting and Sculpture, The Pennsylvania Academy of the Fine Arts, Philadelphia, Pennsylvania, January 19 through February 25, 1945.

Portraits of Today by Painters of Today, Mortimer Brandt Gallery, 15 East 57th Street, New York, March 31-April, 1945.

11th Upper Hudson Annual, Albany Institute of History and Art, Albany, New York, May 1-June 2, 1946.

Prize Winners, 1945-46, An exhibition of seventy-one pictures that have received prize awards during the past season from selected juries in 29 national and regional exhibits, Addison Gallery of American Art, Phillips Academy, Andover, Massachusetts, September 13-October 21, 1946.

9th Annual Exhibition, Artists of the Upper Hudson, Albany Institute of History and Art, Albany, New York, April 26-June 3, 1944.

Annual Exhibition for Michigan Artists, Detroit Institute of Arts, Detroit, Michigan, November 28-December 24, 1944.

8th Annual Exhibition, Artists of the Upper Hudson, Albany Institute of History and Art, Albany, New York, April 29-May 30, 1943.

Adlow, Dorothy. «Quarry with Swimmers: An Oil Painting by Joseph Jeffers Dodge.» *The Christian Science Monitor*, June 8, 1960.

«A la galerie Hirschl & Adler, Joseph Jeffers Dodge.» *France-Amérique*, January 22, 1961, 15.

«A lifetime's collection.» *The Florida Times-Union* (Jacksonville), Sunday, November 19, 1995.

Ambrose, Stephen E. *Eisenhower, Soldier and President*. 1990.

Arbitman, Kahren. «Joseph Jeffers Dodge: A Director's Legacy.» *The Cummer Quarterly*, volume 1, number 1, Winter, 1997, 12.

Arenz, Peggy. «The Two-Hour Landscape.» *American Artist*, February, 1993, 36-41, 75-78.

Balliett, Whitney. «Celebrating the Duke.» *The New Yorker*, November 29, 1993,134-147.

Bass, Ruth. «Realism: When a Rose *Is* a Rose.» *Art News*, February, 1996, 93-94.

Benbow, Charles. «'Florida Realists' on exhibit in Bradenton.» *St. Petersburg Times*, Sunday, October 23, 1984, 2E.

Bischof, Günter and Stephen E. Ambrose (eds.). *Eisenhower, A Centenary Assessment*. Baton Rouge, LA, 1995.

Bonte, C.H. «Rattner Winner of the Temple Award At Academy's 140th Annual Exhibition.» *The Philadelphia Inquirer*, Sunday Morning, January 21, 1945.

Bradt, Clif. «Public Picks 'Nude', Oil by Dodge, as Tops in Institute Show.» *The Knickerbocker News*, Albany, N.Y., Thursday, May 14, 1959, 10A.

Breuning, Margaret. «The Cerebral Approach to Portraiture.» *Art Digest*, April 15, 1945, 13.

Brown, Gordon. «Gallery Previews in New York.» *Pictures on Exhibit*, February, 1961, 18-19.

Burk, Robert F. *Dwight D. Eisenhower, Hero and Politician*. Boston, 1986.

Burton, W.C. «It's Realism As High Art In Winston-Salem Exhibit.» *Greensboro Daily News*, Sunday, October 12, 1969, B12.

Caliste, John. «Rising to the Occasion.» *Vue*, December, 1986, 25.
Campbell, Mary. «Hubbard House auction a symbol.» *Jacksonville Journal*, Thursday, June 3, 1982, 8D.

«City Museum Open Today With Special Exhibits.» *Schenectady Gazette*, Tuesday, November 8, 1955, 11.

Clark, Kenneth. *The Nude: a Study in Ideal Form*. New York, 1956.
Codrington, Andrea. «Figuratively Speaking.» *Art & Auction*, June, 1996, 76-81.

«'Collector's Choice' Opens Sunday at the Art Center.» *The St. Augustine Record*, November 4-5, 1967, 2.

Corbino, Marcia. «Joseph Jeffers Dodge.» *American Artist*, 47, June, 1983, 50-54, 95-99.

Covington, Richard. «Balthus.» *Art & Antiques*. November, 1994, 70-77.

«Crowds fill downtown art show in Dyal Upchurch.» *Metropolis*, volume 1, number 2, Wednesday, December 16, 1981, 1-2.

Crowley, Matthew. «Portrait of a Hyde Curator.» *The Post-Star* (Glens Falls, NY), Thursday, October 19, 1995, D-4.

Cummer Gallery of Art, Jacksonville, Florida, 1965.

Davis, Esther, ed. *The Scout*. Finch, Pruyn and Company, Inc., Glens Falls, NY, volume 7, number 2, September, 1962.

Dodge, Joseph Jeffers. *An Introduction to Landscape in French Eighteenth Century Drawing and Painting* (unpublished Honors Thesis submitted to the Department of Fine Arts in Harvard College), April, 1940.

———. *Contemporary American Realistic Painting* (exhibition pamphlet, November 1-15, Albany Institute of History and Art; November 15-31, Crandall Library, Glens Falls; December 1-15, Skidmore College, Sarasota Springs, n.d.).

———. *European Painting of the Twentieth Century on exhibition from March 22 through April 10 at Crandall Public Library*. Glens Falls, NY (exhibition pamphlet, n.d.).

———. «Rubens' *Man in Armor*.» *The Art Quarterly*, 5, 1942, 147.

———. «The Visual Arts: A Chronicle of Humanity.» *Arts Assembler*, Jacksonville, FL, volume 2, Number 8, November, 1976.

———. *Thirteen Paintings From the 15th century to the present time, A loan Exhibition at Crandall Public Library in Glens Falls*, N.Y. (exhibition pamphlet) August 31-September 30, 1946.

———. Unpublished Lecture Delivered at the Jacksonville Art Museum, June 28, 1990.

«Dodge Painting of Kattskill Scene Purchased by Artists' Group.» *The Post-Star* (Glens Falls, NY), Thursday, June 13, 1946.

Downs, Linda Bank. *Diego Rivera: The Detroit Industry Murals*. New York and London, 1999.

Drucker, Peter F. «Japan's Not-So-Secret Weapon.» *The Wall Street Journal*, Tuesday, January 9, 1990.

Edelson, Elihu. «Art Celebration Closes Strong.» *Jacksonville Journal*, Saturday, January 19, 1974, 11.

———. «'Art Celebration' Exciting and Significant Event.» *Jacksonville Journal*, Saturday, December 15, 1973.

———. «'Classical Realism' By Cummer's Director.» *Jacksonville Journal*, Saturday, April 25, 1970, 28.

———. «Dodge's Show At Group Gallery is 'Cool'.» *Jacksonville Journal*, Thursday, April 25, 1968, 14.

———. «JU Exhibits Dodge Art.» *Jacksonville Journal*, Saturday, June 12, 1976, 16.

———. «The 'Human Presence' at Museum.» *Jacksonville Journal*, Saturday, September 21, 1974, 15.

———. «Sesquicentennial Art: Part II.» *Jacksonville Journal*, July 8, 1972.

———. «There are several kinds of realism.» *The Florida Times-Union and Journal* (Jacksonville), Sunday, November 19, 1978, E-8.

———. «Works of Joseph Dodge on Exhibition.» *Jacksonville Journal*, Saturday, May 31, 1975, 7.

Enns, Catherine. «Artist Inspired by Delius.» *The Florida Times-Union* (Jacksonville), Friday, February 24, 1984, D-1 and D-4.

————. «'Twentieth Century American Drawings,' Richness of drawings shows in exhibit.» *The Florida Times-Union* (Jacksonville), C-1 and C-6.

Felton, Nancy Belote. «A Man's Domain.» *Antiques Show Magazine*, December, 1988, Jacksonville, Florida.

Filaroski, P. Douglas. «It *did* happen here, Hurricane Dora destroyed myth of a storm-proof city.» *The Florida Times-Union* (Jacksonville), Sunday, May 30, 1999, D-1 and D-6.

Foley, Bill. «Cummer Gallery Director Named, Joseph Jeffers Dodge to Succeed Late Robert L. Parsons.» *The Florida Times-Union* (Jacksonville), Sunday, March 25, 1962, 17.

————. «Gallery's Director Arrives.» *The Florida Times-Union* (Jacksonville), 1962, 19 and 25.

«Forever Dodge in the gallery.» *Folio Weekly* (Jacksonville), December 3, 1996.

Gaddis, Eugene R. *Magician of the Modern: Chick Austin and the Transformation of the Arts in America*. New York, 2000.

«Gallery Previews in New York.» *Pictures on Exhibit*, May, 1952.

Ginders, James. *A Guide to Napkin Folding*. Boston, 1979.

«Glens Falls Artist Gives Albany Show.» *Knickerbocker News*, Albany, NY, January 19, 1956.

Goffen, Rona (ed.). *Titian's Venus of Urbino*. New York and Cambridge, 1997.

Graham, Judy Wells. «Painting Puts Cummer on Connoisseur's Art Map.» *The Florida Times-Union* (Jacksonville), Sunday, November 7, 1976.

Gristina, M. Campbell. Cummer Gallery of Art brochure and calendar, September, 1992.

————. *The Wark Collection: Early Meissen Porcelain*. Jacksonville, FL, 1984.

Gustafson, Eleanor H. «Museum accessions.» *Antiques*, November, 1993, 612.

Hall, James. *Dictionary of Subjects & Symbols in* Art. New York, 1979.

Hamm, Wayne. «The Corporation collections.» *Jacksonville Journal*, January 3, 1985.

Hardin, Jennifer. *The Lure of Egypt: Land of the Pharaohs Revisited*. Museum of Fine Arts, St. Petersburg, Florida (exhibition catalogue), January 10-June 9, 1996.

Hardwick, Taylor. *Joseph Jeffers Dodge* (videotape made in conjunction with the artist's exhibition at the University of North Florida). Jacksonville, FL, 1996.

Harvard Class of 1940, Fiftieth Anniversary Report. Cambridge, MA, 1990.

Hasse, John Edward. *Beyond Category: the Life and Genius of Duke Ellington*. New York, 1993.

«He 'Zig-Zags' In His Paintings.» *Jacksonville Journal*, February 27, 1964.

Hobhouse, Janet. *The Bride Stripped Bare: The Artist and the Female Nude in the Twentieth Century*. New York, 1988.

Holland & Knight Art Collection, Jacksonville. Florida, n.d.

Hughes, Robert. «Seeing Life in Jazz Tempo.» *TIME*, January 20, 1992, 60-61.

————. «Under the Crack of Reality.» *TIME*, July 17, 1995, 54-56.

Hyman, Ann. «Hint of Mystery Hides Beneath Painter's Realistic Images.» *The Florida Times-Union* (Jacksonville), March 4, 1988, D1-2.

«Infinite Pictorial Variety: The Paintings of Joseph Jeffers Dodge.» *The Hyde Connection*, volume V, number 4, October-December, 1995, 5.

Jablonski, Edward. *Alan Jay Lerner, A Biography*. New York, 1996.

Janis, Sidney. *Abstract & Surrealist Art in America*. New York, 1944.

Jencks, Charles. *Post-Modernism: The New Classicism in Art and Architecture*. New York, 1987.

Jones, Tanja, Hope McMath, Aaron De Groft and Maarten van de Guchte. *Cummer Museum of Art and Gardens*. Jacksonville, FL, 2000.

«Joseph Jeffers Dodge.» *Art Digest*, May 1, 1952, 21.

Joseph Jeffers Dodge, A Ten Year View, The Cummer Gallery of Art, 1975. (exhibition catalogue with essays by Russell B. Hicken and William E. Parker), Jacksonville, FL, 1975.

«Joseph Jeffers Dodge Giving One-Man Show.» *The Post-Star*, Glens Falls, NY, January 19, 1961.

Joseph Jeffers Dodge, Paintings and Drawings, The Cummer Gallery of Art, 1964. Jacksonville, FL, 1964.

Judd, Donald. «Joseph Jeffers Dodge.» *Arts*, January, 1961.

Katchen, Carole. «Exploring Technique, Joseph Jeffers Dodge: Evolving into Simplicity.» *Painting Faces and Figures*, New York, 1986, 54-61.

Karabinis, Paul and Debra Murphy-Livingston. «An Interview with Joseph Jeffers Dodge.» (published in conjunction with the exhibition *Joseph Jeffers Dodge, Paintings and Drawings: 1940s to the Present*. October 17-November 9, 1995), University Gallery, University of North Florida, Jacksonville, FL.

Kettlewell, James K. *The Hyde Collection Catalogue*. Glens Falls, NY, 1981.

Korzenik, Diana. *Drawn to Art, A Nineteenth-Century American Dream*. Hanover and London, 1983.

Koscielny, Margaret. *The M. Anwar Kamal Collection of Art, Twentieth Century Painting* (exhibition catalogue). Cummer Gallery of Art, Jacksonville, FL, November 29-December 31, 1989.

Knight, Ralph. «Money Isn't Everything.» *The Saturday Evening Post*, September 26, 1959, 22-23, 107-111.

Lagerlöf, Margaretha Rossholm. *Ideal Landscape, Annibale Carracci, Nicolas Poussin and Claude Lorrain*. New Haven and London, 1990.

Lambert, Eddie, *Duke Ellington, A Listener's Guide*. Lanham, MD, 1999.

Larson, Robert A. *Hiram Williams, Images of Compassion*. Lanham, MD and New York, 1998.

Lazarus, Lynn. «Jerry Dodge: A time in his life for his own art.» *Times Journal Magazine*, July 16, 1972, 6-9.

Lee, Jane. *Derain*, New York, 1990.

Leighton, Anne. «Best and Brightest.» *Folio Weekly* (Jacksonville), July 17, 1990.

———. «Dodge's Brittany Works Outstanding.» *Folio Weekly* (Jacksonville), October 6, 1992, 14.

———. «Landscapes Sparkle.» *Folio Weekly* (Jacksonville), March 15, 1988.

———. «Museum Men.» *Folio Weekly* (Jacksonville), January 17, 1989, 6-10.

Leymarie, Jean. *Balthus*, New York, 1979.

Ludwig, Harriet. «Artist of Few Words Paints with a Human Touch.» *The Florida Times-Union and Journal* (Jacksonville), Sunday, November 21, 1976, I-6.

McCarthy, Cathleen. «The Problems and Potentials in Painting Nudes.» *American Artist*, April, 1990, 34-39, 68-70.

Malraux, André, translated by Stuart Gilbert. *The Voices of Silence*, New York, 1953.

Marter, Joan. «Dorothy Dehner's Legacy to the League.» LINEA, *The Newsletter of the Art Students League of New York*, volume 2, number 1, Winter, 1998, 1, 7 and 14.

———. *Dorothy Dehner: Sixty Years of* Art. Katonah, New York, 1993.

Martin, Judy Wells. «Art Celebration! will begin on Saturday.» *The Florida Times-Union and Journal* (Jacksonville), 1981.

———. «Cummer Gallery of Art slates exhibit of drawings by Jacksonville artists.» *The Florida Times-Union and Journal* (Jacksonville), Sunday, June 7, 1981, G-9.

———. «Egyptian motif is featured at art gallery.» *The Florida Times-Union* (Jacksonville), December 11, 1986, C.

McCaughey, Patrick. «*The Spirit of Genius*,» *Art at the Wadsworth Atheneum*. New York, 1992.

Mifflin, Margot. «Hughie Lee-Smith, 'It's a Topsy-Turvy World, Isn't It?'» *ARTnews*, October, 1994, 89-90.

Miller, Dorothy C. and Alfred H. Barr (editors). *American Realists and Magic Realists*. New York, 1943 (reprint 1969).

Morris, Donald R. «Thomason U.S.M.C..» *American Heritage*, November, 1993, 52-66.

Morrow, Elizabeth Chase. «Growing by pinks, browns, Hues of recognition color Cummer artist's life.» *The Florida Times-Union* (Jacksonville), Sunday, June 26, 1983, G1-2.

———. «'Twentieth Century Painting' on view at Cummer.» *The Florida Times-Union* (Jacksonville), Friday, December 15, 1989, «Coasting» section, 10.

Murphy-Livingston, Debra. *Joseph Jeffers Dodge: An American Classicist* (exhibition catalogue, September 11-October 25, 1992). Cummer Gallery of Art, Jacksonville, Florida.

———. «Museum has a Jerry Christmas.» *Jacksonville Magazine*, December, 1996.

Norton-Taylor, Duncan. «The Banker in the Budget Bureau.» *Fortune*, March, 1953, 134-136, 138, 144.

Otten, Alan L. and Charles B. Seib. «There Goes the Man who Cut the Budget, Joseph Morrell Dodge has returned to banking but he leaves a heritage of economy-mindedness to the government.» *Nation's Business*, May, 1954, 43, 85-88.

«Outstanding Art Exhibit Featured.» *The St. Augustine Record*, Friday Afternoon, November 7, 1969.

Paige, Pamela. «Dodge of Cummer: The director's first one-man local exhibit goes on display.» *The Florida Times-Union* Sunday Magazine (Jacksonville), February 16, 1964, 12.

«Paintings by Joseph J. Dodge.» *Your Museum*, volume 4, number 2, November, 1955, Schenectady, NY, 5.

Parker, Yvonne. «Man Still Remains Focal Point For Artists.» *Jacksonville Journal*, Thursday, March 5, 1964, 27.

Parks, Cynthia. «Celebration, Flexibility and simplicity helping artists' co-op remain together through the years.» *The Florida Times-Union* (Jacksonville), Thursday, November 17, 1988, C-1 and C-4.

———. «'Art Celebration' is a short sweet, visual treat.» *The Florida Times-Union* (Jacksonville), April 30, 1992, E-1 and E-6.

———. «Coming Home to the Cummer, Former director returns with his own show, collection.» *The Florida Times-Union* (Jacksonville), Sunday, September 6, 1992, F-1 and F-3.

———. «Exhibit honors magic of lines.» *The Florida Times-Union* (Jacksonville), Thursday, June 22, 1989, C-1 and C-4.

———. «Senior artists display treasures, Works by familiar names on exhibit in Ponte Vedra gallery.» *The Florida Times-Union* (Jacksonville), January 20, 1992.

Petersen, Valerie. «Joseph Jeffers Dodge.» *Art News*, January, 1961.

Phelps, Bob. «Bob Phelp's people.» *The Florida Times-Union* (Jacksonville), Monday, February 22, 1993, B-1.

———. «Classical music has rich history in Jacksonville, Frederick Delius tops century of ties.» *The Florida Times-Union* (Jacksonville), June 20, 1999, D-1 and D-3.

Phelps, Bob and Sharon Weightman. «Dodge Collection at Cummer.» *The Florida Times-Union* (Jacksonville), Sunday, November 24, 1996, F-3.

Pignatti, Terisio. *The Golden Century of Venetian Painting*. Los Angeles, 1979.

«Presidential Adviser Joseph Dodge, Man with a Puzzle.» *Time*, January 24, 1955, 12-15.

«Preview of Art Show at Fort Edward.» *The Post-Star*, Glens Falls, NY, June 1, 1960.

Rattenbury, Ken. *Duke Ellington, Jazz Composer*. London, New Haven. 1990.

Rhoades, Shirrel. «He's Drawn Toward the Golden Beach.» *The Florida Times-Union* (Jacksonville), Entertainment Showcase, April 17, 1966, 16.

Rome (Knopf Guides), New York, 1994.

Rothschild, Jane. «City Art Comes out of the Closet; Meet a Few of Our Artists....» *Folio Weekly* (Jacksonville), April 7, 1987, 6.

Russell, John. «Centuries of Blue Skies O'er a 'Pastoral Landscape.'» *The New York Times*, Sunday, November 13, 1988, H35-36.

Saunders, Gill. *The Nude: A New Perspective*. New York, 1989.

Sawin, Martica. *Surrealism in Exile and the Beginning of the New York School*. Cambridge, MA, 1995.

Schaffner, Ingrid and Lisa Jacobs (eds). *Julien Levy, Portrait of an Art Gallery*. New York, 1998.

Schilling, Richard. «Coping with Color Blindness, Practical ways to compensate for-and create with-color impairment.» *The Artist's Magazine*, March, 1994, 36-38.

Shapiro, Doris. *We Danced All Night, My Life Behind the Scenes with Jay Lerner*. New York, 1990.

Sheriff, Mary D. *Fragonard, Art and Eroticism*. Chicago and London, 1990.

Shrum, L. Vance. *Jacksonville Artists Drawing Exhibition* (exhibition catalogue). Cummer Gallery of Art. «Joseph Jeffers Dodge.» Jacksonville, FL, n.d. (1981).

Smith, Griffin. «A Solid Look at Major Florida Painters.» *The Miami Herald*, Sunday, January 23, 1972, 2M.

Steed, Janna Tull. *Duke Ellington, A Spiritual Biography*. New York, 1999.

Suter, Noel. «The Surprising Hyde Collection.» *Museum Magazine*, September/October, 1982, 23-26.

Sutton, Denys. *André Derain*. London, 1959.

Tashjian, Dickran. *A Boatload of Madmen: Surrealism and the American Avant-Garde, 1920-1950*. New York, 1995.

Taylor, Joshua c., et al., *Perceptions and Evocations: the Art of Elihu Vedder*. Washington, 1979.

«The Report Card From Glens Falls Schools.» *The Post-Star*, May 14, 1948, 17.

Travis, Dempsey J. *The Duke Ellington Primer*. Chicago, 1996.

Tucker, Mark (ed.). *The Duke Ellington Reader*. Oxford and New York, 1993.

Vance, Joel. *Ain't Misbehavin: Fats Waller, His Life & Times*. New York, 1979.

Verne, Jules. *20,000 Leagues Under the Sea*. With illustrations by Milo White, translated by Philip Schuyler Allen, Chicago, 1922.

Vincent, Steven. «The Crimson.» *Art & Auction*, January, 1996, 80-81, 112-113.

Ward, Geoffrey C. and Ken Burns. *Jazz: A History of America's Music*. New York, 2000.

Weeks, Ted. «Classical Realism, Cummer Museum pays homage to its guiding spirit-Joseph Jeffers Dodge.» *Folio Weekly* (Jacksonville), August 6, 1996.

———. «Three of a Kind.» *Folio Weekly* (Jacksonville), November 7, 1995, 38.

Weightman, Sharon. «Artist, lecturer, author and educator ... Joseph Jeffers 'Jerry' Dodge.» *The Florida Times-Union* (Jacksonville), Sunday, August 14, 1994, E-1 and E-4.

———. «Chosen to become an artist's muse.» *The Florida Times-Union* (Jacksonville), Sunday, August 14, 1994, E-1 and E-4.

———. «Arts supporters honored, Cultural Council hands out awards.» *The Florida Times-Union* (Jacksonville), April 26, 1996, B-3.

———. «Ex-Cummer art director Dodge dies.» *The Florida Times-Union* (Jacksonville), March 7, 1997, B-1 and B-3.

Wells, Judy. «The Wells Watch.» *The Florida Times-Union* (Jacksonville), Sunday, November 2, 1997, D-2.

Wheeler, Robert G. «Art in Albany.» *Sunday Times-Union* (Albany, NY), October 9, 1949, D-5.

Williamson, Judith. «The Art of Modeling.» *Jacksonville Today*, March/April, 1990, 30-31.

Wilson, Elizabeth B. «Who Needs The Big City?,» *Art & Antiques*, November, 1998, 84-91.

Wood, Wayne. *Jacksonville's Architectural Heritage*. Gainesville, FL, 1998.

Yau, John. *Robert Birmelin: Opening the Door* (exhibition catalogue). Contemporary Realist Gallery, San Francisco, California, November 2-December 2, 1995, New York, 1995.

Concept of the catalogue	Kym Staiff, DOC design consulting
Text edited by	Jeanne M. Theriault
Graphic design, typesetting, Composition & photo work	Kym Staiff and Pierre-Yves Gadina DOC design consulting Vers le lac-1813 St-Saphorin-Switzerland
Photo credits	John Faulkner Michael Fredricks Erik Gould Walter Larrimore Raymond Marinot Robert Paull James Quine Pablo Rivera L. Vance Shrum SuperStock, Inc. Tim Thayer TIMEPIX
Photolithography Printing	CDM - Torino ItaliArt Printing Corso Galileo Ferraris 110 10129 Torino-Italy
Typefaces, paper & print run	Composed in ITC Leawood & Futura typefaces 1000 copies hardback & 1000 softcover on 170 gm^2 Gardamat

ISBN 0-915135-13-2
Printed in Italy

Cummer Museum of Art & Gardens
829 Riverside Avenue
Jacksonville, FL 32204
www.cummer.org